Fraud

Crime and Society Series

Series editor: Hazel Croall

Published titles

Sex Crime (second edition), by Terry Thomas
Burglary, by R.I. Mawby
Armed Robbery, by Roger Matthews
Car Crime, by Claire Corbett
Street Crime, by Simon Hallsworth
Hate Crime, by Nathan Hall
Fraud, by Alan Doig

Fraud

Alan Doig

WILLAN
PUBLISHING

Published by

Willan Publishing
Culmcott House
Mill Street, Uffculme
Cullompton, Devon
EX15 3AT, UK
Tel: +44(0)1884 840337
Fax: +44(0)1884 840251
e-mail: info@willanpublishing.co.uk
website: www.willanpublishing.co.uk

Published simultaneously in the USA and Canada by

Willan Publishing
c/o ISBS, 920 NE 58th Ave, Suite 300,
Portland, Oregon 97213-3786, USA
Tel: +001(0)503 287 3093
Fax: +001(0)503 280 8832
e-mail: info@isbs.com
website: www.isbs.com

Hardback
ISBN-13: 978-1-84392-173-8
ISBN-10: 1-84392-173-1

Paperback
ISBN-13: 978-1-84392-172-1
ISBN-10: 1-84392-172-3

British Library Cataloguing-in-Publication Data

A catalogue record for this book is available from the British Library

Project managed by Deer Park Productions, Tavistock, Devon
Typeset by GCS, Leighton Buzzard, Bedfordshire, LU7 1AR
Printed and bound by T.J. International Ltd, Padstow, Cornwall

Contents

Abbreviations and acronyms

ABI	Association of British Insurers: the representative association for UK insurance companies
ACFE	Association of Certified Fraud Examiners: an industry professional body based in the USA, with national chapters
ACPO	Association of Chief Police Officers: the organisation that represents chief constables
APACS	Association of Payment Clearing Services: the body that represents cheque and credit card issuers
ARA	Asset Recovery Agency: the law enforcement agency with responsibilities which include confiscation work and training officials in relation to the Proceeds of Crime Act
ATM	Automatic Teller Machine: machine dispensing banknotes
BBA	British Banking Association: the representative body for UK and other banks
BSA	Building Societies Association
C&AG	Comptroller and Auditor General: the head of the National Audit Office
CAB	Criminal Assets Bureau: an Irish law enforcement agency dealing with asset confiscation
CAP	Common Agricultural Policy
CBI	Confederation of British Industries
CC	Competition Commission
CFIS	Counter Fraud Investigation Service, part of the Department for Work and Pensions
CFS	Counter Fraud Service: now the Counter Fraud and Security Management Service of the NHS
CFSMS	Counter Fraud and Security Management Service: a unit within the NHS dealing with fraud
CHIS	Covert Human Intelligence Source

CIB	Company Investigations Branch: part of the DTI
CIFAS	Credit Industry Fraud Avoidance Scheme: a body funded by its members to exchange information for fraud prevention and detection
CIPFA	Chartered Institute of Public Finance and Accountancy: the professional association for public sector auditors
CML	Council of Mortgage Lenders
CPIA	Criminal Procedure and Investigations Act
CPR	Civil Procedure Rules
CPS	Crown Prosecution Service
CSG	Corporate Services Group
DCPCU	Dedicated Cheque and Plastic Card Unit: the police unit that deals with organised crime and cheque and credit card fraud
DEFRA	Department for the Environment, Food and Rural Affairs
DFAU	Defence Fraud Analysis Unit
DFES	Department for Education and Skills
DoH	Department of Health
DPP	Director of Public Prosecutions: head of the CPS
DSS	Department of Social Security
DTI	Department of Trade and Industry
DVLA	Driver and Vehicle Licensing Authority
DWP	Department for Work and Pensions
EC	European Commission
ECHR	European Convention on Human Rights
ES	Employment Service: former government department that dealt with unemployment benefit and job centres. Now merged into the DWP
FE	Further Education: deals with education between secondary school and universities
FIG	Fraud Investigation Group: staff within the CPS who dealt with complex fraud cases
FSA	Financial Services Authority: the statutory body that supervises the regulated sector
FSMA	Financial Services and Markets Act: the Act that set up the Financial Services Authority
GP	General Practitioners: doctors
HMCE	Her Majesty's Customs and Excise (merged into HMRC and SOCA in 2005 and 2006)
HMCPSI	HM Crown Prosecution Service Inspectorate
HMIC	Her Majesty's Inspector of Constabulary
HMRC	HM Revenue and Customs (a new agency from 2005 comprising Inland Revenue and part of HMCE)
HMSO	Her Majesty's Stationery Office
IB	Intervention Board
ICAEW	Institute of Chartered Accountants for England and Wales: the professional body for accountants

ILA	Individual Learning Account: a government initiative to encourage a return to education, beset by fraud
IR	Inland Revenue (is now merged with part of HMCE to form HMRC)
IRA	Irish Republican Army
IS	Insolvency Service
IT	Information technology
KPMG	Klynveld, Peat, Marwick, Goerdeler: A tax, audit and management consultancy
KYC	Know Your Customer: a requirement for the regulated sector imposed by the FSA
LACORS	Local Authorities Coordinators of Regulatory Services
LF	Long Firm Fraud: a fraud committed by obtaining credit, selling goods and failing to repay the credit
LOC	Letter of Credit
MLRO	Money Laundering Reporting Officer
MOD	Ministry of Defence
MOT	Motor vehicle test
MP	Member of Parliament
NAO	National Audit Office: the UK state audit
NCIS	National Criminal Intelligence Service: the law enforcement agency that collects and collates information for use by other law enforcement agencies. Now integrated into SOCA
NCS	National Crime Squad: the law enforcement agency that deals with serious and organised crime. Now integrated into SOCA
NDPB	Non-Departmental Public Body
NERA	National Economic Research Associates; a consultancy
NHS	National Health Service
NIM	National Intelligence Model: current investigation framework used by law enforcement
OCE	Organised Crime Enterprise
OECD	Organisation of Economic Cooperation and Development
OFT	Office of Fair Trading
PAC	Public Accounts Committee
PACE	Police and Criminal Evidence Act
PAYE	Pay as you earn: the method for deducting tax at source by employers for employees
PBI	Prime Bank Instrument
PEACE	Planning, Engage, Account, Closure and Evaluation: an interviewing method
PIDA	Public Interest Disclosure Act: more commonly known as the Whistleblowing Act
PIN	Personal Identification Number: used for credit and debit card. 'Chip and Pin' – an electronic chip and the PIN – are the two features that describe the new anti-fraud measures built into the cards

POCA	Proceeds of Crime Act
PPA	Prescription Pricing Authority: part of the NHS that pays the bills for medicines
PSA	Property Services Agency
PwC	PricewaterhouseCoopers: a tax, audit and management consultancy firm
RART	Regional Asset Recovery Team
RCPO	Revenue and Customs Prosecutions Office
RIPA	Regulation of Investigatory Powers Act
SAR	Suspicious Activity Report: also known as the STR – Suspicious Transaction Report
SCO	Special Compliance Office: a department within HMRC
SDT	Solicitors' Disciplinary Tribunal: an independent body that hears cases brought to it by the Law Society about the conduct of solicitors
SFO	Serious Fraud Office
SIB	Securities and Investments Board
SIO	Senior Investigating Officer
SOCA	Serious and Organised Crime Agency
SRO	Self Regulating Organisation: once the bodies working within the SIB framework
TEC	Training and Enterprise Council
TSO	Trading Standards Officers
TSO	The Stationery Office
VAT	Value Added Tax

Acknowledgements

This book is dedicated to the students (and their assignments) and the lecturers (and their course material) involved in the MA Fraud Management programme. Since all are employed in the prevention, detection, investigation and prosecution of various aspects of fraud and financial crime – from employee fraud through to money laundering, organised crime, and terrorist finance – from corporate, law enforcement, and public sector perspectives, the programme has provided a wealth of expertise and experience from each of them and for myself. I only hope that they feel that they have received as much benefit and enjoyment from the programme as I have and that this book in some way reflects many of the themes and issues of the programme.

I should like to thank members of the Certificate Steering Committee for their time and commitment: Stephen Low (SFO); David Middleton (Law Society); Ruth Shelley (Nationwide); John Armstrong (Aviva); Sterl Greenhalgh (PricewaterhouseCoopers); and Nikki Heasley (PricewaterhouseCoopers) for looking after the details. I should also like to thank: Mike Adlem; Martin Baldwin; Alan Batey; Andrew Becconsall; Alan Blaney; Robin Booth; Phil Bottomer; Nick Briggs; John Brougham; Alex Brown; Phil Butler; Lee Cadman; Dave Churchill; Bill Cleghorn; David Clough; Lee Cadman; Barry Cotter; Roger Crotty; Gavin Cunningham; Alex Deane; Noel Dennis; Barry Dickinson; Les Dobie; Darryl Evans; Paul Fredericks; Malcolm French; Matt Gilham; Martina Hogg; Graham Hooper; John Howell; Fred Hutchinson; Jim Jolly; Gareth Jones; Stuart Kent; Michael Macaulay; Dick Mead; Alan Merrett; Stephanie McIvor; Frank Nesbitt; Emma Porter; Steve Power; Derek Purdy; John Rosenbloom; Peter Ramsay; Dave Rowson; Tim

Salt; Terry Street; Tony Thomas; Peter Tickner; Mike Trigg and Cary Whitmarsh.

I should like to thank Hazel Croall, the series editor, for her comments. Particular thanks go to Dave Crinmon, Paul Cottam, Malcolm Driscoll, Dave Hepworth, Martin Lindsay, Nick Mattock and Kieron Sharp for their studies, to Jim McCartan and David Morrison (for Scotland), and to those who took time to be interviewed and comment on drafts of the book: Sterl Greenhalgh (PwC); Clive Barnes (South Yorks Police); Paul Worth (Eversheds); Charlie Dickin (ARA); Stephen Low (Serious Fraud Office); Richard Kitchen and Dave White (DWP); Jon Edwards (Companies Investigation Branch, DTI); William Amos (FSA); Dave Graves (MOD); John Conyngham (Control Risks); David Moore (Newcastle Building Society); Steve Phillips and Jim Gee (NHS); Derek Elliott (District Audit); Paul Archer (DFAU), Colin Gibson (Durham Constabulary), Ken Farrow (City of London Police). Further thanks go to Lew Tassell, Martin Harvey and John Fothergill, not only for their comments but also for agreeing to read the whole draft (in Lew's case, part of it twice).

Finally, there are those I'd like to thank who have been as immersed in the world of fraud and fraud investigation as I am and who are always ready to talk about it: Norman Wise, Monty Raphael, Matthew Cooper, Peter Sproat, David Watt, Denis Clark, Mike Levi, and Ann ('I'll be glad when that bloody book's finished') Lockhart. And to Chris and Natalie, enjoy the future.

A brief introduction to fraud

Fraud is listed by the 2003 UK Threat Assessment issued by the National Criminal Intelligence Service (NCIS 2003) as one of the seven most significant threats facing the United Kingdom, along with firearms and Class A drugs trafficking, but is not currently in itself a specific criminal offence. Fraud is reckoned to be responsible for almost half the estimated value of all criminal activity investigated by the police but the police devote less than 3 per cent of their staff to its investigation. In terms of agencies or units, the police resources devoted to the detection, investigation and prosecution of fraud amount to approximately 5 per cent of the total number of staff dedicated to fraud in other agencies or units within both the public and private sectors. Those who perpetrate fraud range from university students to individuals involved in organised crime. They and others have exploited government policy to steal millions of pounds. On the one hand, the Lord Chief Justice has called for convicted offenders not to go to prison, but despite this it is one of the few crimes that successive official inquiries want removed from trial by jury because it is assumed that the complexity of the detail results in too many acquittals.

As a topic of concern, fraud has moved up and down the scale of corporate priorities over time. In 1991 a police working party on cheque and credit card fraud noted that 'corporate interest was drifting away because it was assumed that fraud was being addressed.' By 2004, the British Banking Association (BBA) and the Association of Payment Clearing Services (APACS) had developed a raft of committees, working parties, warnings, websites, PINs, retailer liability and other initiatives as the cost of credit card fraud continued to climb, with organised crime, the internet and marketing departments all helping to make the card both ubiquitous, accessible and exploitable.

It has now arrived on the Labour government's agenda, some 10 years after the 1997 election manifesto offering to 'crack down' on tax avoidance, dishonesty in the benefit system, and the fraudulent use of birth certificates (in the context of bogus asylum seekers), as well as address the possibility of fraud in the Common Agricultural Policy. Marginalised in terms of ministerial ownership or priorities thereafter, fraud has slowly re-emerged on to the agenda, not in the least because it is seen there as a resource for terrorism and organised crime. In September 2003 the Attorney General made a speech proclaiming: '[Let us] explode the myth sometimes spread that economic crime is somehow less evil than other criminal activity because it does not damage people. I reject this argument. Economic crime fuels terrorism. Money laundering is essential to serious and organised crime. Revenue fraud ... is one of the major threats to the UK from organised crime. The cost to the UK economy of fraud has been put at £14 billion a year, which is the equivalent of £230 for each member of the population. It is not victimless but is indiscriminate, hitting both rich and poor. Fraud may involve no violence ... but it can be devastating in its effects.' In May 2004, Baroness Scotland, junior minister at the Home Office, produced a consultation paper on the introduction of a single offence of fraud. In it she announced that the cost of fraud was £14 billiion. The same document mentioned, in passing, the links fraud has (or might have) to money laundering, corruption, identity 'theft' (as the Home Office has kept calling it) and cybercrime (as everyone keeps calling it).

In October 2005 the government finally got round to doing something about it; some might say that they had to. The imminent passing of the Fraud Bill and the use of the National Crime Recording Standards rules would reveal the full extent of offences and their value, with some suggesting they could reveal the now-defined offence of fraud as the single most costly acquisite crime in the UK. The Attorney General announced that 'our response to fraud must be strengthened further. To facilitate that an interdepartmental review of fraud has been established which will report jointly to me and the Chief Secretary to the Treasury, by late spring 2006. The review will consider the prevention, detection, investigation and prosecution/ punishment of fraud. It will consider the scope for improving the current arrangements with the objective of reducing the amount of fraud and minimising the harm it causes to the economy and wider society.' A month later he drew attention to the impending Fraud

Bill and the introduction of non-jury fraud trials. In December 2005 the Home Office invitation for research into fraud noted that not only was the cost around £14 billion per annum but there is a lack of data on the nature and scale of both public and private sector fraud, without which 'it is not possible to develop a true picture of the amount of fraud and the economic impact it causes', nor ensure that 'fraud receives the prioritisation that it deserves in the resource allocation process'. In the meantime the interdepartmental review was underway. Comprising major public sector and private sector representatives and with a number of industry working parties, it promised 'to take a holistic view of fraud and develop an anti-fraud culture throughout society', dividing its work into four areas covering: preventing and deterring fraud; investigating fraud; prosecuting and penalising fraud; fraud trial management. Its Final Review, discussed below, was published in July 2006.

This book explains why fraud is a rising cost to the country, but why it is difficult to measure. It describes who commits fraud, how and why, and provides a comprehensive overview of who investigates fraud, and how, as well as the issues relating to investigation and punishment. It answers many of the questions that the Review is (or should be) asking, mixing practitioner issues with academic analysis to provide a textbook that will look at these and many other issues. It offers a conceptual, contextual and contemporary overview of fraud, the law, the offences, the causes of fraud, and the agencies and procedures involved in the prevention, detection, investigation and prosecution of fraud. While there are many more laws, agencies and cases than even this book can cover, it seeks to provide a representative picture of those laws, agencies and cases that offer a range of perspectives on fraud. It is written as a book that may be used by students and practitioners, from those interested in fraud to those working in a fraud environment.

Chapter I

Fraud – the academic and practitioner contexts

The origins of white collar crime and the study of fraud

Fraud has been a defined subject of academic study since the mid-twentieth century but its location within an academic discipline has fluctuated depending on the enthusiasm of individuals or the disciplinary perspectives of groups of academics. Persuading people to part with their money by using deception or misrepresentation through words and documents rather than threats or violence by means of a weapon or physical intimidation, has, to put it simply, been seen as a crime that assumes some sort of relationship between the perpetrator/persuader and the victim/persuaded. That relationship also assumes that one is, for example, the client, customer, contractor, or colleague of the other. In other words, unlike the conventional view of theft, offender and victim (whether persons, public bodies or corporate entities) were not unknown to each other – or at least had some notional basis on which to have a relationship (bogus or genuine).[1] This would usually involve the offender having something the victim wants (or can be persuaded they want), or is eligible to (or satisfies the conditions to be eligible to) secure something from the victim. Again, put simply, that contact or relationship was seen as normally taking place in a work or organisational context involving people dealing in paper and working at desks – hence its general description as an aspect of white-collar crime and its inclusion as a subject of study within that context.

The genesis of the study of white-collar crime lies in the pioneering criminological study of business deviance (Sutherland 1983; he first used the term 'white-collar crime' in a conference address in 1939 and then in the title of the subsequent academic journal paper the following year; his book, minus a few names, appeared in 1949 and the full version in 1983). Sutherland's investigation of business or corporate crime was based on studying what might loosely be termed occupation, class and social status as the determining characteristics, with a particular permutation – people in senior positions as managers, executives and officers – used for the basis of his term 'white-collar.' The term denoted the offenders rather than the offences although, here, these were also limited to the defining context of the offender. Thus a senior manager could shoot a neighbour but that would not make him or her a 'white-collar murderer.' The investment broker who stole his neighbour's savings would be a 'white-collar embezzler.'

Sutherland's argument was that the prevailing theories – such as poverty or genetic disposition ('social and personal pathologies') – were not an adequate explanation for certain types of criminal behaviour. He argued that criminal behaviour might also be linked to wealth and power, and in the hands of those senior enough to make the necessary decisions. (This also meant that, because such criminals could afford good lawyers, punishment rates were much lower and thus they were less likely to show up in the crime statistics as an identifiable group over and above the usual suspects.) His thesis was that 'persons of the upper socioeconomic class' also engaged in criminal activity. This activity he termed white-collar crime, loosely defining it as 'a crime committed by a person of respectability and high social status in the course of his occupation' (Sutherland 1983: 7). What Sutherland also argued at the time he was writing (in 1949), was that such crime could also encompass a wide range of activities – for example, procurement, banking, car repairs – and groups – for example, doctors – and that the cost of such crime was probably several times as great as the financial cost of all the crimes which are customarily regarded as the 'crime problem' (1983: 9). His focus, however, was very much on corporate wrongdoing in its widest sense (such as restraint of trade, unfair labour practices and stock manipulation)[2] which he clearly distinguished from financial crime against the corporation – he called embezzlement by a low-level employee 'the most foolish of the white-collar crimes' (1983: 237).

Sutherland's themes have been developed, expanded and adapted by academics subsequently (see Geis 1968; Geis and Meier 1980; Geis and Stotland 1980; Johnson and Douglas 1978). In their 1980 edited book, Geis and Meier included material on corruption while in the same year Geis's edited book with Stotland discussed computer-related crime and management fraud (including fraud by managers against the company). The post-Sutherland US work tended to avoid too much attention to definitions, devoting more pages to motivations, deterrence, criminality (including the concept of the criminogenic nature of business as a consequence of the need to deliver sales and profits), and an expanding range of offenders (including pharmacists and nursing home owners). The overall trajectory of the research has stayed generally within the sociology/criminology academic disciplines, with white-collar crime increasingly researched through the business organisational deviance perspective. Here the areas of actual or potential criminality now included any form of misrepresentation for profit, and extending to include charities, home improvements, food and academic qualifications as areas where white-collar crime also occurred.

There was, as a consequence of the developing research, a recognition that Sutherland's 'wealthy and powerful' distinction was too restrictive for such a range of perpetrators and that the focus should be on the crime – 'white-collar crime' as opposed to the 'white-collar criminal.' As Edelhartz (1978) noted, the character of white-collar crime should focus on the crime rather than the perpetrator: 'The character of white-collar crime must be found in its modi operandi and its objectives rather [than] in the nature of the offender' (1978: 45). In the 1980s and into the 1990s, the range of research in the US did look more at the crime, extending further into the fields of corruption and organised crime where many of those involved would clearly not fit into Sutherland's definition of 'a person of respectability and high social status.' The expansion of academic study – much of it based on fieldwork – was matched by an extensive and detailed tradition of investigative journalism, both mainstream and alternative. Primary source material was provided by publications and reports from a strong Government Accountability Office (the USA's equivalent of the UK National Audit Office, dealing with the accounts of Federal government departments). There was a congressional committee system that regularly exposed fraud, waste and corruption in the Federal public service. Further material emerged from a range of *ad hoc* official inquiries at national and state level.

Writing on fraud by both practitioners and academics is extensive and often an integral part of the study of white-collar crime. Even before the raft of books explaining the Enron and other corporate collapses, books were published on investment banking corporate self-interest (Auleta 1986), loans fraud (O'Shea 1991) and practitioner approaches to fraud (see, for example, Albrecht *et al.* 1995). At the same time, the academic focus on white-collar crime includes fraud because the former is 'committed through the use of some combination of fraud, deception, or collusion' (Weisburd and Waring 2001: 12). Further, white-collar crime itself no longer solely encompasses those at the top of the corporate structure but all of those for whom 'changes in our society … have placed the opportunity for white-collar crimes in the hands of a much broader class' as a consequence of the increase in white-collar jobs and of the expansion in public sector bureaucracies, the changes in technologies, and the development of the credit economy (see Weisburd and Waring 2001: 9). What is noticeable about the academic perspective, is the range of research and debate on fraud, often with a practitioner focus, from the investigation of fraud in the Federal public sector (Light 1993), through specialised issues such as the prevention and detection of financial statement fraud (Rezaee 2002), to developing ethical environments (Cooper 1998).

Contemporary research also continues to analyse motivation, with one contemporary piece of empirical research arguing that, on the one hand, evidence from some white-collar criminals might indicate that their crimes are not always 'aberrations on unblemished records' (i.e. that white-collar crime is not always a one-off occurrence) but, on the other, 'their criminality may reveal little more than they have committed a crime' (i.e. profiling white-collar criminals does not throw up a distinctive 'type' – see Weisburd and Waring 2001: 144, 145). What the authors suggest is that circumstance or context and necessity lie at the centre of white-collar crimes:

> Situation plays a central role in explaining participation in crime for most offenders in the sample. The lives of those we have termed opportunity takers and crisis responders do not seem to be characterized by instability and deviance, and there was little in their records that indicated a predisposition to criminality. A specific crisis or special opportunity appears to have drawn otherwise conventional people across the line to crime. Even for those described as opportunity seekers, situational opportunities play an important role in defining why offenders commit crimes at specific junctures. (2001: 145–146)

> Many of these white-collar criminals maintain positive attitudes toward conventionality and legality even when participating in crime. Many of those labeled crisis responders are, by and large, conformists, but, in a specific situation, they feel the need to do something they define as wrong in order to deal with

some perceived crisis that threatens them, their families, or their companies. Even when committing crime, they accept the fact that they should conform to legal norms, but believe they cannot. People we have defined as opportunity takers also accept more generally legal and conventional norms. Arguably, such people would not have violated the law in the first place if a specific opportunity had not confronted them. Although they do not seek out criminal opportunities, once they appear, opportunity takers decide that conventional norms are holding them up in a specific circumstance. (2001: 146–147)

Generally, however, the authors suggest that seeking to establish the 'chain of causal events' which led up to the point of criminal action for either group was not always possible, making the use of systemic pre-emptive, or over-intrusive, controls debatable for a crime that might thus be both deliberate and opportunist. Further, the findings suggested that financial penalties rather than imprisonment would be more effective inhibitors on either group.

The study of fraud in the UK

There remains a limited investigative journalism tradition in the UK[3] but despite this, and the much more detailed material available from the public auditors, these are not drawn upon in any significant way for academic study into white-collar crime which has not moved too much from its original sociological/criminological roots, nor has it shifted towards a more empirical focus. Academics in these fields have tended to address the subject on three areas. The first concerns white-collar crime in its broadest sense, developing an elasticity of definition which has moved the subject away from its financial focus. Here it is the range of criminal activity in the workplace or by the organisation that becomes the focus, from pollution to dangerous products. Hazel Croall (2001), for example, lists categories that include: theft at work, fraud, corruption, employment offences, consumer offences, food offences, environmental crime. The breadth of her interest, however, takes a mainstream approach to white-collar crime in its wider sense in that it reflects both US and UK publications where workplace violence, espionage and theft are also now included (see Gill 1994; Giacalone and Greenberg 1997; Davies *et al.* 1999).

The second area concerns organisational deviance, focusing on two aspects. One aspect is occupational or organisational deviance which has broadened out the subject from the issue of class or status to a more general theme of self-regarding activity by low-status employees, whether stealing stock, manipulating the opportunities presented at the workplace, or defrauding the company or customers in an organisational context (see, for example, Ditton 1977 and Mars 1983). The other aspect continues to focus on business as an aspect of organisational deviance in providing a 'criminogenic arena' – 'the organisation as a weapon, a target, an offender, a scene of crime, a justification, an opportunity, a means, and as a victim' (Punch 1996: 271). Here managers and executives may not only act deviantly on behalf of the organisation, but also against it. As Clarke (1990: 7) puts it in introducing his book on business crime: 'It is maintained in this book that crime and misconduct are endemic in business … '. Some of the literature has sought to look at corporate scandals – ranging from corporate killing through financial depredation to specific disasters – through the context of both organisational culture and institutional control (see Clarke 1981, 1986, 1990; Drummond 2003). Others have taken an approach influenced by what Slapper and Tombs describe as 'partisan scholarship' (Slapper and Tombs 1999: 232), sometimes termed 'radical criminology', where the framework is shaped by what might be termed the crimes of the rich and powerful within a capitalist context.

The third academic area relates to certain areas of social study. Thus criminologists, social policy academics and sociologists touch on benefit fraud (see Dean and Melrose 1995 and below, pp 88). It attracts academics interested in the nature of control and sanction – where there may be a marked contrast between tax and benefits sanctions (Cook 1989) – and those interested in the informal or shadow economy as a sociological or anthropological activity (see Henry 1978). Finally, there is an even smaller subset within this area; these are the economists and econometricians who work on the informal economy. Their work is largely in terms of where does the money go if it is not going in VAT and tax. One of the few contributions came from Stephen Smith (1986) who has argued that the informal economy embraces not only the traditional informal economy activities of moonlighting or tax evasion, but also the wide range of ordinary household activities such as washing up, baby-sitting, and DIY.

Outside these broad categories, there have been a handful of academics – usually with sociology/criminology or legal backgrounds – who have focused more specifically on fraud, and taken a more orthodox legal and crimino-legal perspective. There is also a small (and sometimes high-quality) market of practitioner authors writing on the prevention, detection, and investigation of fraud (see, for example, Comer 1985, 2003; Huntington 1992; Huntington and Davies 1994; Brown *et al.* 2004; Jones 2004; and Hyland 2005). Academic interest in fraud tends to be focused on the law and institutions, sometimes with empirical research and often in areas where practitioners are interested in the outcome of the research. Clarke's work in the decade from 1980 focused on business scandal and then business crime (1981, 1986 and 1990). It sought to look at both within their contexts which covered the City deregulation and Big Bang era. The work is useful in that it draws attention to a number of phenomena associated with corporate crime. One concerns the concept of anathematisation – the individualisation of the cause of such crime – and of 'identifying it with the personal character and motivation of those individuals named. The explanation is seen to lie there, rather than in the institutions in the midst of which the offence took place, and which are and will be administered by the rest of the elite' (1980: 151). Another is the emphasis on the imprecise nature of business regulation, using the 1980s reforms to the City to point up the delicate balance between scandals as drivers for reform, and governments' reluctance to go too far beyond pumped-up self-regulation to avoid alienating business.

Leonard Leigh's book (1982) was a straightforward description of corporate financial offences – theft, corruption, conspiracy to defraud, fraudulent trading, etc. – and those institutions responsible for regulating, investigating and prosecuting them. Leigh acknowledged that he had ignored the impact on society, the causes of the crimes and the psychology of those who committed them in favour of a grounded study of compliance and control environments, in terms of what should be taken seriously by law enforcement and regulatory agencies. He took a sideswipe at the criminologists for their undifferentiated assumptions about capitalism and economic crime, and their apparent failure to distinguish between absorbable criminal activity, and criminal activity likely to damage the economy. He emphasised the perennial issues relating to the cost of fraud, the fragmented nature of the agencies dealing with it, and the issue of sanctions.

Most of the empirical work has been single-handedly addressed by the leading-edge research of Michael Levi, probably the outstanding researcher of his generation in this area whose capacity to operate at, and transfer knowledge across, the practitioner and academic boundaries has resulted in a body of work that has shaped and continues to shape the contemporary study of fraud (see Levi, 1981, 1987, 1993, 1999) at academic and practitioner levels. In two publications, the Royal Commission Study (1993) and his earlier book (1987), Levi has raised through both academic and practitioner perspectives a number of core issues relating to the study of fraud:

- The limited academic interest in fraud in the UK, as well as the absence of empirical study;
- The changes to economic activity which result in shifts in patterns of crime (which also move them in and out of the radar of certain academic disciplines);
- The cost of fraud against the cost of crime, and in particular at the higher end of the value scale where fraud easily outstrips armed robbery on a case-by-case basis;
- Fraud may be linked to a number of other crimes, such as money laundering, and involves the use of professionals to facilitate them;
- The multiplicity of agencies and the variations in powers of the agencies dealing with fraud;
- The trial process and the issue of jury trials.

Generally, however, academic study in the UK has barely begun to touch such subjects. This may be considered a matter of surprise and concern, given the practitioner attention now accorded to fraud as it has established itself on the agenda in both private and public sectors over the past 25 years.

The emergence of fraud as a private sector practitioner issue

Fraud as a practitioner issue began to attract attention at the beginning of the 1990s, when it was suggested that the sum lost through management fraud was double that lost in household burglaries and that the financial value of fraud was greater than that relating to other crimes. Police forces in England and Wales reported 123 robberies, 419 burglaries and 819 thefts over £50,000, very few of which 'would have been significantly over that amount' noted Levi in 1991–92 for his study for the Royal Commission (1993). In that year, the CPS dealt with fraud-related cases involving £3.9 billion 'at risk'; the corresponding figure for the SFO for 1992–93 was £4.5 billion.

It is worth pointing out that there have always been fraud-related scandals in both public and private sectors (see Doig 1984; Searle 1987; and Robb 2002, for example, on corporate and political misconduct up to the middle of the twentieth century) to suggest that fraud has long been a feature of corporate and public life. The 1980s provided a number of controversies in both public and private sectors, including the Crown Agents, Johnson Matthey Bankers, John Poulson, London and County Securities, London Capital Group (see Clarke 1986 and Doig 1984), but these were often seen – to emphasise Clarke's comment about anathematisation – as either the consequence of predatory individuals or misjudgments by those involved. They were not seen as symptomatic of corporate misconduct, regulatory failure or changes in organisational culture. This was a perception that in the private sector was reversed with major early 1990s scandals, which – apart from the audit and regulatory issues surrounding the collapse of the Bank of Credit and Commerce International (BCCI; see Hemraj 2005; Adams and Frantz 1992) – included:

Polly Peck: Polly Peck was a small clothing manufacturer taken over by another clothing manufacturer, Asil Nadir. His ability to spot companies and products with potential profit, his tax-efficient location in North Cyprus, and his exploitation of the produce-growing and export markets from Cyprus and Turkey turned Polly Peck into an international conglomerate. By the end of the 1980s, it was capitalised at £760 million, an increase by a factor of 100 since Nadir took it over, with a turnover of £700 million and pre-tax profits of some £100 million (see Barchard 1992). Buying the Del Monte brand and a 51 per cent stake in the Japanese electronics company Sansui in 1989 made Polly Peck a significant multinational.

Nadir's enthusiasm for more planned takeovers – car manufacturing, hotels, travel, etc. – was not matched by the company's liquidity, nor helped by rumours of investigations into family trusts, irregular share dealing, the actual worth of some of the companies in the conglomerate and its tax position. The rumours hit Polly Peck's over-inflated share price. Nadir's announcement of his plan to take Polly Peck into private ownership saw its shares continue to fall until it was suspended on the London Stock Exchange. This was followed by various creditors starting to end their loan facilities and demanding existing loans be repaid. In the end Polly Peck was found to have debts that exceeded its asset value by some £300 million and went into administration. Nadir was charged by the SFO with theft and false accounting to the value of some £150 million (money allegedly siphoned out of the company into a byzantine group of privately controlled offshore trusts). Asil Nadir fled to Northern Cyprus where he remains to this day.

Robert Maxwell: A Czech émigré who joined the British army and fought in the Second World War, Maxwell began his business career in scientific publishing, book and journal distribution, and ultimately general printing (the British Printing Corporation, later to be named the Maxwell Communications Corporation). He served as a Labour MP for a number of years until 1970, although a judge was to comment about him in a court case that 'it is questionable in my view whether that averment taken by itself provides any indication of a person's standing in public life.' Indeed in 1971 his business dealings, merger and takeover tactics, and company management relating to a takeover bid for Pergamon Press from Leasco, an American financial and data processing group, were severely criticised by a DTI report. The report concluded that 'he is not in our opinion a person who can be relied on to exercise proper stewardship of a publicly quoted company.'

Nevertheless, with the profits from his existing companies, Maxwell bought the Mirror newspaper group (comprising the *Daily Mirror*, *Sunday Mirror* and *Sunday People*) in 1984. The newspaper suffered the usual overmanning and restrictive practices that bedevilled Fleet Street at that time (see Martin 1981). Maxwell pruned costs and staffing levels but still could not emulate the success of the Murdoch-owned *Sun*. Maxwell then insisted on setting up a short-lived rival – the London *Evening News* – to the *Evening Standard*, part of the *Daily Mail* group, as well as undertaking newspaper ventures in France, Australia, the USA and Israel. Overstretched on loans linked to a percentage of the share value of the hub of his business empire, the Maxwell Communications Corporation, Maxwell took to selling assets, share manipulation, window-dressing company accounts and ultimately looting the newspaper's pension fund, to keep his empire financially solvent. Maxwell fell from his yacht in 1991, shortly before the collapse of the share prices of the Corporation and Mirror Newspaper Group and the uncovering of multi-million-pound company debts. His sons, Kevin and Ian, were later charged, along with two other directors, and acquitted of complicity in the pension fund theft and risking pension fund shares as collateral for loans. The sons' defence was less about what was happening and their involvement than that their father demanded agreement to all his business decisions (see Bower 1991; Thompson and Delano 1991).

Guinness: Both Guinness the brewers and the Argyll Group (one of the UK's largest supermarket groups) were seriously acquisition-minded in the late 1980s. The whisky-focused Distillers Group (owners of the Gordons Gin, Johnnie Walker and Dewars brands) was targeted by both but favoured the drinks-based Guinness company over the more food- and retail-focused Argyll Group. Argyll bid £1.87 billion, Guinness followed with an offer of £2.2 billion. Both bids comprised offers of shares in the two bidders' companies. Both companies therefore realised that it was important to ensure that their own share prices held up (although of course there were laws and rules governing this practice, as well as the practice of buying shares in the company to be taken over, in order to influence its decision over whose bid to favour). The subsequent takeover battle involved visits to the courts and investigations by various agencies (including the DTI and the police). During the investigations, it was alleged that Guinness's Chief Executive Ernest Saunders authorised company payments to friends and supporters to maintain the value of Guinness shares during the takeover. He also allegedly agreed to cover any losses incurred by others who bought Guinness shares during the bid, but found the share value dropping once the share price settled after the bid. Other supporters were allegedly funded to buy blocks of Distiller shares to later support the Guinness bid.

After Guinness won the bid in 1986, and following boardroom changes, Saunders was suspended when the financing arrangements of what was termed the Guinness 'supporters club' came to light. The Board went to court to begin getting some of the outlay returned and Saunders was arrested on charges of perverting the course of justice, and destroying and altering documents. Subsequently, Saunders was one of eight people charged with offences relating to the bid – primarily conspiracy to defraud in relation to the share support for Guinness shares; theft; and false invoicing. Over four different trials, four of the defendants were acquitted but Saunders was found guilty; this was then reduced on appeal. He was freed after claims by three defence doctors that he was suffering from early onset Alzheimer's (the prosecution expert witness refuted the claim but the court accepted the formers' evidence). Saunders was later to be one of the very few people to recover from the symptoms of the illness and go on to a new career as a management consultant (see Bose and Gunn 1989; Kochan and Pym 1987).

Barlow Clowes: Barlow Clowes was a Manchester-based company that moved from being an investment broker to managing its own investments through gilts – government-issued bonds – for which the company offered either capital growth or an income with a guaranteed return on the investment amount. His claims to be able to exploit varying rates and his appearance on the BBC Radio 4 *Money Programme* pushed up the levels of investment into the company. Clowes moved his business offshore (to Jersey and then on to Gibraltar) and used new income to pay the fixed (and unrealistic) returns promised to existing customers. He spent much of the rest – nearly £100 million – on a lavish lifestyle which he shared with the former wife of a member of the Hollies pop group (whose ex-husband also acted as the couple's chauffeur).

The government regulator, the Licensing Unit, was a small section in the Financial Services Division of the DTI. It first wanted to close Barlow Clowes down but, with the Conservative government keen to promote business and loosen regulation, it then moved to license Clowes to trade, although one official noted that he 'had no concrete reason to worry although one naturally tends to look in askance at business controlled from Gibraltar and harbour unworthy thoughts about the real motives in moving there' (see Lever 1992). Equally suspicious concerns by others, including a neighbour, the Bank of England, the police and the DTI, led to the latter undertaking an inquiry that, among other things, uncovered basic and obvious document forgery. The company was closed down in 1988, owing over £100 million (apart from theft to fund the exotic lifestyle, much of the money was used for the traditional scam of paying dividends to existing policyholders from the deposits paid by new policyholders). Clowes got 10 years for theft, making false statements for gain, and conspiracy to deceive. Under pressure from MPs, many of whom represented the small middle-class investors who had put the Conservatives in power and had chosen to invest their pensions and life savings with Clowes, the government set up an inquiry – the Le Quesne Inquiry. The criticisms of the DTI contained in its report allowed MPs to call for the Parliamentary Ombudsman to investigate allegations of maladministration. This was duly proved and the government paid over £150 million in compensation.

The emergence of fraud as a public sector practitioner issue

In the public sector fraud began to emerge as an issue as part of a wider concern about controls, cultures and the threats in central government departments, government bodies and local government in terms of the potential for fraud. The cases included:

Forward Catering: this was the Civil Service's central catering organisation. The possibility of privatisation in the early 1990s focused its management's attention on the need to be in a position to take advantage of the opportunity – 'the need to gain new business and safeguard its existing business against competitors' – rather than 'the very important matter of financial control.' This included shifting staff onto cash salaries to drive down costs, awarding contracts without tenders as well as allegedly asking suppliers to hold back on various discounts until after the buy-out (worth several hundred thousand pounds), among a number of activities which were later described in an PAC report (1993) as reflecting 'poor control, mismanagement, irregularity, malpractice and fraud ... a serious failure in the proper conduct of public business in what is – or should have been – a straightforward trading operation.' Among other malpractices was the failure to pay tax and other statutory costs, which was somewhat ironic since the organisation was nominally under the control of HM Treasury.

The Property Services Agency: an executive agency of the Department of the Environment, the Property Services Agency (PSA) designed, managed and maintained buildings and property for government departments. The lack of supervision of, and low priority given to, the parts of the organisation responsible for minor works and maintenance (involving a multi-million-pound annual expenditure) was exacerbated by growing pressure on those areas to make savings, to quickly fulfil the needs of client departments, to deal with an increasing volume of paperwork and to assume, untrained, an increasingly managerial role with the shift of work to the private sector. The sense of detachment from the higher levels of PSA management was matched by the closeness to private sector contractors and reinforced by shared backgrounds and a shared interest in work completion. This in turn provided the basis to encourage some contractors to exploit social relationships, work dissatisfaction, procedural inadequacies and organisational indifference in order to corruptly acquire contracts and to overcharge on those contracts.

A number of critical references by the PAC to levels of corruption and misappropriation triggered an inquiry – the Wardale Report – which acknowledged the procedural, cultural and management weaknesses. The Departmental Action Plan was, however, somewhat tarnished by newspaper allegations of widespread corruption on works maintenance in London, with PSA staff holidaying abroad on the basis of points awarded according to the value of contracts allocated to contractors. These were followed by yet more internal inquiries and critical PAC reports which confirmed the entrenched and resilient internal organisational or procedural weaknesses, including: weak guidance on standards of conduct or non-compliance with procedures; management indifference or ignorance; inadequate financial and management information systems; lax working practices; poor staff relations; no separation of functions; excessive discretion; inadequate recruitment, promotion and training policies; and, crucially, the increasing contact with private sector values, personnel and practices which could result in the exploitation of weak public sector procedures and standards as well as persuading public officials of the acceptability of personal financial gain (Doig 1997).

Lambeth Council: the five-page £250,000 report by Elizabeth Appleby QC was published in July 1995. In the report, commissioned in April 1993, Appleby blamed Lambeth's predicament up to April 1991 firmly on the Labour council whose intent to obstruct the implementation of Government policy resulted in the creation of significant financial and staffing problems. The party was riven with turbulence, the Directorates were independent of and jealous of each other, council meetings were unruly and unproductive, staff were unqualified, inexperienced, often totally unsuitable for the job given to them. There were signs of nepotism, a large number of the management were either incompetent or incapable, contributing to a disorganised and chaotic administration, an 'appalling' management and 'the perfect atmosphere for abuse' (Appleby 1995).

The report listed 45 District Audit reports (from 1979 to 1993) that drew attention to its collapse in income from housing rents (1979), its deteriorating financial position (1980), its lack of accounting systems and financial control (1980), and failure to know its financial position (1985). It then noted that the policies and actions of the council had been the 'contributing factor in creating the perfect atmosphere for abuse of the system ... Lambeth has suffered at the hands of dishonest employees, dishonest members of the public and dishonest contractors.' While unable to identify the cause – Freemasonry, a 'Mafia' and a pornographic ring were all proposed to the inquiry – Appleby pointed to unbelievably bad management that allowed huge over-runs on contracts but where the absence of any documentation created the perfect atmosphere for abuse with all the hallmarks of fraud. The inquiry also noted that there could be a significant number of officers fraudulently claiming housing and social security benefits – some officials remained on the payroll when identified as actually having done so to the tune of several thousand pounds. It also claimed an established sale of keys fraud (allocating council property for cash payments, or renting out the property by pretending to be private sector landlords and fixing council records to ensure the property did not show up as available for rent).

The practitioner responses

The reaction to the apparent rise in levels of fraud and corruption in both public and private sectors prompted significant (and in many areas, continuing) official reviews, not only of the cases and their circumstances, but also of the legal, institutional and regulatory contexts in which fraud (and corruption) had taken place.

In the private sector, the early 1990 corporate scandals, and other issues such as the rise of concern over insider trading (see Ashe and Counsell 1990), provided the context for the establishment of the Cadbury Committee which reported in 1992. Given that the scandals involved senior management, involved conduct that was visible (and on occasion had been raised as matters of concern but was not picked up by regulators or auditors), there was pressure for a review to address the organisational context – what was to be termed corporate governance (see Box 1.1).

The Cadbury Committee (Committee on the Financial Aspects of Corporate Governance) (1992) was set up in May 1991 by the Financial Reporting Council, the London Stock Exchange and the accountancy profession. Its format followed a not unusual reaction to organisational misconduct: there is a problem of standards; standards are generally high; there should be a reiteration of standards and a delineation of responsibilities; there should be improvements to various controls to deal with the problem.

Cadbury proposed a range of measures on the roles and responsibilities of the executive and non-executive directors, the transparency and accuracy of corporate information, the role of remuneration and audit committees, the use of codes of conduct throughout the business. Cadbury was the first of a number of similar reports on corporate governance (Greenbury, Hempel and Turnbull; see p 97). It was also one aspect of attempts to deal with fraud in the private sector through self-regulation. Another was the establishment of a dedicated agency – the Serious Fraud Office (see p 97). Overall, the early 1990s corporate fraud scandals did bring private sector fraud firmly into the public domain and probably accelerated the progress of reform which, while started in the 1980s, was found to be deficient in a number of aspects and resulted in further reforms during the

Box 1.1 What is corporate governance?

From a brief analysis of the many international and national codes of good corporate governance it is possible to summarise the guiding principles and best practices as follows:

- Governance structures need to be designed with clear delineation of power, responsibilities, checks and balances including the establishment of board committees to look at complex and detailed areas (such as financial reporting).
- Accountability and control are fundamental but they can only be safeguarded if sufficient disclosure and transparency are guaranteed when reporting to the market.
- The members of the board must be selected according to the principles of professionalism and ethical behaviour. Non-executive directors should also be independent.
- There should be formal and transparent arrangements for maintaining an appropriate relationship with the company's auditors, who help to safeguard shareholders' interests.

Corporate governance is important because it is concerned with both the effectiveness and the accountability of boards of directors. The effectiveness of boards, which covers the quality of leadership and direction they provide, can be measured over time by performance in earnings and the share price. Accountability, which is key to corporate governance, will include the issues surrounding disclosure and transparency of communications to shareholders.

Source: ICAEW Website: www.icaew.co.uk. Accessed 12.12.04

1990s and beyond, culminating in the establishment of the Financial Service Authority (FSA: see p 153).

In the public sector, the official reaction was equally blunt to evidence of fraud, misconduct and negligence in the early 1990s. On the other hand, the sector had been here before, and had anticipated the Cadbury tripartite approach to problem, standards and improvements. In the 1970s, after the Poulson corruption scandal,[4] there were four official inquiries. Two were parliamentary committees looking at, in one case, the MPs involved with Poulson and, in the second, generally at MPs' financial interests, to make recommendations about a new regime of registration, disclosure and inquiry. The other two inquiries were official public inquiries which looked at local government (the 1974 Redcliffe-Maud Inquiry) and standards of conduct in public life (the 1976 Royal Commission into Standards of Conduct in Public Life). The latter two inquiries noted that the problem lay with money, discretionary power and planning, but that standards were generally high and that what was needed was responsible management, codes and organisational procedures, as well as reviews of the law, external scrutiny, the role of the media and political parties (few of the recommendations from either inquiry were implemented). Fifteen years later, the perspectives from the Audit Commission, the National Audit Office, the Committee of Public Accounts and the Committee on Standards in Public Life were not too dissimilar from the Cadbury approach, with an acceptance of generally high standards but concerns over a changing environment and management practices, which would require a range of reforms, including codes and standards of conduct, risk assessments, audit committees, whistle-blowing, control environments, training and monitoring.

Summary

The practitioner reactions to fraud and misconduct up to the mid 1990s have not been reflected to the same extent in academic study, where the study of fraud from its low pre-1990s base continues to be a specialist or niche interest. The reactions were both significant and the trigger for on-going reform in both public and private sectors. The amounts at stake, the variety of organisations and companies involved, the mainstream backgrounds of the senior managers and directors involved, the ease with which controls and procedures were bypassed or ignored, all contributed to the perception that fraud is, and continues to be, a serious threat to public and private sector activity. This book takes forward both the concerns and the responses – what is fraud, what is the cost and impact, who commits fraud and how, and who deals with fraud today – but asks firstly: what exactly is fraud?

Notes

1 In trying to emphasise the difference between theft and deception, Shute and Horder suggest: 'Whereas the thief makes war on a social practice from the outside, the deceiver is the traitor within.' (quoted in Herring 2004: 506)

Chapter 2

What is fraud?

Definitions of fraud

One of the problems with fraud is that it does not exist as a coherent or single activity or statutory offence[1] although the common law offence of conspiracy to defraud is much valued by police fraud officers and has been described as 'one of the most versatile and effective weapons in the armoury of the fraud prosecutor' (Kirk and Woodcock 2003: 269). There is no one piece of legislation that criminalises fraud (at the time of writing the Fraud Bill has had its second reading and when enacted will for the first time define what constitutes an offence of fraud; see below, p 38) and there is no one agency, apart from possibly the Serious Fraud Office, that devotes its time and resources primarily to dealing with fraud. There is no one academic discipline that is devoted to the study of fraud. Fraud occurs in relation to many activities where it has only a tangential relevance to a number of mainstream issues, and often does not have sufficient relevance to be a mainstream focus in its own right. Fraud is a subject and a word that, in itself, is both very broad and appears in some guise in a range of laws, but does not have a single definition. What the law does possess, however, 'is a *concept* of fraud, a broad notion (broader, indeed, than the layman's) of what it means to defraud someone' (Arlidge and Parry 1985: 1).

Thus, as will be noted, fraud is often about persuading someone to part with something but the substantive law has tended to focus on the receipt as theft – that is, the law has often concentrated on the outcome rather than on how the perpetrator achieved this. Second, fraud has been associated with a range of orthodox activities or transactions covered by various laws, with the word 'fraudulently' added to legislation to distinguish between lawful and unlawful aspects of the same activity. Third, fraud often means persuading someone to do something or hand over something as a result of the words or conduct of the persuader: 'We may, then, regard as a paradigm of fraud the case of a deception which induces the victim to act to his own detriment and to the deceiver's profit' (Arlidge and Parry 1985: 22). On the other hand, an action may be interpreted as being done with criminal intent, or as being reckless, or as the persuaded taking a risk, or being careless, so the term fraud may be used in a range of situations, of which the legal definitions are but one. In the view of a 2002 Law Commission report:

> At present, the criminality or otherwise of a fraudulent act depends whether it falls within one of a multitude of offences of varying degrees of specificity. The fact that it is fraudulent will not necessarily mean that it is an offence. (Law Commission 2002: 7.5)

It could be argued that one of the reasons why there is no one single definition or offence of 'fraud' is because much of the attention is on a process – the deception that precedes the theft of someone else's assets, for example – that may well be called theft-with-lies or theft-with-cover-up. Indeed, the purpose of fraud is not the process itself but the acquisition or gain that it is intended to achieve. Certainly in relation to the law, there is no one single offence of 'fraud' but defrauding or fraud-related activity is mentioned in over 50 pieces of extant legislation. Although many of these will be repealed with the enactment of the impending Fraud Act (see Box 2.1 for the Acts currently used for Home Office crime statistics classifications for fraud and forgery categories), the range of legislation has also caused difficulties in quantifying the cost of fraud, as each offence is recorded separately under the National Crime Recording Standards (NCRS).

The laws and offences

The law may, as Denis Clark[2] notes, be divided generally into two, evidential and substantive:

> The law of evidence is that body of rules, which regulate the means by which facts may be proved in a court of law, and in the context of criminal evidence that means a criminal trial. The law of evidence is adjectival rather than substantive law.

Box 2.1 Home Office statistics – fraud and the laws

51. Frauds by company directors, etc	Theft Act 1968; Companies Act 1985
52. False accounting	Theft Act 1968; Companies Act 1985; Detection of Depositors Act 1963
53A. Cheque and credit card fraud	Theft Act 1968; Theft Act 1978; Theft (Amendment) Act 1996; Criminal Justice Act 1987
53B. Other frauds	Theft Act 1968; Criminal Justice Act 1987; Fraudulent Mediums Act 1951; Public Stores Act 1875; Post Office Act 1953; Stamp Duties Management Act 1891; Agricultural Credits Act 1928; Gaming Act 1845; Law of Property Act 1925; Land Registration Act 1925; Theft Act 1978; Criminal Justice Act 1993; Criminal Justice Act 1988; Theft (Amendment) Act 1996; Social Security Administration Act 1992; Computer Misuse Act 1990; Social Security Act 1998; The Enterprise Act 2002; Prevention of Corruption Act 1906
55. Bankruptcy and insolvency offences	Deeds of Arrangement Act 1914; Insolvency Act 1986; Company Directors Disqualification Act 1986
60 Forgery of drug prescription	Forgery and Counterfeiting Act 1971
61. Other forgery etc	Forgery and Counterfeiting Act 1981; Mental Health Act 1983; Coinage Act 1971; Hallmarking Act 1973; Protection of the Euro Against Counterfeiting Regulations 2001
814. Fraud, forgery etc associated with vehicle or driver records	Road Traffic Act 1988; Public Passenger Vehicles Act 1981; Road Traffic Act 1988; Vehicle Excise and Registration Act 1994; Transport Act 1968; Goods Vehicles (Licensing of Operators) Act 1995; Road Traffic Regulation Act 1984

Source: Home Office Counting Rules (see www. homeoffice.gov.uk)

The substantive law is the criminal law, murder, manslaughter, theft, burglary, rape, violence to the person and other crimes that define the conduct and mental element that is required for the particular crime. The law of criminal evidence is the law that governs how these criminal offences are to be proved.

This chapter deals with the substantive law (Chapter 10 deals with the evidential issues). While not comprehensive, this chapter seeks to identify the main themes and issues relating to law and fraud.

Criminal law: theft

Fraud is usually dealt with by the Theft Acts because dishonesty is 'commonly regarded as the core of fraud' (Ormerod and Williams 2005: 1/6). The central piece of legislation is the 1968 Theft Act. This Act consolidated an extensive range of legislation and may be divided here into three sections: theft, deception and corporate offences. Section 1 of the Theft Act provides the basic definition of theft and Sections 2–6 define the component terms of that definition:

(1) A person is guilty of theft if he dishonestly appropriates property belonging to another with the intention of permanently depriving the other of it; and 'thief' and 'steal'; shall be construed accordingly.

(2) It is immaterial whether the appropriation is made with a view to gain, or is made for the thief's own benefit.

The elements of the offence under Section 1 are dealt with in Sections 2–6 which cover the five core components of any theft, however perpetrated:

- a dishonest
- appropriation
- of property
- belonging to another
- with the intention of permanently depriving the other of it.

Dishonesty is dealt with in Section 2 which states that the appropriation (the taking) of property belonging to another is *not* dishonest if the person appropriating the property believes he has a right to it in law. Further, it would not be dishonest when the other person would agree to the appropriation if he or she knew about the appropriation or where it would be difficult to find out who owned the property in the first place. Since the Act does not actually say what 'dishonesty' or 'dishonestly' mean, a number of court cases have shaped their meaning. Of particular importance are the *Feely* and *Ghosh* cases. In the former case, a betting shop manager was charged with taking money from the shop safe which he said he intended to repay, but knew his employers would not condone such practice. The case established that the objective test for dishonesty – the defendant's state of mind and not his conduct – 'was to be judged according to the standards set down by the jury, rather than his or her own subjective estimation of his or her conduct' (Goldspink and Cole 2002: 151).

The 1982 *Ghosh* case concerned a locum hospital consultant who tried to persuade a patient to hand over money for himself and an anaesthetist for a private abortion. His defence was that they were legitimate fees; he was convicted, with the trial judge directing the jury that they were to set the standards of honesty, and that having heard the evidence they had to consider contemporary standards of honesty and dishonesty in the context of what they had heard (see Westlaw, accessed 22 February 2005). On appeal the court laid down two tests for dishonesty. The first is the objective test – 'whether according to the ordinary standards of reasonable and honest people what was done was dishonest.' If the jury decided that the answer was 'yes' then a second, subjective, test follows where it is for the jury to ascertain not just what they thought was dishonest but whether they also believed that the perpetrator would know that what he or she were doing would more than likely also be considered dishonest by others.

Appropriation used to mean that the property passed from the control of the owner to the person appropriating it. This raised issues about the point of transfer (for example, is it possible to be arrested for shoplifting in a store or must the offender actually leave the store and thus deliberately ignore the pay counters to be apprehended for theft?). In 1985 there was a case that involved switching price labels in a supermarket. It dealt with that issue by indicating that appropriation took place at the point of switching the labels. Thus the owner's rights – the price at which they wanted to sell the goods – were being interfered with even though the property – the goods – had not yet been appropriated, or taken from the owner, by the perpetrator actually paying the lower price or absconding without paying. Later cases confirmed the issue of a person's rights to a property as the basis of appropriation.

The other issue with appropriation concerns the absence or otherwise of the owner's consent; what if the owner appears to agree or, rather, not object to the transfer of control over his or her property, or does not know that the property is now within the possession of another? The 1972 case of a London taxi driver who helped himself to £6 from an Italian student's wallet on the grounds that the (50p) ride was more costly than the £1 the student offered, was based on the taxi driver's claim that the student had agreed to his taking the money. The House of Lords quashed the taxi driver's appeal on the grounds that consent was irrelevant, overruled by the issue of dishonesty (that is, the taxi driver knew that what he was doing was dishonest). Indeed this was confirmed in the 1993 case of *Gomez* (who got his electrical goods store manager to agree to his supplying goods to two accomplices by convincing the manager that their cheque was valid). In a later case of *Hinks* (2000) even a gift, given with the consent of the owner, may be seen as an appropriation if (and here the donor of a series of building society withdrawals totalling £60,000 was known to be mentally handicapped) the receiver knew it was wrong (i.e. dishonest) to accept such a gift (see Herring 2004: 469–476).

Property is classed as everything or anything – except (apart from a limited number of exclusions) land, and encompasses everything from plants to 'intangible' property (the Act itself applies dishonesty to abstracting electricity). The question of 'invisible' or 'intangible' property is important. For example, when a fraudster arranges the transfer of funds from one bank to another, the 'money' does not physically exist and also does not physically move. Indeed, any transfer (or payment of bills and so on) is simply a change of the record of ownership. The 'ownership' of property that has no physical entity is termed a 'thing in action' or 'chose in action'. It relates to the issue of ownership itself rather than to the object, or whatever, that is owned. It is 'a known legal expression used to describe all personal rights in property which can only be enforced against another person by an action in law and not by taking physical possession' (Phillips *et al.* 2001: 65–66).

This has had significant implications for bank or credit fraud (see below, p29). Generally 'things in action' include something of value, even if there is no physical existence (such as copyright or trademarks) but there are limitations to what may be classed as 'stolen.' Thus stealing advance notice of examination questions (taking the paper, reading it and returning it prior to the examination) is not theft and nor is (necessarily) stealing commercial data, such as client lists, for sale for gain to competitors (although, of course, other criminal, civil and disciplinary redress may be available).

'Belonging to another' refers to whoever has legitimate possession or control over the property, or having any right in, or an interest in, it. For example, this would apply to a garage owner repairing a car, who is owed money for repairs and finds the car taken away by the owner who is trying to avoid paying the bill; the garage owner has an interest in the car because he is owed money in relation to his work on it. It also explains why the Theft Act covers the abstraction of electricity by fixing the meter; the electricity is intangible and has no physical entity but the supplying company clearly has possession and rights over its supply.

Nevertheless the question of property and possession has caused confusion; one area concerned bank fraud – see the *Preddy* case, below p 29. Even where 'property' is understood, being deceived into handing it over to another does not necessarily mean that an offence may automatically follow. Whether or not a person may be accused of theft of that property may well depend on the basis on which the money, for example, is handed over. In the case of a travel agent, it is not an offence under the Theft Act if deposits are taken for a holiday and then lost if the agency goes out of business – the money is paid into the company accounts but not held for a particular purpose (*Hall* in 1973). On the other hand, the *McHugh* case (in 1993) held that theft of investment funds is clearly possible since that investment is for a particular purpose and should not be mixed in with general company or other accounts (see Westlaw, accessed 19.06.06).

An intention 'permanently to deprive' does not just mean the gain or benefit to the taker but refers to the fact that the owner loses their right to ownership of or control over their property. 'Permanent' is a relative term and taking and returning may not be theft although the 1978 Theft Act would cover such circumstances. The case of *R. v. Fernandes* (1996) made it plain that using other people's money as their own is an intention to permanently deprive. Fernandes was a sole solicitor convicted of theft and procuring the 'execution of a valuable security' by deception, and of two counts of theft. In financial difficulties, he raised a building society mortgage on his house but lost it on an investment. He then raised a much bigger mortgage, with false information on the application form, used some of it to repay the existing mortgage, and some of it on personal expenditure. He then used money from a client's account to invest in his book-keeper's firm of licensed backstreet money lenders. The money disappeared and this was one aspect of his appeal, on the grounds that he did not intend to deprive the owner of the money 'permanently.' The trial judge directed the jury that he could be regarded as having the requisite intention if he treated the money as his own to dispose of, regardless of the other's rights. On appeal, the court agreed with this, and added that 'a person in possession or control of another's property who, dishonestly and for his own purpose, deals with that property in such a manner that he knows he is risking its loss' is intentionally permanently depriving the owner under the meaning of the Act (see Westlaw, accessed 19.06.06).

Criminal law: deception

The deception offences[3] are contained in Sections 15 and 16 of the 1968 Act:

- obtaining property by deception;
- obtaining a pecuniary advantage by deception.

How deception is perceived in a legal context is shaped by a 1903 case involving London and Globe Insurance Corporation. The judge indicated that deceit involved inducing someone to believe that something was true when it was not, and the deceiver also knows it to be untrue.[4] Deceiving by falsehood induces a state of mind, and thus deception is using deceit to induce a course of action (e.g. handing over property to another). The two offences involve the following terminology: *'A person who by any deception dishonestly obtains property belonging to another, with the intention of permanently depriving the other of it.'*

The Sections add 'deception' to the components under Sections 1–6. The purpose relates to the word 'obtains.' The previous Sections 2–6 deal with appropriating – taking – while Section 15 is about persuading someone to give something by misrepresenting the reasons why they should hand over ownership, or what they might gain in return. For example, *R v. Lambie* in 1982 involved the defendant using a credit card knowing that it was over its limit. Thus by her silence she was inviting the shop member of staff to enter into a contract that would be binding on the credit card company, and inducing the shop to hand over the goods. The court held that the member of staff would not have continued the transaction if they had known the 'true position'. For deception to be the basis of an offence, the person deceived is 'genuinely' deceived, and property changes hands without the true consent of the owner. Examples include (see Phillips *et al.* 2001):

- dressing as a student to obtain discount on books;
- ordering a meal (implying an ability to pay and seeking to evade liability for eating it);

- arranging for a council grant to benefit an elderly relative who subsequently dies but not notifying the council of this, as a consequence of which the grant-related work was still completed.

Section 16 makes it an offence to *'dishonestly obtains for himself or another any pecuniary advantage'* by deception. This would cover presenting false qualifications to obtain a job (or a higher grade) available only to candidates with appropriate qualifications – see Box 2.2 – or using a bogus credit card or cheque to obtain goods or services. Thus it would even cover payments by cheque when there is not enough money to cover the transaction, even though payment is guaranteed by the cheque card and paid by the bank to the company to whom the cheque had been given for the goods or services provided. The case that raised this issue was that of *Kovacs* in 1974. The defendant bought a train ticket and a Pekinese dog after the bank had told her she was overdrawn and couldn't use her chequebook. This raised the question of who was deceived by the cheque – the people asking for it in return for the dog and the ticket but who suffered no loss since the cheque was covered by the card, or the bank, who did suffer loss but were not deceived. Here the court decided that the person being deceived did not have to suffer any loss but that the bank did and, since the two events were related (between the deception used and the advantage gained), the person was convicted of obtaining an advantage by deception.

Criminal law: revisions to the law relating to theft and deception

The 1978 Act came into being as a consequence of the recommendations of the Criminal Law Revision Committee in their Thirteenth Report. The Committee was asked to look at Section 16 of the Theft Act 1968 (obtaining pecuniary advantages by deception) and suggested that the Section should be replaced with new provisions. It was felt that, in its existing form, the Section had given rise to serious problems of interpretation, such as in the situation where a debtor obtains, by deception, further time to pay a debt, then makes off without payment. There were also new areas where offences of deception needed to apply (see www.bopcris.ac.uk/bopall/ref19287.html)). The Act adds three new offences:

- obtaining services by deception;
- evasion of liability by deception;
- making off without payment.

Box 2.2   The CV

The chief executive of an NHS trust admitted yesterday that he landed the £115,000-a-year job by faking his CV. Neil Taylor claimed he had a first class degree from Nottingham University and produced a bogus degree certificate to support his application to run Shrewsbury and Telford Hospitals NHS Trust. In fact, he had only 'one or two' A-levels. Shrewsbury magistrates' court heard that he successfully ran Birmingham's Royal Orthopaedic Hospital and the Royal Shrewsbury Hospital, where he cut waiting lists and helped the hospital achieve the highest, three-star status.

When the RSH merged with the Princess Royal Hospital in Telford in October 2003 to form the new trust, Taylor was the unanimous choice to take the chief executive's post. But a salary review in April last year uncovered his lies. Taylor claimed he had a BA in business administration and economics, was a graduate of the Institute of Personnel Management and had a postgraduate diploma in forensic medicine, all from Nottingham.

John Snell, prosecuting, said: 'The authorities were pressing him to produce his degree certificate and qualifications. He took the line, "They are on my aged parents' wall." Taylor, 42, then produced a certificate but it was clear the logo was made up. He is thought to have taken a copy of the university's logo from the internet. Checks showed he had never studied there. Mr Snell said: 'The untruths he had told were that he was a graduate and he had a first-class degree, which he had not, and that he had a graduate diploma from the same university.' Magistrates were told that Taylor, from Solihull, West Midlands, had merely attended a two-day course in Nottingham to assess whether he could take the diploma. He could not have graduated from the Institute of Personnel Management because it does not exist. Mr Snell said the offences were very serious because of the amount of money Taylor had earned and because a truly qualified candidate was denied the post.

Taylor, who is married and has a child, admitted one charge of obtaining a pecuniary advantage by deception and one of attempting to commit the same offence. A charge of obtaining a pecuniary advantage by deception over his appointment as head of the RSH Trust in 1999 was dismissed.

Source: *Daily Telegraph*: filed 18 August 2005[5]

Not unnaturally, subsequent court cases pointed to further gaps in interpretation. In particular, the Court of Appeal decision in *R v. Halai* (1983) decided that the simple making of a mortgage loan could not amount to a service. This meant that the prosecution chose to deal with the 1995 *Preddy* case – which involved obtaining a mortgage advance on the basis of false information, with the money being electronically transferred from the banks to the solicitor organising the applications – under Section 15. The House of Lords decided that crediting a bank account did not amount to appropriating the property of another because nothing physically existed and nothing moved; the moment of transfer shifted one 'thing in action' to another 'thing in action' (i.e. the nature of the transfer altered the 'thing in action' rather than transferred property from one person to another). This meant that, although there were other remedies that the bank could use, a straightforward charge of theft was procedurally avoided: 'the lending institution's credit balance was a chose in action (the debt owed to the institution by the bank) which was *extinguished* and subsequently the defendant obtained something different, namely the chose in action constituted by the debt owed to him by his bank as represented by a credit in his own bank account. This asset was created for him and had therefore *never* belonged to anybody else. Thus the prosecution could not show that the borrower defendant had obtained property "belonging to another"' (Law Commission 1996: para 1.5).

This in turn led to Sections 1 and 2 of the Theft (Amendment) Act 1996 which closed the *Preddy* decision in relation to money transfers by inserting offences that clarify obtaining a money transfer by deception and dishonestly retaining a wrongful credit, as well as a Section which extends 'services' so that obtaining of services now includes another party being 'induced to make a loan, or to cause or permit a loan to be made, on the understanding that any payment (whether by way of interest or otherwise) will be or has been made in respect of the loan.' This also encompasses situations where banks or building societies are induced (persuaded or satisfied as to the eligibility of the applicant) to make a mortgage advance acting on false information contained in mortgage application forms.

Criminal law: forgery and misrepresentation

There are a range of other offences that reflect elements of deception or misrepresentation and which are worth noting. The 1981 Forgery and Counterfeiting Act covers forgery – the making of an instrument purporting to be that which it is not (a false instrument). A false instrument is any created document – these are 'formal' in the case of official documents such as a passport, or 'informal' in the case of cheques, as well as stamps and other items – which is 'used to induce someone to accept it as genuine' (and in accepting it, to do or not to do some act to his own or any other person's disadvantage). Here it is important to note that forgery is about the actual document and not about a genuine document containing lies. For example, a person who writes a CV in which they state they have more or better qualifications than they have is not committing a forgery but a deception (see above). A person who designs a diploma on his or her PC, and signs it with the signature of the principal of the college he or she allegedly attended, is producing a forgery (put another way, the CV contains lies but the diploma is a lie in itself). Section 2 of the Forgery and Counterfeiting Act 1981 creates the offence of copying a false instrument.

The area of product misrepresentation and deception – as opposed to that perpetrated by individuals or companies – is also written into a range of legislation, implicitly or explicitly, primarily with the intention of protecting the consumer's or public's interests. Most fall within the statutory responsibility of Trading Standards departments employed by local councils (by requiring the Inspector of Weights and Measures to enforce the terms of the Act). How many staff are employed is the responsibility of individual councils (there are about 2,300 in England and Wales). The profession is divided by qualification and responsibilities into Trading Standards Officers and Enforcement Officers whose professional interests are represented by the Trading Standards Institute; wider policy issues are addressed through LACROS (Local Authority Coordinators of Regulatory Services). Depending on the legislation, officers have rights of entry, inspection and copying of documents, inspection and seizure of goods, and to suspend provision of services or activities. The duty to enforce under the legislation[6] relates to the area of the local authority but the sanctions remain limited, which leads to joint working to pursue criminal conduct.

Corporate offences

Industry is covered by four main regulators – the Department of Trade and Industry (DTI), the Financial Services Authority (FSA), the Competition Commission (CC), and the Office of Fair Trading (OFT). The latter two primarily have responsibility for ensuring market conditions and honest practices although the legislation they work under – the 1998 Competition Act and the 2002 Enterprise Act

– does impinge on fraud or economic crime. The OFT also puts out fraud awareness information for consumers on its website. The 1968 Theft Act itself does specify a small number of false accounting and corporate offences. These include:

- false accounting (faking, altering, and hiding accounting documents);
- liability by company directors and others for deception committed in the name of a company (so long as it can be shown that the offences were committed by those in 'real authority' – or 'controlling' or 'directing' mind – within the company);
- false statements by company directors or others (e.g. faking the value of a company to ensure a good price for shares held by a director could cause that director to be charged under the Act, and also applies to any other director agreeing to such a course of action);
- destroying, defacing or concealing any document with a value for gain;
- procuring the execution of a valuable security for gain (for example, faking a letter of credit).

False accounting is concerned with the altering, falsifying or hiding of any account or document necessary to carry out the deception. Exactly what constitutes an account or a document is interpreted widely. It can include anything that provides the record of the action or transaction that would form part of any accounting process. Thus falsifying or altering a housing benefit application form or a home loan application form would fall within this Section. Even though by itself it would not be an accounting document, such a form could be used in any audit or reconciliation process. The document itself does not have to be produced; the omission of information required by a document could count as falsification, so long as the intention was dishonest. What counts as 'valuable security' may be any document that appears to indicate control over, or ownership of, or involving payment in relation to, property. This dates back to a 1964 case under the old Larceny Act 1916 which described a valuable security as *'a document imposing liability on the person defrauded, or someone at any rate other than the accused, to pay money or to perform any other obligation to the advantage of the defrauder, or some person whom the defrauder desires to benefit'*.

In relation to corporate fraud the aspects of other relevant legislation include:

- The 1985 Companies Act which deals with fraudulent trading (where it is an offence to be 'knowingly' involved in any business being run to defraud its creditors or the creditors of any other person, or for any fraudulent purpose), companies buying their own shares, and supporting others buying their shares;

- The 1986 Insolvency Act includes a number of offences mentioning fraudulent behaviour for company directors and others whose businesses are running out of money, including: the provision of false information to creditors; selling property obtained on credit; concealing, destroying or falsifying company documents; making any gift or transfer of, or any charge on, their property; obtaining credit without disclosing current circumstances; increasing the debt by gambling or by 'rash and hazardous speculation';

- A number of consumer protection laws. In addition to those noted above that are usually covered by Trading Standards departments, these include the Consumer Credit Act 1974 (provides for control of consumer credit and hire and provides certain safeguards to consumers who purchase goods and services on credit) and the Consumer Protection Act 1987 (which primarily deals with unsafe goods and allows for powers of seizure and forfeiture, and the powers to suspend the sale of suspected unsafe goods);

- The 1986 Company Director (Disqualification) Act which bans those who formerly have been responsible for: an insolvent company; are deemed unfit to manage a company; have been convicted of an offence involving setting up or running a company; or are in default of requirements on filing company information. Two specific grounds relating to fraud are concerned with fraudulent trading or fraud relating to actions as a liquidator, receiver or manager;

- The 1993 Criminal Justice Act which covers insider trading in terms of three offences – possession of inside information; encouraging others to trade on the basis of the information; disclosure of the information;

- The 2000 Financial Services and Markets Act (FSMA) now provides for a range of offences by business, including: market abuse (which includes insider trading); carrying out a 'regulated' activity (such as investment broker) without authorisation; falsely claiming to be authorised (or exempted from authorisation); promoting investments unless authorised; providing false information to auditors; providing false information to the market (market rigging);

- Cartels were prohibited by the 1998 Competition Act but in 2002 the civil provision was complemented by its criminalisation in the Enterprise Act. Cartels are agreements between businesses not to compete with each other. The agreement is usually secret, verbal and often informal and may cover: prices; output levels; discounts; credit terms; which customers they will supply; which areas they will supply; who should win a contract (bid rigging).

Other fraud offences

There are a number of public agencies whose legislation also contains responsibility for and powers relating to fraud and fraud-related offences. For example, the Rural Payments Agency is primarily responsible for the £2.2 billion spent on Common Agricultural Policy (CAP) and other schemes for which the complexity and range of subsidies for, and levies on, a range of products, activities, import/export schemes, and foods offer opportunities for both error and fraud (see Box 2.3 for an example of the latter; the Intervention Board was the Agency's predecessor) and for which the Agency has a number of scrutiny and investigative staff.

HMRC also has an interest in this area – movement of goods between countries within the EU to exploit VAT arrangements generates fraud worth over £2 billion annually (see NAO: 2004) – and the 1979 Customs and Excise Management Act contains a range of related offences. These include the impersonation, bribery and obstruction of a customs officer, or the making of untrue declarations in relation to goods. It also creates offences of counterfeiting, falsifying or altering documents while Section 72 specifically makes it an offence to be knowingly involved in the 'fraudulent' evasion of VAT; and Section 170 specifically mentions 'fraudulent' conduct in relation to handling goods, or avoiding paying duty on goods on which duty should be paid. There is a statutory offence of fraudulently evading the payment of VAT in the 1994 VAT Act.[7] There is a wider common law offence of cheating the revenue which is concerned with any form of fraudulent conduct which results in diverting money from the revenue and depriving the revenue of money to which it was entitled (and thus does not need deception as a necessary ingredient of the offence). The Inland Revenue (IR) also used the 'cheating the public revenue' common law offence where the offence does not have to be positive; it is possible to cheat by omission – failing to provide information, for example. The Inland Revenue used Theft Act offences or, under the 2000 Finance Act, the statutory offence of fraudulent evasion of income tax.

Box 2.3 Farming the waves

Most of the charges were in respect of claims between 1994 and 1996 under the Arable Area Payments Scheme, administered by the Ministry of Agriculture, Fisheries and Food (the Ministry); or the Fibre Flax Subsidy Scheme, administered by the Intervention Board Executive Agency (the Board). Joseph Bowden submitted claims or declarations under both schemes for harvested crops, which in part covered the same areas of land. In respect of fibre flax, he made declarations through different contractors covering areas of land that in part were the same. According to the grid references he included in his documentation, some of the areas of land claimed for were not on the UK mainland.

The Arable Area Payments scheme is the largest of the Common Agricultural Policy schemes operating in the United Kingdom. The total amount paid to around 40,000 farmers under the scheme in 2000–2001 was some £860 million. In any one year, the amount falsely claimed under the scheme by Mr Bowden amounted to some £40,000.

In addition the North Devon Swede Group, of which Joseph Bowden was the leading partner, submitted an ineligible claim for a grant under a European Union structural funds programme, the Objective 5b scheme, for encouraging business in rural areas. The claim involved a grant for building new premises, which Joseph Bowden had already rebuilt using the proceeds of an insurance claim following the destruction of a barn by fire. This charge was one of the three which were ordered to lie on the Court's file.

Source: NAO, 2002a

In relation to the payment and receipt of welfare benefits, the main pieces of legislation are the Social Security Administration Act 1992; the Social Security Administration Act 1997; and the Social Security Fraud Act 2001. The 1997 Act deals with the offence of dishonest representation for obtaining benefit (which includes statements and documentation; and failure to report, or allowing another to fail to report, changes in circumstances). The 2001 Social Security Fraud Act provides powers to improve the investigation of fraud (including the legal basis for exchange of information between government agencies) and enables more severe punishment for repeat offenders. These include: powers to obtain information about customers suspected of committing benefit fraud from their banks, building societies and other organisations; penalties for people convicted twice of a benefit offence; and penalties for employers who know that their employees are committing benefit fraud. The Department of Work and Pensions also uses: the Theft Act 1968; the Criminal Law Act 1977; the Criminal Justice Act 1987; the Accessories and Abettors Act 1961 (under which 'any person who aids, abets, counsels or procures the commission of an indictable offence[8] shall be guilty of an offence'); the Magistrates' Courts Act 1980; the Criminal Attempts Act 1981; and the Forgery and Counterfeiting Act 1981.

Conspiracy, attempts and incitement

There are both statutory and common law[9] offences relating to the planning of fraud (and other crimes). Incitement is encouraging or persuading others to commit a crime where the inciter knows that the offence is a crime, intends the person to commit the crime and where the person could commit the crime but does not necessarily do so (although there could be an issue about whether the inciter does so for dishonest purposes or to draw attention, for example, to poor controls). Planning crime alone or together is covered by two Acts.[10] The 1981 Criminal Attempts Act criminalises the intent to commit an offence (which, in so doing, goes beyond what the Act terms an act which is 'merely preparatory to the commission of the offence'). It is also an offence to attempt to do so, even when actually carrying out the offence would be impossible. The common law conspiracy to defraud concerns an agreement by two or more persons to dishonestly deprive someone of something which belongs to that person or in which they have rights, as well as a dishonest agreement between two or more persons to 'defraud' another by deceiving them into acting in a way contrary to his or her duty. There is also a statutory offence of conspiracy to commit other offences, such as deception, under Section 12 of the 1987 Criminal Justice Act, and that, rather than the more general common law conspiracy to defraud, is expected to be the basis of any charge (see Arlidge and Parry 1985: 2). It remains an offence to have an agreement to commit a crime even if the crime itself could turn out to be impossible to commit, so long as there was an agreement and that those involved knew that they were planning something that was an offence. Such conspiracies may take place without personal contact so long as there is a common plan, and it involves intending to commit an offence.

The common law offence is wider than the statutory offence in that planning to commit a crime becomes an offence in its own right, and does not require an agreement to commit a statutory offence as the intended outcome to justify a prosecution. For fraud the value of the common law offence is where the course of conduct pursued will not lead to a crime as defined by law, nor be a crime when committed by one person, and this is why commentators such as Kirk and Woodcock note its value to prosecutors. For example, in the 1975 case of *Scott v. The Metropolitan Police Commissioner*, Scott agreed with the employees of a cinema that, in return for payment, they would secretly remove films from the cinema so that he could copy them for the black market. This was clearly done without the consent of the cinema owners, and with the intention to defraud the owners of the copyright (their proprietal rights) to the film, so that, even though Scott returned the films (that is, there was no appropriation of property), it was held that, although there was no offence of theft in borrowing the films, there was still a conspiracy to defraud. The essence is an agreement (even if nothing is done in pursuit of the agreement). Repentance, lack of opportunity or failure are all immaterial although the fact that a person withdraws from an agreement may be used as mitigation in any subsequent court case.

Thus conspiracy to defraud remains a common law offence and has the advantage of being used to charge two or more people[11] with something that one person cannot be charged with as a statutory offence, and including: the unauthorised acquisition, disclosure or misuse of confidential information, which does not count as 'property' for the purposes of the law of theft; obtaining a service dishonestly but without deception – this includes obtaining a service by giving false information to a machine, which in law cannot be 'deceived' other than by provisions in certain specific legislation; 'fixing' an event on which bets have been placed; conduct on the part of an agent which is contrary to the interests of the agent's principal, where bribery cannot be proved; intentionally providing assistance towards the commission of a fraud which is not in fact committed (see www.cps.gov.uk: offences of dishonesty).

The Law Commission reforms

The fact that fraud is not defined in a single offence, nor addressed by a single piece of legislation, but is recognised as an area of growing criminality and financial loss, has meant that there have been attempts to review, revise and consolidate its legislative context. The Law Commission is the public body with a remit to review law where, for example, the passage of time, legislative amendments that tinker with major pieces of legislation, etc., suggest the need for more substantive legislative reform. The Law Commission has looked at fraud twice. In 1999 the need for reform was driven by:

> parliamentary debate on the Theft (Amendment) Act 1996 which prompted the government to indicate 'it would refer the issue of fraud' to the Commission; criticism from the judiciary in a 1994 Court of Appeal which stated that 'the law of theft [is] in urgent need of simplification and modernisation'; concerns that advances in modern technology meant that 'certain acts of dishonesty might not be effectively covered by the present legislation'; comments from the Jack Committee on Banking Services drawing attention to 'various acts of dishonesty which were not covered by the existing legislation'; the Lord Chancellor's claim that 'the ability to respond effectively to major fraud is of the highest priority to the government'; public concern that 'those responsible for major crimes in the commercial sphere have managed to avoid justice'; and a view that, 'even when fraud is detected, the present procedures are often cumbersome, and difficult to prosecute effectively (see Law Commission 1999: paras 1.2–1.4).

On this occasion, what was exercising the Commission was whether or not there should be a general offence of fraud, rather than continue to rely on essentially three aspects of criminal law – theft, deception, and conspiracy to defraud – and thus what should, or should not, be done about specific existing offences (1999: para 1.16). The Commission's view then was that a single fraud offence would not be welcome on the grounds that it would criminalise acceptable behaviour that 'factfinders' (including juries) could label as dishonest or fraudulent (1999: para 5.31). From this decision followed proposals from the Law Commission to tighten up and amend existing legislation.

This approach was overturned within three years when its next report decided that an offence of fraud *was* required (Law Commission 2002). The Commission noted in its 2000 Report that it was returning to the issue of definition because:

> In April 1998, the then Home Secretary asked the Law Commission as part of their programme of work on dishonesty, to examine the law on fraud, and in particular to consider whether it: is readily comprehensible to juries; is adequate for effective prosecution; is fair to potential defendants; meets the need of developing

technology including electronic means of transfer; and to make recommendations to improve the law in these respects with all due expedition. In making these recommendations to consider whether a general offence of fraud would improve the criminal law. (2000: para 1.1)

This time, and on the basis that 'the inexhaustible ingenuity of fraudsters' and 'the bewildering variety of methods they employ' may lead to some frauds being difficult or impossible to prosecute for any offence other than conspiracy to defraud, and 'where no conspiracy can be proved, it may be difficult or impossible to prosecute at all', the Law Commission decided that there should also be new offences to address conduct which:

(a) currently falls within conspiracy to defraud (if done in concert) but no other offence, *and*
(b) is thought sufficiently culpable to justify the imposition of criminal liability.

Arguing that the dishonesty test should not be the sole arbiter of criminal conduct, but nor should the law continue to be amended as previously proposed, the Commission proposed that:

the key to defining such an offence ought to be the ordinary (non-legal) usage of the word 'fraud'. At present, the criminality or otherwise of a fraudulent act depends whether it falls within one of a multitude of offences of varying degrees of specificity. The fact that it is fraudulent will not necessarily mean that it is an offence. Most non-lawyers would think this an extraordinary state of affairs. It was therefore a matter of simple common sense for the courts to recognise that 'fraud', in the ordinary sense of the word, was an objective which could not be pursued by two or more people in combination without infringing the criminal law (2000: para 7.5).

The test of 'fraud' would be that, first, the conduct in question would be regarded by factfinders as dishonest according to the *Ghosh* criteria and, secondly, that it is intended to, and does, cause actual financial loss to another. One key element would be misrepresentation:

We have therefore concluded that this form of the new offence should be defined in terms of misrepresentation rather than deception. For most practical purposes, however, the distinction is immaterial. The concept of fraudulent misrepresentation is well established in both the civil and criminal law. It may be defined as an assertion of a proposition which is untrue or misleading, either in the knowledge that it is untrue or misleading or being aware of the possibility that it might be.

There would also be:

two further kinds of 'secret' conduct, not involving misrepresentation, which can properly be described as fraud and should be sufficient for the new fraud offence. They are (a) non-disclosure (deception by omission), and (b) secret abuse of a position of trust (an abuse of an existing position of trust, even if there is no question of the victim's thereby being induced to act or omit to act).

Together with separate offences of obtaining services dishonestly, fraudulently trading, and offences relating to making, possessing and using the means to commit fraud, the new offences of fraud by misrepresentation (which could also apply in relation to a machine), failing to disclose information and abuse of trust[12] would require the abolition of all the deception offences under the Theft Acts 1968–1996, although conspiracy to defraud is currently reprieved. As the government stated in its 2004 consultation paper, it intended to leave the law on theft (and specialist legislation such as tax and benefits fraud) alone but pursue the Law Commission's proposal: 'the main proposal is for a general offence of fraud which can be committed in three different ways: by false representation, by wrongfully failing to disclose information, or by abuse of office. In each case the behaviour must be dishonest, and must aim at securing a gain for the defendant or a loss for another. But the gain does not actually have to take place,[13] as it does under the existing statutory offences, which would be repealed' (Home Office 2004a: 6). The Fraud Bill that should be on the statute books sometime in 2006 will simplify the offences of fraud and its definitions. Offences of possessing, making or supplying articles for use in fraud could also cover developing issues such as identity fraud. A side effect of the Bill will be that it will change recording methods under the National Crime Recording Standard (NCRS) rules. This will mean that, for the first time, the cost of fraud at all levels will be quantifiable in police statistics. This may have a greater effect than any other single measure on the investigation of fraud by the police, by providing the basis for appropriate resources being made available.

Summary

One of the drivers for law reform was not only the need for a definable statutory offence but also the increasing cost of fraud. The Law Commission's 1999 report noted that 'we are very conscious of the level of fraud, and this shows the importance of this review' and referred to two Institute of Chartered Accountants reports. One in 1998 concluded that 'business fraud is a growing problem that affects everyone both in the private and the public sectors … The cost to the country is huge in terms of those who have to pay for it and the loss of reputation as a safe place to do business' while another pointed out that in 1992 'losses of reported fraud totalled £8,500 million whereas the figures for reported burglaries totalled just under £500 million, retail crime £560 million and vehicle crime £700 million' (1999: para 1.9). The next chapter looks at the cost of fraud, how assessments of the cost of fraud are made and what impact fraud has on those affected by it.

Notes

1 This book deals primarily with England, Wales and Northern Ireland, whose legal and investigative procedures are similar. Scotland's legal environment is somewhat different (see Annex: Scotland).
2 Denis Clark is author of *The Investigation of Crime* (Butterworths, 2004).
3 The 1906 Prevention of Corruption Act also has a clause making it an offence 'If any person knowingly gives to any agent, or if any agent knowingly uses with intent to deceive his principal, any receipt, account, or other document in respect of which the principal is interested, and which contains any statement which is false or erroneous or defective in any material particular, and which to his knowledge is intended to mislead the principal.'
4 In the House of Lords appeal in the 1889 case of *Derry v. Peek* (involving the directors of the Plymouth, Devonport and District Tramways Co. Ltd and the wording of a shares issue), one of the Law Lords stated that, 'in order to sustain an action of deceit, there must be proof of fraud, and nothing short of that will suffice. Secondly, fraud is proved when it is shown that a false representation has been made (i) knowingly, or (ii) without belief in its truth, or (iii) recklessly, careless whether it be true or false. To prevent a false statement being fraudulent, there must, I think, always be an honest belief in its truth. And this probably covers the whole ground, for one who knowingly alleges that which is false obviously has no such belief. Thirdly, if fraud be proved, the motive of the person guilty of it is immaterial. It matters not that there was no intention to cheat or injure the person to whom the statement was made.'

5 The sentence was 12 months imprisonment, suspended for 2 years, and a fine (NHS CFSMS press release, 23 September 2005).

6 See the Trading Standards Institute's website (www.tradingstandards. gov.uk) for over 20 pieces of legislation they police (from the 1988 Educational Reform Act which restricts the ability to award degrees to certain authorisied bodies to the 2002 Copyright etc. and Trade Marks (offences and enforcement) Act which establishes a criminal offence to combat counterfeiting). The government is currently considering transferring powers to the proposed Consumer Trading and Standards Agency following the 2004 Hampton Report.

7 The offence under the Act includes 'knowingly concerned in' and 'taking of steps with a view to.' Both allow charges to be brought against those working in an enterprise with potential criminal intent, and being involved in work setting up the enterprise (see Finnerty 2005: 8/25).

8 All criminal offences currently fall into one of three categories. Summary offences which include most motoring offences and other relatively minor matters such as drunkenness, common assault and prostitution, are triable only in a magistrates' court. 'Either-way' offences, including theft, drugs offences and some involving violence against the person are triable by either a magistrates' court or by the Crown Court. Indictable-only offences, such as murder, rape and robbery, must be tried by the Crown Court (Auld 2001). The SOCA legislation took away the distinction between an arrestable and a serious arrestable offence which has meant that an arrest for an indictable offence (one that can be tried either-way or as an indictable-only offence) now widens the powers of the police to exercise certain of the more extensive powers under PACE, such as extended detention, the taking of intimate samples, delay in permitting access to legal advice, etc., at the start of an inquiry, irrespective of which court the case will actually be tried in.

9 Unwritten law developed through court decisions.

10 The Acts are two which deal with what are called 'inchoate' offences where the defendants have planned or are beginning a crime. Inchoate offences may loosely be termed 'conduct' offences as opposed to 'result' offences (see Goldspink and Cole 2002: 198).

11 This could effectively mean trying one person if at least two are named but one could be deceased or be unavailable, having fled abroad. A company could also be charged as a co-conspirator to prove a 'guiding' or 'controlling' mind.

12 This brings the criminal law closer to the legal rules relating to civil fraud cases which cover common law fraud – an action for deceit or fraudulent misrepresentation – and equitable fraud (a breach of fiduciary duty): see Goldspink and Cole 2002: 79.

13 Hence the wording of the Bill which discusses the 'intention' by the perpetrator to make a gain for himself or another, or to cause loss to another or to expose another to a risk of loss.

Chapter 3

The cost of fraud

One obvious problem with having no single definition of fraud is that there is no single source for the number of fraud cases and the cost of fraud. With numerous pieces of legislation focusing on specific offences, and with a number of agencies reporting on 'fraud', there are no clear figures on the definition, type, volume and value of fraud. Part of the problem of determining losses through fraud is a consequence of how the figures are calculated and recorded; a further consequence is that evidence of the impact of fraud is both diffuse and specific. This chapter looks, firstly, at the cost of fraud and, secondly, at its impact.

The official statistics

Statistics reveal various issues: most (48 per cent) reported fraud involves cheque and credit card fraud; at 6 per cent of all recorded crime, fraud is, in volume terms, an insignificant proportion of overall crime statistics; what is reported by agencies illustrates the number of agencies involved in fraud work; the volume of fraud cases (apart from cheque and credit card fraud) are not handled by the police; the value of fraud cases varies according to definitions and methodologies used, and also varies according to the source. Of particular importance is the issue of the volume of fraud in terms of recorded offences for the Home Office statistics. Under the old and new counting rules the volume of recorded frauds has remained relatively constant in the decade from 1991 (around 200,000 under the old rules and between 300,000 and 350,000 under the new rules). Up to the end of 2005, the estimated total number of crimes in England and Wales was around 11 million; the recorded crimes were 5,500,000. Of these (emphasis added):

1,171,000 related to criminal damage;
1,057,000 related to violence against the person;
714,000 related to vehicles (taking, and stealing from);
653,000 were burglaries;
254,000 were fraud and forgery offences;[1]
155,000 related to drugs;
71,000 related to robbery (with force);
69,000 were classed as 'other' (from rioting and other public order offences, to race crimes, blackmail, dangerous driving, indecent exposure, etc.);
62,000 were sexual offences.

Even allowing for the volume of cases, fraud does not itself fall into an obvious category, ranging from the high-volume, low-cost crime of card fraud or welfare fraud to multi-million pound high-yield investment fraud. Even though fraud accounts for more offences than some other crimes, the public and political concerns over the nature of the numerically smaller categories, such as sex crimes or drugs, means that fraud has not received significant police resources, been the subject of media campaigns, or (until recently) attracted the attention of governments. Further, what the Home Office statistics do not cover are the number of fraud cases that fall outside their remit – which relates only to cases reported to, *and* recorded by, the police. Thus, the other agencies with prosecuting powers, such as the DWP, local authorities, HM Customs and Excise, and Inland Revenue, have not had their figures included (the DWP currently issues 26,000 prosecutions, financial penalties and cautions). The Home Office statistics also do not cover the values (monies lost or at risk from being lost) of the cases of reported fraud.

The first overview of the cost of fraud

The first contemporary cross-sector snapshot of the cost of fraud was the 2000 report prepared for the Home Office and the Serious Fraud Office by the National Economic Research Associates (NERA 2000). It listed the value of fraud for a range of public and private sector agencies – see Table 3.1.

Table 3.1 The cost of fraud

Agency	Number of cases	£ million	
		Low estimate	High estimate
Home Office police statistics	312,151	No data	No data
SFO	94	512	1,281
DWP/Local authorities	1.5 million	2,000	3,000
Civil service	580	3	–
Audit Commission/			
Local authorities	638	10.8	–
NHS	–	4.7	6.0
HMCE	–	885	2,500
IR	–	1.8	19.4
ABI/Insurance	430,000	645	650
Financial fraud (cheque, credit card and other frauds)	–	221.7	–
Retail fraud	393,000	147.2	–
		4,431.2	7,838.1

Source: NERA 2000

Overall, the report stated that discovered and undiscovered fraud could each range from £5 billion–£9 billion, giving an overall upper range of some £18 billion. It also included in the figures staffing and other costs associated with prevention, detection, investigation and prosecution which it assessed at: criminal justice system costs, £500 million; public sector organisation costs, £521 million; private sector organisation costs, £114 million.

The moving totals

The NERA figures were collated from material published by various agencies in both public and private sectors, with no review of the methodology used or the robustness of the data. This leads both to revision and variation. To take one example, the NERA study assessed the estimated cost of Inland Revenue fraud at between £1.8 and £19.4 million, using figures from IR Intelligence and Special Compliance Office (SCO) activities, and SCO estimates. In its 2003 study, the

NAO stated that between 1998–99 and 2001–02 the Office 'recovered £1.4 billion in tax, interest and penalties.' The issue here is what is fraud and what is not. The IR did not calculate fraud loss because of the 'absence of any measure of the difference between 100 per cent compliance and actual compliance (the 'tax gap'), and the proportion of this that is explained by tax fraud' (NAO 2003b: 15). The IR argued that even for the totality of what could be owed it would be unrealistic to establish a meaningful single aggregate estimate of the 'tax gap' because:

- no independent baseline exists to assess the level of income or profits that should be declared and the level of tax due;
- there are no known reliable and practical methods to assess the scale of unknown activity within the shadow economy and its effect on the tax gap;
- there are no known reliable and practical methods to assess the scale of income and assets concealed by known taxpayers.' (NAO 2003b: 15)

The NERA study, furthermore, overlooked the value of frauds dealt with by the police and the police's costs in investigating the cases (but not the SFO). Yet the minimum value for even the smallest fraud reported by any UK fraud squad in the 1998 and 2000 surveys on behalf of the National Working Group on Fraud was £40,000.[2] Further the survey put the total value of cases handled by police fraud squads at between £3–4 billion, spread over some 2,000 cases, investigated at that time by around 700–800 officers. Clearly, then, it is important to ensure a comprehensive overview.

Organisations are now spending more time and effort refining figures which either suggest that fraud is increasing or that the original NERA figures were under-estimates. For example, the APACS 2004 card fraud figures are now broken down by category, and are more specific in terms of value – almost a doubling since the figures produced by NERA four years earlier. The total of over £504 million contrasts with the £189 million recorded in 2000 by the NERA report. This is reflected in a review of fraud figures and values by the Home Office's Research, Development and Statistics Directorate Measuring Crime Programme (Wojciechowski *et al.* 2001/2002) which both converges with and diverges from the NERA figures. These, as well as those recently published by various institutions such as the NAO, and by the 2006 Fraud Review, are noted in Table 3.2.

Table 3.2 Moving millions?

Agency	Number of cases		[£Million]					
	NERA (2000)	Home Office (2001/02)	Law Commission (1999)	NERA – low (2000)	NERA – high (2000)	Home Office (2001/02)	NAO and other sources	2006 Fraud Review
Home Office police statistics	312,151	317,399	–	–	–	–	–	–
SFO	94	70	–	512	1,281	1,630	2,006	2,000
DWP	1.5 million	402,000	1,400	2,000	3,000	2,095	2,000	900
Civil service	580	539	–	3	–	2	–	–
Local authorities	638	1,600	–	10.8	–	10	–	–
NHS	–	300	70–100	4.7	6.0	6	–	79
HMCE	–	–	–	885	2,500	6,400	4,000 at risk	HMRC – 4,870 to 5,650 (VAT and Excise only)
Inland Revenue	–	–	–	1.8	19.4	1.8	At least 1,400 at risk	–
ABI/Insurance	430,000	430,000	30	645	650	645	–	–
Financial fraud (cheque, credit card and other frauds)	–	567,718	122	221.7	–	372	504	–
Retail fraud	393,000	–	560	147.2	–	171	–	–

New methodologies for old

Any attempt to assess the true cost of fraud will continue to be hindered by the various reporting sources and the criteria they use. Thus, activities that fraud squads report as fraud may, when reported by detectives, be classed differently because both the detectives and the fraud squads are reporting under the same sections of the Theft Act, but interpreting the offender and offence differently. Methodological and interpretative confusion increases when reviews or data from other agencies are also involved. For example, the recent Audit Commission survey on the police reporting of crime in general concluded that: 'the results do, however, also indicate that 60 per cent of authorities and forces have not yet reached the Home Office good practice standard. In some cases, crime recording performance has deteriorated, without any improvement in management arrangements to address difficulties' (2004: 33). When the private sector seek to assess fraud levels, much of the figures are 'extrapolated' – calculated upwards on the basis of structured telephone and postal surveys but without any effective verification of the methodology or data sources underpinning the corporate guesstimate of losses.

Even different methodologies can throw up variations. Thus HM Customs and Excise's estimates of a growing level of spirits fraud, which formed part of the basis for a government proposal in the Pre-Budget Report 2003 to introduce 'tax' stamps on bottled spirits from 2006/07 turned out, as the Committee of Public Accounts reported, to be five times higher than the figures from the Scotch Whisky Association: 'using the methodologies of both Customs and the Scotch Whisky Association, the National Audit Office found that the resulting fraud estimates lay within a broad range of uncertainty. This work showed that Customs' estimate of spirits fraud in 2001–02 should be presented as falling between £330 million and £1,080 million. Scotch Whisky Association estimates fell within a range of £10 million to £260 million, though the Office of National Statistics did point to an error in its analysis of underlying data which could affect this estimate. The National Audit Office concluded that the underlying data used and the modelling undertaken by both Customs and the Scotch Whisky Association in estimating spirits fraud were defensible in their own terms. But neither method can be deemed reliable when they result in such widely different estimates' (Committee of Public Accounts 2004: 8).

Estimates of levels of fraud outside formal statistical or criminal justice recording categories may be even more susceptible to definition and interpretation. Thus the 1995 internal Benefits Agency assessment of levels of Housing Benefit fraud relied on the subjective judgements of DWP investigators in assessing the presence of fraud as 'established or strongly suspected' or 'possible' fraud. A review in the same year of Income Support and Unemployment Benefit widened the tests for fraud beyond 'confirmed fraud' to include four levels of suspicion of fraud: 'could be genuine'; mild suspicion 'but no proof'; strong suspicion but 'no proof'; 'certain that a fraudulent situation has been discovered but insufficient information to establish fraud.' The recent Robson Rhodes survey claimed that the levels of suggested fraud from 108 companies with a combined turnover of £500 billion was around 3–5 per cent (a figure not dissimilar to the findings in the NHS) but then extrapolated that to mean over £32 billion actual losses in the corporate sector.[3] While a more valid assumption may have been funds 'at risk', even a claim of losses to that level might prompt greater analytic work to drill down into what is clearly an expensive and recognised threat, which has a range of consequences.

The impact of fraud

Many public sector agencies now carry information and warnings about fraud (for example, see the ACPO website on fraud prevention – http://www.uk-fraud.info; the Metropolitan Police website – http://www.met.police.uk/fraudalert). Others (as in the case of DWP) run sustained advertising campaigns on the risk of being caught committing fraud, or (as in the case of the private sector) on the threat of a compromised credit card as a result of identity theft (as some banks and others did during 2005). The interesting point about this growth in information on fraud is that it parallels the continued growth in fraud, and organisations' wish or need to respond but within their own resources. The reason for the attention given to credit card fraud, for example, concerns the first impact – as the resources devoted to detection, investigation and prosecution decline (see p 105 for the police response to card fraud) so the likelihood of fraud increases.

From this issue comes the second impact – the threat posed to the trustworthiness and suitability of a ubiquitous product as the public find themselves more likely to be a victim of fraud. Losses through card fraud are a small percentage of turnover – both volume and value. Neither card issuers nor retailers want its use compromised – not so much in terms of losses (which fall on the company, rather than the cardholder since in most cases cardholders' losses are capped) than in public suspicion about possible adverse consequences of its use, including 'identity theft'.

The third impact relates to how far can or should an individual or organisation go to guard against fraud in normal commercial or financial relationships or, indeed, at what point could they identify when fraud might be a risk or a reality. As Croall notes:

> Some offences, such as the sale of short weight goods or abstracting small amounts of money from a large number of customers', investors', or clients' accounts, lead to small losses to individual victims. Victims may not be aware of any harm ... The *ambiguous legal and criminal status* of white-collar crimes is a further characteristic, which is also related to their treatment in the criminal justice process. In many offences, there is an apparent *lack of intent*, particularly where a diffusion of responsibility is involved, and where, although a regulation may be broken, the consequences of that violation, such as injury, is not intended. This means that the moral element so important to the definition of crime is absent. Victims' lack of awareness and the invisibility and complexity of offences makes them difficult to detect, and difficulties of attributing responsibility and obtaining evidence also make offences difficult to prosecute. (Croall 2001: 8, 9)

Here, as Levi argues, whether an action can be attributed to fraud, or even whether the victim (or investigators or prosecutors) can disengage risk, error or negligence from fraud becomes problematic: 'fraud does present some special problems, because it offers the possibility of inducing into the victim some erroneous interpretation of what has happened. The victim may believe that he or she has been unfortunate or has made a commercial misjudgment: capitalism, after all, is taking risks and profiting or losing by one's risk-taking. Victims may even remain unaware that they had lost money at all. How does a commodities investor or a member of Lloyd's know that the best risks have been siphoned off into the dealer's own account or the re-insurance channelled to a firm beneficially owned by the underwriter? This can happen whether or not the primary investors actually *lose* any capital: the result may be merely that they fail to make as much money as they would have done had they not been defrauded' (Levi 1987: 27–28).

This begs the question of how far anyone other than the investors themselves – *caveat emptor* – should be responsible for the consequences of their decisions and rely on their ability to invoke civil proceedings to secure restitution.[4] On the other hand, ensuring a level playing field in terms of information and awareness, instilling confidence in normal commercial relations, is something that government agencies and regulators, such as the OFT, the DTI and the FSA, seek to promote. This also has political implications where the public is being persuaded to invest money as official policy and might be entitled to expect a duty of supervision and the availability of a safety net on the part of the state. Thus, while government is not so interested in credit card fraud, it is aware of the need of some supervisory role to protect the integrity of the pensions marketplace, particularly after the Maxwell case debacle, and thus consumer trust, as well as provide cover when schemes collapse.

A fourth area of impact relates to business failure, although not all alleged frauds collapse a company and, even when they do have a detrimental effect, do not always mean the end of the business. As the Guinness case and others demonstrate, there is not always a direct relation (unlike some other impacts) between alleged fraud, business continuity and shareholder protection. In 2002, a number of former directors of Wickes, the DIY chain, were acquitted of fraudulent trading and making a false statement to auditors between January 1994 and June 1996 by introducing a two-letter scheme with wholesale suppliers. One letter stated the actual position with wholesale suppliers in terms of the fees they paid for guaranteed future sales. The other, intended for the auditors and prepared by someone in Wickes on suppliers' letterheads, allowed fees by suppliers to be classed as relating to past deals. Thus they could be included in the profit accounts for that year, rather than for future sales whereby they would have to be spread in the accounts over a number of years. The scheme was discovered by the auditors for one of the suppliers who was also the auditor for Wickes. One of the defendants – the former finance director – claimed that these 'were clearly accounting irregularities and inconsistent letters which resulted in the possible overstatement in the accounts', a concern confirmed by the others although no one was to be identified in the various trials as responsible for the arrangement. The acquittal of the last defendant, the former group buying director (whose QC stated in court that 'there is no dispute on behalf of Mr Rosenthal that the two-letter system existed and was used for several years within Wickes and between the company and its suppliers'), meant that none had 'been convicted although all accepted that there was a fraud' (*Daily Telegraph*, 27 June 2003).

However, fraud can and does lead to business failure – see Box 3.1.

Box 3.1   Fraud and jobs

Universal Bulk Handling was formed in 1958. In 1990 the company was acquired by, and became a wholly owned subsidiary of, Hadleigh Plc ('Hadleigh'), a firm based in Suffolk. In 1990 Christopher Freeman was appointed financial director of Universal Bulk Handling and in 1991 Alan Hodgkinson became its managing director. During the early 1990s the tank container industry generally experienced adverse trading conditions resulting from increased foreign competition and increased cost of raw materials. It is clear that Hadleigh were a demanding company and in order to present a more favourable financial picture of Universal Bulk Handling to the parent company, Freeman began to falsify the accounts. Consequently, both Freeman and Hodgkinson concealed the true position and state of affairs of the business from Hadleigh and from the auditors.

It was no doubt their intention to trade out of the difficulties eventually and to restore accuracy to the accounts. However, this was not achieved and the situation deteriorated from year to year. Eventually in early 1999, a worsening cash flow at Universal Bulk Handling caused Hadleigh to carry out a detailed investigation into the accounts and this in turn led to the discovery of the true state of the finances of its subsidiary. In the trading years from 1995 onwards, the accounts of Universal Bulk Handling showed an apparently profitable company making an average annual profit of some £2 million. When the true position was discovered it was clear that no profit was being made. Instead there was an overall discrepancy of not less than £11.5 million between what the accounts declared to be owing to the company and what in fact the company owed to both its suppliers and its customers. As a result of this discovery it was clear to Hadleigh that continued business at its subsidiary was untenable and it was placed into receivership causing the closure of the factory, the loss of 270 jobs and the demise of a number of creditors.

Source: SFO website (25 July 2003)[5]

The collapse of the Facia group threatened thousands of High Street jobs while the Barings case illustrates how a single fraud can collapse an international operation (see Fay 1996). In February 1995, a young stock-option trader, Nicholas Leeson, fled Singapore (and was arrested later in Frankfurt) for trading that left his employer, Barings PLC, the

UK's oldest merchant bank, with over $1 billion in losses. Leeson was later tried and jailed in Singapore for six years on charges of forging documentation and misleading the Singapore Exchange. The losses from high-risk futures dealing, including differential rates changes between Stock Exchanges, eventually reached $1.4 billion, and led, on discovery, to the bank's collapse, with investors losing their savings and over 1,000 employees losing their jobs. Barings was purchased by the Dutch bank/insurance company ING for the nominal sum of £1 (it no longer has a separate corporate existence but its name lives on in Baring Asset Management and Barings Trust).

Finally there are those who are victims of fraud (see Fraud Advisory Panel 2005) and those who are involved in fraud. It is relatively easy to see how the former react to fraud. Because victims have personal knowledge of the person, or some contact with the company defrauding them, they feel both shock as victim but also a sense of betrayal. Many have reacted like Scott Mead, the Goldman Sachs banker defrauded by Joyti De Laurey (see below, p 63) who claimed, 'She hasn't just violated my life once, but twice. Not only did she steal my money, but she took away all my privacy' (*Daily Telegraph*, 21 April 2004). In relation to accusations of benefit fraud, many claimants 'accepted the inevitability of prosecution [but] were still very upset by the process ... other respondents were also surprised and upset at the way they were treated. They were willing to admit that their activity had been illegal but they did not feel that it had been "criminal". They were angry at being treated in exactly the same way as "real criminals" such as murderers' (Rowlingson *et al.* 1997: 114, 116).

For those where innocence was an issue, both their sense of personal shock and their experiences of the investigative process were significant in terms of impact at an individual and occupational level. In 1992 Monty Don the media gardener went bankrupt after his design business failed. Signing on for unemployment benefit, he was called to the local benefits office for a fraud interview after the Benefits Agency had received an (erroneous) complaint that he was 'living off the state when he has a fortune in the bank.' Later Don said that the allegation 'blighted our lives for months, lost us nearly six months of benefits we were entitled to at a time when we were almost starving and, worst of all, sowed seeds of suspicion within a small community ...' (*Sunday Telegraph*, 11 August 1996). In 2004 the Inland Revenue offered compensation to Gordon Maynes whose house and bus company was raided in his absence over VAT some eight years earlier and records seized in what the Inland Revenue apparently admitted was a case subject to 'various faults, mishandling and delays.' In a report on the raid, Ernst & Young wrote that 'the officers used foul and abusive language and searched in a manner which left much disturbed.' They were also critical of the treatment of the Maynes' bookkeeper, an elderly lady whose home was visited by inspectors on three occasions without an appointment. Offered £3,000, the Maynes claimed legal and accountancy costs of over £34,000 and also argued that the company had lost up to £500,000 after their case was subsequently thrown out of court (*Sunday Telegraph*, 25 January 2004).

Summary

Fraud lacks a single definition; it also lacks a single impact or a single value. As noted by Leigh, it also remains in general an absorbable cost: a Barings or a Maxwell is the exception rather than the norm. Guinness is still drunk, Wickes is still a DIY store and the *Daily Mirror* still is widely read. In the public sector, the NAO may qualify the DWP's accounts in 2005 because of levels of fraud but that does not impact on benefits paid. Hardly any public sector institution or activity has been stopped because of fraud (although some – such as the Individual Learning Account (ILA) scheme – have collapsed: see below, p 66). On the other hand, the cost of fraud appears to be on the rise, raising the question of just how widespread is fraud; who commits fraud and how, but also who commits fraud and why – the subjects of the next two chapters.

Notes

1 Of the eight categories under which fraud cases are recorded, 'other' accounts for over 50 per cent of cases. Cheque and credit card fraud accounts for most of the other 50 per cent. In 2004/05, forgery involved over 10,000 cases; vehicle/driver document fraud involved nearly 5,500 cases. Frauds by company directors involved 50 cases; bankruptcy offences totaled 11 (Fraud Review Team 2006: 28).
2 Although this may be varied in specific circumstances, such as public sector corruption or voting fraud where the offence rather than the value becomes the basis for a decision to investigate.
3 On the other hand, to illustrate just how easy it is to extrapolate beyond robust methodologies, the Fraud Review Team (2006) quoted a 'most recent estimate of UK corporate fraud' as £72 billion. This figure was quoted in a report by a firm of London solicitors, Mishcon de Reya, who

used a US figure of corporate losses estimated at 6 per cent of GDP, to suggest equivalent UK losses. The US figures came from a membership organization, the Association of Certified Fraud Examiners, who based its figure of 6 per cent on reviews of 508 cases (30 per cent of which involved public sector and not-for-profit organizations) by its own members.

4   In October 2004, John Palmer, the architect of Britain's biggest time-share fraud, was ordered to pay £3.25 million into court to meet potential claims by 200 victims who were tricked into buying shares in holiday apartments in an action brought by them. Under recent High Court reforms, a party can be ordered to lodge money in court if he has failed to comply with a ruling. Irwin Mitchell, the claimants' solicitors, said that it was the first time that a defendant had been ordered to make a payment into court as security for damages. They had already obtained a default judgment against Palmer and explained that the court had acted because of his 'deliberate and flagrant' breaches of earlier orders relating to disclosure of assets (*Daily Telegraph,* filed 25 February 2004).

5   Freeman was sentenced to two years' imprisonment and disqualified from acting as a company director for 10 years. Hodgkinson was sentenced to nine months' imprisonment and disqualified from acting as a company director for five years. A number of staff who had been employed at Universal Bulk Handling submitted to the receiver a bid to buy the assets of the old business. The bid was accepted and the new business now trades as UBH International Ltd, albeit with a reduced workforce.

Chapter 4

Who commits fraud, and what types of fraud?

Introduction: who and what?

There are, somewhat obviously, no simple answers to the questions of who commits fraud, how or why, but there are many examples to consider that may offer possible explanations. This chapter is essentially descriptive. However, to try and bring some perspectives to the many different types of fraud, it studies those most commonly investigated by police fraud squads (reported in two surveys in 1998 and 2000). It then unpicks a number of cases in more detail where the information has been available to do this, to consider whether or not any common issues or themes emerge. The chapter provides the context for Chapter 5 which looks more closely at possible motives – why fraud is committed.

Cases investigated by the police

The only surveys of police fraud squad cases were undertaken in 1998 and in 2000 for the National Working Group on Fraud (Doig *et al.* 1998; Doig *et al.* 2000, unpublished; see summary in Doig *et al.* 2001). It asked fraud squads to list the distribution of types of cases by force and by volume (see Table 4.1); in this chapter a number of illustrative examples are given from some of the categories.

Table 4.1 Police fraud squad cases

Category	Cases	Number of UK forces with a case in the category (total response: 47)
Advanced fee/investment fraud	262	40
Deception	238	26
Bank/building society fraud	171	28
Company/fraudulent trading	149	32
Public sector fraud	104	24
Long firm fraud	93	23
Computer	92	17
Embezzlement	87	25
Corruption	66	30
Mortgage	56	24
Solicitor fraud	53	23
Forgery/counterfeiting	52	21
Offences under insolvency legislation	39	18
Factoring/leasing	23	18
Doctor/pharmacy fraud	20	12
Procurement	17	6

Source: Doig *et al.* (unpublished)

Types of fraud

Advance fee fraud   This is also known as 419 fraud, named after the Section in the Nigerian Criminal Code that specifically makes such a fraud an offence and, as such, has been identified as originating among Nigerian professional criminals. The basis of the fraud is a letter (or, today, an email) purporting to have identified the recipient as willing to help access monies that are locked up as, variously, surplus government funds, in bank accounts belonging to people with no traceable relatives, and so on, for which an overseas bank account is needed and for which the provider will receive a percentage of the millions of dollars to be transferred.

The purpose used to be to acquire bank account details in order to execute a fraud against the account, but increasingly this fraud is intended to coax facilitation fees and other expenses – the advance fee – from the victims with the expectation of a share of a large sum of money. This, essentially, and ignoring the '419' dimension, is the core of the fraud and it relies on the victims' expectations – the 'quick win', as one put it – and the ability of the fraudster to persuade the victim to hand over the fee (and this is often done face to face) in anticipation of the delivery of the larger amount (for an example, see the case of Steen (see p 73).

High-yield investment fraud is a similar offence, predicated on offering significant benefits in return for an initial advance or investment. It may differ from a 419 fraud in that it appears to suggest a spurious legitimacy to the activity; most 419 frauds invariably indicate that the funds are to be accessed illegally. High-yield investment fraud involves persuading people to part with their money for high-yield investments, often with an international dimension to explain away the absence of the central bank base rates and tax regimes that might make the returns seem unrealistic. Those with the international dimension also claim to explain the rates, to involve dealings in realistic-appearing but counterfeit international banking drafts, and take advantage of multiple jurisdictions to work successfully. They often appeal to those with substantial funds who think they have the financial acumen[1] to spot investment opportunities, especially when they think they are being allowed into some inside high-finance world (for an example, see the Salvation Army case below, p 70).

Bank/building society fraud It is self-evident that financial institutions are obvious targets for fraud, and this is not helped by the enthusiasm with which they compete to sell mortgages, loans and other financial services, their provision of services through third parties (such as supermarkets), and by their own use of telephone and web-based services. Fraud is prevalent, and obvious, ranging from applications for current accounts in order to establish a financial profile for frauds elsewhere, to mortgage fraud. Most frauds depend on false application details that bypass appropriate application, surety and vetting procedures intended to confirm the eligibility of the applicant and the likely security of repayment. Invariably, collusive support from employees can be a central part of such frauds, whether it is knowing the on-screen score-card points system for telephone loans or ensuring the paperwork is processed (see example 4.1).

Fraudulent trading This involves operating a company in breach of various pieces of company legislation and in particular continuing to profit from a company when knowing the company cannot pay its creditors (see example 4.2).

Example 4.1   Defrauding a bank

Philip Ashley was jailed for a total of two and a half years at Leeds Crown Court today after pleading guilty to his part in a fraud perpetrated against United Mizrahi Bank. He was a client of the bank and conspired with bank employees to defraud the bank through dishonest loan applications, the purpose of which was to avoid the bank's rules on lending limits. Loans were obtained totalling £3.7 million; almost twice the limit permitted by the bank's own rules. The sentence for that offence was two years. He received an additional sentence of six months to run consecutively for contempt of court in relation to breach of bail conditions; namely residence and travel restrictions.

Philip Martin Ashley was a property entrepreneur. He was a client of the London branch of United Mizrahi Bank ('UMB'), an Israeli bank with a head office in Tel Aviv. All his dealings were with the London office, in particular with senior bank employees John Doherty and Rafael Kellner. His relationship with the bank revolved around loan facilities. UMB had internal rules on the limits set on loans, requiring referral to Tel Aviv for approval to lend a client more than £2 million and evidence that suitable security was in place to cover the exposure. Between May 1994 and December 1995 Ashley conspired with Doherty and Kellner to circumvent the bank's lending rules. Loans amounting to more than £3.7 million were structured in such a way by the two bank employees that the aggregate lending limit appeared not to have been exceeded. These loans were made to shell companies that appeared to have no connection with Ashley but were in reality controlled by him. Because the lending was masked in this way it did not come under the scrutiny of Tel Aviv.

For their part in the conspiracy, Doherty and Kellner received money from Ashley. For example, in one loan transaction of £1.1 million, a sum of £65,000 was paid into an account held at Credit Suisse in Zurich for their benefit. Though Ashley made some repayments to UMB, by December 1995 when he and his companies were declared bankrupt, loans amounting to £3 million remained outstanding and to date, the bank has still not recovered £2 million of the debt.

Source: Serious Fraud Office press archive website, 22 January 2003[2] (www.sfo.gov.uk)

Example 4.2 Fraudulent trading

Two brothers who plundered their company's stock before it went into liquidation have been sent to prison for 12 months each following a DTI prosecution. Darren Robin Young, 35, and Robin Gary Young, 41, of Hungerford, Berkshire took over as directors of Evencray Ltd, a company selling white goods to large retail stores and the public, when their father retired from the business.

The company ran into financial difficulties and ceased trading in May 2002. The company's debts at the time of liquidation were £199,237. During the course of the winding-up procedure it was discovered that the brothers had stolen money from the company while failing to pay their debts, and had carried on making sales when the company should have ceased trading.

Both brothers pleaded guilty to two separate offences of theft at Peterborough Magistrates Court, admitting stealing £29,500 between them. Both said that they had been stealing independently of each other. Since the liquidation of the company Darren Young has repaid the money stolen to the liquidator. The DTI has instigated confiscation proceedings against Gary Young to recover the money he has stolen.

Evencray Ltd was incorporated on 29 December 1980 and went into creditors voluntary liquidation on 15 May 2003. The investigation into the actions of the Young Brothers commenced following a report by the company liquidator to the Insolvency Service. They were convicted on 19 May 2004 in the Peterborough Magistrates Court on two offences of Theft contrary to S1 Theft Act 1968.

Source: DTI website, filed 28 April 2005 (www.dti.gov.uk)

Public sector fraud This involves the misuse of position or official resources for personal use. The discretionary powers available to councillors and officials, the position of councils as large contractors of services, and the availability of funds from a variety of sources to promote economic and social regeneration, often with private and non-profit sector partners, does provide a range of opportunities for personal gain, corruption and fraud (see example 4.3).

Example 4.3 Public sector fraud

A former Labour councillor who spent money from an anti-poverty charity on prostitutes, drinks and lavish meals was jailed for three years yesterday by a judge who demanded that the 'cancer of local government corruption' be rubbed out.

Garvin Reed betrayed every principle of the National Local Government Forum Against Poverty to swindle £172,000, in a systematic fraud with the group's national co-ordinator, Bob Bone. Reed, 54, a long-serving councillor in Rotherham, South Yorkshire, admitted stealing the money to put up friends, relatives and political associates at luxury hotels. Research funds intended to alleviate poverty in the former coalfields were diverted to a 'stable' of prostitutes. Sheffield crown court heard that meetings of the group were arranged to coincide with race meetings and football matches, with tickets provided from the stolen funds.

Judge Patrick Robertshaw said that the operation, the ramifications of which are still being investigated by police, was evil, corrupt and deeply damaging to local democracy. 'This was not dishonesty to relieve some urgent financial necessity,' he told Reed. 'It was greed, pure and simple. With breathtaking hypocrisy, you lived a lavish lifestyle.' Judge Robertshaw sentenced Bone, 47, of Wakefield, to two years' jail and ordered Reed's driver and personal assistant John Cook, 54, of Rotherham, to do 220 hours community service for conspiracy to defraud.

The three-day trial heard that Reed's deceit came to light during interviews with other women after the murder of a prostitute in Hull. One, Jayne Frangopulo, described a 'sugar daddy who had something to do with politics' and eventually named Reed. Detectives found that the former deputy council leader had toured the country pretending to be a millionaire between 1996 and 1998. Fake travel claims disguised the spree in the accounts of the Forum, which was launched in 1993 and paid for by subscriptions from local councils across the country.

Source: *The Guardian*, 26 November 2002

Long firm fraud (or LF) has a long history (Levi 1981), often favoured by professional criminals (the Krays and the Richardsons, leaders of two 1960s London gangs, all worked this fraud). Essentially it involves setting up the façade of, or buying into, a legitimate commercial company, developing lines of credit with suppliers until such time as

Example 4.4   Long firm fraud

Dennis Michael Cook and his associate Paul Leslie Lester operated a classic long firm fraud, based in Worcester between 1995 and 1997. They obtained over £1 million worth of goods from over 50 suppliers before the scheme was stopped. Cook operated with three trading names: Megatoys International, Central Meat Trading Company, and Boss Commodity Contracts. Each of these businesses was purported to be involved in a market trade in commodities purchased from suppliers and Cook used them to build up the confidence of suppliers and banks. Then, between May and December 1996, Cook and his associates used the businesses to obtain goods that they had no intention of paying for. Several bank accounts were opened with five separate High Street banks so no single account manager had a clear picture of the business activity.

One of the main deceptions practised on suppliers, to induce them to supply or persuade them to wait for payment, was to produce bogus VAT returns for a rebate of more than £200,000 worth of VAT allegedly paid on goods exported to the Ukraine. Other deceptions, often used in combination, were as follows:

- Post-dated cheques which were stopped.
- Promises of payment which were not kept.
- Promises that payment would be made when the Customs & Excise paid large VAT refunds to the businesses.
- Assurances that the businesses were financially sound. These assurances were supported by falsified accounts and trading forecasts that were provided to suppliers.
- Falsely claiming that a freezer had broken down, ruining the contents supplied, and seeking to defer payment until an insurance claim had been processed.
- Claiming that goods supplied were faulty when they were not.

Cook and Lester were charged with an offence of conspiracy to defraud the creditors. Cook was additionally charged with two offences of fraudulently evading VAT. In July 2000 Cook was convicted of both offences and sentenced to five years' imprisonment. Lester was also convicted and sentenced to 21 months imprisonment. A third defendant was acquitted. In February 2001 the Crown Court ordered the confiscation of the

> assessed proceeds of £1.3 million which Cook was ordered to
> pay, or serve an additional five years' imprisonment in default.

Source: ACPO website (Fraud Reduction website, published by
the National Working Group on Fraud on behalf of the UK
Association of Chief Police Officers (ACPO) – www.uk-fraud.
info.

those running the fraud think they can order sufficient goods to sell
on, without then paying for them, as well as not paying VAT, tax, etc.
(see example 4.4).

Computer-based fraud illustrates some of the advantages and
disadvantages of computers: the facility they provide to do business
but also the difficulties of detection and investigation. The growing
use of the Internet to do business leaves payers vulnerable to fraud as
pre-payment, cross-border jurisdictions and lack of personal contact
increase the risk. One fraud that is on the increase is the boiler-
room fraud – net-based bogus share-dealing schemes – carried out
in foreign countries whose financial regulators and law enforcement
agencies tend to ignore such schemes as long as they do not target
their own nationals (see example 4.5).

Example 4.5   Computer-based fraud

Robert Damon-Aspen was sentenced to two and a half years'
imprisonment after pleading guilty to 81 offences of deception
and nine offences of forgery. Through his business, CFT Group
Insurance Services based in Canary Wharf, he advertised on the
internet as an insurance intermediary. His advertising focused
on small IT companies that needed professional indemnity
insurance cover. Applicants completed on-line application forms.
Around 5,000 applicants paid about £1.3 million in premiums.
However, the defendant did not place any insurance contracts;
instead he forged insurance certificates. Administrative errors
in his dealings with clients prompted some of them to contact
Lloyds of London which then notified the regulator, the Financial
Services Authority. The case was referred to the SFO and a
criminal investigation began in November 2001. In February
2004 Damon-Aspen was charged. On 3 September 2004, before
his trial began, he pleaded guilty.

Source: Serious Fraud Office Annual Report, 2004/05.

Case studies in fraud

The following cases[3] look in more depth at the contextual circumstances that may give some insights into how the frauds occurred. The case studies make no claim to be representative of particular types and themes relating to fraud. On the other hand, they go beyond the brief descriptions in the media to explore in more detail the who and how of frauds.

Private sector insider fraud

In 1998 Joyti De Laurey went to work as a PA for Jennifer Moses at Goldman Sachs, the investment banking and securities firm that expects 'our people to maintain high ethical standards in everything they do, both in their work for the firm and in their personal lives.' De Laurey, however, was more interested in the cash-rich lifestyle of those around her and, when Moses left to become an independent consultant and wanted to take the efficient and hardworking PA with her, De Laurey declined. Moses then recommended De Laurey to another long-serving Goldman Sachs manager – Scott Mead. De Laurey, whose mother was a GP and whose ex-Royal Navy husband was working as a chauffeur, never earned more than £37,200 at Goldman Sachs (she also owed £24,000 and was the subject of a strict creditors' agreement order after the failure of a sandwich bar she had run with her husband, until she used stolen money to pay off her debts).

As a partner in the firm, Mead was said to have received around $50 million when Goldman Sachs went public in 1999 and, as head of Goldman Sachs's media and telecoms corporate finance team, to have been paid up to $20 million annually in salary and bonuses in his peak earning years. He received a request in 2001 to make a donation to his old university (Harvard) and asked De Laurey to get his account statements from an account he held in New York. When De Laurey kept failing to produce the statements, he ordered them himself. He found a significant discrepancy between the amount he had thought was in the account and what he found – which included one transfer out of over £2 million to a person named Schahhou. Goldman Sachs soon ascertained that this was De Laurey's mother's name and notified the police; De Laurey was arrested with air tickets to Cyprus in her possession. Her husband was also arrested on grounds of handling stolen goods and money laundering (assisting in the retention of the proceeds of criminal conduct); her mother was also charged with money laundering.

The investigation was to claim that De Laurey had started stealing from Moses (over £1 million) and, by the time she began on Mead's account, had developed an organised system (the prosecution case was helped by SFO-prepared graphics that demonstrated the organised and planned flow of the stolen assets) to use forged and genuine signatures sent by fax to 'authorise' transfers of over £3 million. She was able to do this because, with their busy lives, her employers often asked her to undertake similar, legitimate activities for them and gave her full access to their account details. De Laurey spent the money on cars (Saab convertible, VW Golf, Chrysler Voyager, Aston Martin), Cartier jewellery, a powerboat and property in Cyprus and England. She was charged with a range of offences including using a false instrument under the 1981 Forgery and Counterfeiting Act, and obtaining a money transfer by deception. She was found guilty of all but one of the offences and sentenced to seven years in prison (her husband was sentenced for 18 months and her mother received a six months' suspended sentence).

The defence case centred on De Laurey's claim that she had 'permission' to help herself as thanks for her efforts but was unusual because of the presence of counsel for the firm and its staff oversee their interests. This may not be surprising, given any issues that could arise about monitoring account transactions, possible adverse media comment about staff not checking their accounts sufficiently regularly to notice missing millions and, of course, allegations about Mead's private life. Joyti's defence was that she organised everything for her bosses, from children's parties to holidays, and told by them to help herself to as much money as she wanted, as a 'reward for being me.' For Mead, she alleged she went further, lying to his colleagues and his wife at his request about meetings with his mistress. The judge dismissed her defence as from someone for whom 'lying was woven into the fabric of your being'.

Public sector insider fraud

The film plans for a comedy entitled *The Laird* stalled in 1999 after two years' discussion between Mel Smith as director and Phoenix Pictures. (There was the small issue of a convicted person whose life was to be the subject of the film benefiting from his crime.) The life was that of a Surrey-based public official, Anthony Williams, who in 1986 fell for the Banffshire village of Tomintoul, a few miles from the Glenlivet distillery. First buying a rundown cottage (on which he spent over £200,000), he went on to buy and refurbish a large number of properties, including the Gordon Arms hotel on which he spent an estimated £1.5 million.

Another £500,000 was spent on the nearby Clockhouse restaurant. In the village he was known as the Lord: 'the villagers believed that Lord and Lady Williams were landed aristocracy. The couple played the part perfectly and were invited to open a church sale of work. Williams bought fishing rights on the River Avon and the couple, who visited the village about once a month, arrived by Jaguar XJS or Land Rover Discovery with personalised number plates' (*The Times*, 20 May 1995). In all, he was supposed to have spent over £3 million on the village (which was later transferred at a loss by the police to his unsuspecting business partner). Apart from his purchases in the village, there were also purchases of property in London – including a four-bedroom house complete with bluebell wood in Haslemere – and Spain, as well as £60,000 for an ancient title (the barony of Chirnside). He was caught 'by a Scottish bank that was struck by the scale of property refurbishment expenditure by the man who publicly paraded about the Highlands as the "Laird of Tomintoul". Ironically, the bank reported its suspicions to the police under the terms of the Drugs Trafficking Offences Act' (*Finance Director*, 4 November 1999). In August 1994 he was arrested, and admitted to 19 charges of theft and asked for 535 similar offences to be taken into account. He was jailed for seven and a half years in May 1995.

The problem was that Williams had been the Deputy Director of Finance for the Metropolitan Police. In 1986, while working in the Finance Department, he was asked to take on responsibility for ordering and dispersing funds for informant and covert work relating to terrorist activities; the initial tranche of money was said to be to run a Cessna light aircraft to watch suspected IRA terrorists. The plane, based at a Surrey airfield, was registered in the name of a London company to disguise its true ownership. Williams was the cut-out inside the organisation, with all the details in his head. He was never asked to account for the requests for funds drawn from central funds (over £7.4 million in six years, of which he stole over £5 million), nor where he held the funds for disbursement, and nor on what the money was spent. Operational officers never complained to their superiors because Williams made sure their requests were funded.

Such was the organisation's faith in Williams (he was not the sole signatory but his was the essential signatory for any disbursement) that when he moved jobs, his request to take responsibility for the fund with him was happily granted. Williams – who apparently stole £6,000 on his first day managing the account – said: 'It felt as easy for me to write one of their cheques as it was to write one of my own … it was so easy. Nobody was watching me. It sounds bad if I say that it was easy because that suggests I'm pointing the finger at somebody else. I'm not. I did it. Nobody else. Just me. I discovered this bloody great bucketful of money. I went from the need to pay off a few debts to what can only be described as greed. There are no excuses' (*The Times*, 20 May 1995).

Public sector fraud

Widening access to education, and encouraging skills training among the young and the unemployed, has been a policy which both Conservative and Labour governments have pursued, particularly in the further eduction (FE) or vocational education areas. The FE sector was itself subject to reforms during the 1980s and early 1990s with the freeing-up of colleges from local council control and the encouragement of enterprise and maximum use of their resources. At the same time, successive governments have sought to bring education and training to the non-traditional and young unemployed markets through various schemes. In line with the 1980s Conservative governments' enthusiasm for encouraging competition among a range of public services, the preferred funding regime for non-traditional and young persons' provision has been based on the purchaser–provider split. FE would offer courses to students whose fees would come through a range of funding agencies and arrangements, despite concerns over documentation, self-certification and the quality (and existence) of courses (NAO 1989; Committee of Public Accounts 1994b; NAO 1995a). The budget for this area is around £8 billion.

In 1997 the Labour party issued a manifesto that promised education as a central policy objective, with an emphasis on lifelong learning and widening the participation in education for non-traditional learners, especially in the core skills of literacy, numeracy and IT skills. Part of the process to overcome any financial barriers would be the introduction of Individual Learning Accounts (ILA) through (to use its current name) the Department for Education and Skills (DfES). This would use a process that owed its design to a New Labour faith in the Thatcherite purchaser–provider split. The ILA was thus essentially a consumer-driven scheme, whereby anyone who opened an ILA could 'buy' a course with a fee of £250. The government would reimburse the holder with a subsidy of £200; it would support the provider where the fees exceeded the ILA holder amount. The presence of large numbers of ILA holders would stimulate the provision of courses (the learning providers) who would act competitively to ensure a quality service.

The scheme was to be tested in 1999, and opened to the public in 2000. By 2002, there were 1 million ILA holders on what was, the Department claimed, a successful 'light-touch, non-bureaucratic programme' spoilt by a 'minority of unscrupulous learning providers acting against the ethos of the programme.' In 2002 the programme was precipitately closed by the Department with subsequent fraud losses doubling the £100 million legitimately spent by genuine ILA holders.

Interestingly, the ILA concept had been dismissed by the preceding Conservative government who had looked to loans and tax relief to stimulate non-traditional learning. Nevertheless, the incoming Labour government had promised in its manifesto that it would take £150 million from existing Training and Enterprise Council (TEC) resources to encourage a million people to acquire skills for the labour market. Anyone willing to put up a small amount of their own money (£50) would get the government contribution (£200) paid into an account. In the initial trial run, the ILAs were handled by TECs but there were concerns that people would not save the necessary investment and that financial institutions were not keen to set up accounts for the £200 payment.

The alternative to keep the scheme going was the equivalent of a voucher system. A person would register with a body designated by the government to become the ILA holder. If that person then signed up for a course, the amount they would pay would be discounted by the government to reduce the person's cost to £50, and the learning provider would then reclaim the 'balance' between the individual's contribution and the cost of the course (within defined limits and for stipulated subjects) directly from the designated body. In other words, the potential for four frauds was now being introduced: genuine or non-existent persons registered but not attending courses so fees could be claimed; non-existent courses; non-eligible courses; eligible courses with inflated fees. Further, the system allowing people to sign up with a learning provider claiming to be an ILA holder was committing the government to paying up the balance retrospectively (and thus uncapped both in terms of the likely number of ILA holders and the overall cost of the fees). Fraud was not discussed, and nor did the Department respond to concerns expressed in 2000 about the potential for abuse, or about the absence of any quality assurance.

The DfES retained policy control over the scheme. In 2000 it appointed Capita (the only company to bid for the work) as the designated body with whom people would register. Capita would be responsible for signing up and running the ILA holders' accounts, calculating the fees and informing the DfES what to pay the provider, operating through a dedicated call centre. The contract was for five years and worth £55 million. The enabling legislation – the Learning and Skills Act – came into force in July 2000. ILAs were activated from October 2000 and by May 2001 1 million accounts were opened. Despite later criticism, Capita was not tasked with checking the eligibility of ILA holders, the genuineness of providers, the courses being offered by the learning providers (either whether they existed or were eligible), the validity of the fees being charged. Its role was essentially the administration of the registration of holders and providers, and providing information about the former to trigger payments to the latter.

As the numbers of ILA holders and the level of expenditure climbed, the Department were congratulating themselves that both were indicators of success. From a September 2000 base of 100,000 ILA holders, and 2,200 learning providers, within a year these figures had grown to nearly 2.4 million holders, nearly 8,500 providers, and over £180 million in expenditure (finally reaching £226 million). In the months up to October 2001, the Department were receiving an increasing number of complaints about account hijacking, mis-selling, aggressive marketing, unauthorised access to the system, poor courses and fraud.

The frauds were able to operate because:

- learning providers were given a user ID and a password that allowed them to access all ILA accounts. One fraud consisted of trawling accounts to see whose account had not used up its government contribution and placing claims against it;

- there were no software controls that, for example, monitored the number of students 'registered' with a learning provider;

- there were no checks as to whether a student attended or completed the course after first registration (and there was nothing in the provider agreements to say that a student had to finish a course);

- learning providers registered the learners – the ILA holders – onto the Capita website where staff simply checked the completion of the application forms;

- learning providers set up, bought and sold blocs of bogus account numbers among each other (in one case there were nearly 6,000 ILA holders within one post code);

- there were no checks on the learning providers (the Department's own *learndirect* database was only a listing scheme);

- there were no checks on whether any learning was actually provided, nor on whether course costs (such as the provision of a CD-Rom for IT training) justified the fee charged, nor on whether the courses fell within the approved list (and skiing and body massage would not);

- there were no checks on applicants. Providers canvassed in the streets or cold-called people to set up ILAs, even providing the ILA holder with the money for their contribution;

- there were also no checks to verify the authenticity of applicants, nor to investigate the increasing use of bulk applications;

- the registration system did not differentiate between registrations generated through personalised application packs sent to specific individuals and bundles of non-personalised packs sent out to providers and others to promote demand (requests, real and bogus, to set up an ILA increasingly came through the providers as the scheme continued).

The Department finally reacted with a series of measures – setting up a Compliance Steering Group, deregistering providers, blocking the distribution of blank application forms, undertaking fraud work – during mid-2001. In September 2001 it suspended the registration of new providers and refused to accept completed non-personalised applications. None of these measures was sufficient to stop the frauds and, in October, just after the Department had learnt of a bulk sale of 1,000 registered but bogus accounts,[4] the scheme was closed (although initially the Department claimed it was a victim of its own success, with demand outstripping the available funding, with the issue of fraud relegated to 'concerns' of abuse in terms of 'low value, poor quality learning').

Inquiries by the Department's Special Investigations Unit and various police forces continued over the next few years. In 2002 this involved nine police forces, over 200 providers and some £5 million – the year the Commons Education and Skills Committee reported that the ILA 'was a disaster waiting to happen' (Select Committee on Education and Skills 2002: para 97). A further inquiry by the PAC noted that the Department now had 70 staff working on investigations, over 700 providers were the subject of inquiries, that the fraud losses were over £67 million and 60 people had been arrested. The Committee was tart about the Department: 'The Accounting Officer was frank in acknowledging the shortcomings of the scheme, and in regretting that they had occurred. He was however less able to assist the Committee in getting at the specific reasons why they had been allowed to occur' (Committee on Public Accounts 2003: para 3; see also NAO 2002b).

The final loss associated in the ILA scheme is now estimated at about £110 million with some 60 per cent of opened ILAs subject to or used for fraud. Large payments – running into millions of pounds – were paid to some bogus providers; both ethnic organised crime and animal extremist groups were alleged to have exploited the scheme. By February 2004 the Department had formally referred 108 cases, where fraud or other criminal activity had been involved, to the police who had made 91 arrests. This in turn resulted by the end of 2004 in charges being brought against 34 individuals (six had been convicted and 21 were awaiting court appearance). By 2005 14 police forces continued active investigations involving 37 officers, 100 cases and losses of some £63 million. The Department itself claims that it is continuing to investigate complaints made against providers although staff have been moved and the current resource devoted to the original ILA fraud is small. The Department is still seeking the recovery of any payments made on accounts that do not comply with the rules for the programme. As a result of complaints to the Parliamentary Ombudsman, the Department is also compensating ILA holders who incurred further costs after their accounts were hijacked, as well as providers whose income was hit by the sudden closure of the scheme. The full cost of the fraud is not yet known. A variant of the scheme was reintroduced in 2005.[5]

Voluntary sector fraud

In April 1997 a self-styled financial adviser, Stuart Ford, was acquitted after a second jury failed to reach a decision on his involvement in a scheme to defraud the Salvation Army of £6.6 million. The High Court had previously ruled that Ford had no defence against the charity's claim that he took £2.2 million but, after the juries failed to agree on a verdict, the CPS said it was not prepared to hold a third trial. Judge Gerald Butler, QC, stated he had no choice but to acquit Ford, 'saying he regretted that the Scottish legal system did not apply. "In their jurisdiction the judge asks the jury if they find the defendant guilty or not guilty or if the case is not proven. If we had a not proven verdict here it might assist in a case of this kind. The Scots as here and in many other cases are so much more sensible"' (*Daily Telegraph*, 17 April 1997).

The case revolved around raising money for a major housing initiative by the Salvation Army in 1993 to refurbish derelict houses for London's homeless. They needed to raise about £35 million and to do so, decided to invest some £6.6 million of their capital in the alleged trade in various banking documents. There are a number of these; some are fraudulent and some are not. The genuine ones include banker's drafts or the equivalent, a common document is a standby Letter of Credit (LOC). Bogus documents include Prime Bank Instruments or Guarantees (usually termed PBIs) which are purported to be LOCs or bank drafts that circulate between the world's major banks to support each other in terms of liquidity or other requirements under various banking jurisdictions. Such documents are claimed to be traded in great secrecy among a chosen group trusted by the banks, and rely on their apparent ability to 'mimic legitimate financial instruments and transactions. They draw credibility from reference to such transactions. Inevitably, however, they involve a distortion of these legitimate financial vehicles either by falsifying them or intermingling their characteristics in a manner that distorts them. To successfully do so, they rely on ignorance or confusion regarding the true characteristics of these vehicles' (Byrne 2002: 16; see also Hyland 2005).

A Salvation Army officer, Grenville Burn, was introduced through a fellow officer to Ford who claimed to be able to invest funds through a banker with the Islamic PanAmerican Bank (IPB), based in South America and duly recorded in the banking reference book, the *Bankers' Almanac*. Ford was 'mandated' by Burn as a Salvation Army fundraiser on 2 per cent commission and began approaching banks for loans. After little success he convinced a Salvation Army investment committee that PBIs existed. The Salvation Army's Finance Board then agreed to hand over £6.6 million ($10 million) to invest in a 'secret' trading programme involving PBIs, with the help of the banker. Money was transferred to a Belgian bank where it was still under Salvation Army control through the signatories to the account. The Salvation Army was then persuaded to transfer the funds to a Luxembourg bank, to facilitate involvement in the programme, and to relinquish control over the new account. $200,000 was immediately remitted with the claim that this was the first profit from the programme. It was to be the last.

Burn, who had authorised the transfer to Luxembourg, firmly believed in the 'investment' and was reluctant to force his partners – Ford and senior IPB staff – to produce evidence both of the security of the Salvation Army funds and of the supposed traffic in PBIs. They in turn kept insisting that the trading programme could not be interrupted once the money had been invested. Mounting concern forced Burns's superiors to call in the fundraisers who now started to produce various documentation to prove the money was both safe and sensibly invested. These included 'Bank Guarantees' from a German bank, a PBI from ABN Ambro, an LOC from a Polish bank that did not exist, a proposed purchase of an LOC from the Islamic PanAmerican Bank, a false LOC from someone Ford bumped into in a Tokyo bar who had heard that the Salvation Army were looking for LOCs and happened to have one for sale for £1.67 million, a Certificate of Deposit from Arab-Gulf Finance House Corporation, based in Uruguay, whose President was also the Chair of the IPB, a forged LOC from a genuine bank, etc. Unconvinced, the Salvation Army called in their accountants and then a firm of solicitors, followed by the Charity Commission and then the police.

The money was, of course, no longer in the Luxembourg account, but scattered around the world through 13 countries and used for, among other purposes, the purchase of a profitable pub in Scotland (over which the Salvation Army later had a charge as a frozen asset), and properties in Malibu, Santa Monica and Hollywood.[6] Prosecuting counsel alleged that Ford's own financial position became precarious during 1992 when he owed more than £400,000 and faced being evicted from his office and home. Counsel was to allege that, as a consequence, he stole £800,000 of the Church's money to pay off his debts and to buy a new house and car. He allegedly also stole a further £400,000 to provide a loan to another client and kept £60,000 as his arrangement fee (see also Howson 2005).

Ford himself argued that he had, despite the absence of any qualifications or track record in investment, acted with the Salvation Army's best interests at heart, spending a significant amount of time and his own money seeking funds for them but had been duped by others. Later inquiries showed the main vehicles for the transactions were fronts, at least two of which were the subject of regulator attention in the USA. Despite his acquittal – the only person charged with any offence relating to the fraud – he 'was one of the parties to the civil action commenced by the army's solicitors, Slaughter and May. In December 1993, judgment was entered against him for $3.3 million. That judgment was subsequently upheld in a ruling by the

Court of Appeal' (*The Times*, 17 April 1997). The Salvation Army had also used Slaughter and May to begin recovery proceedings against the various banks and institutions holding the money or through whom it had passed. So successful were they in recovering the money, plus costs and interest, that the Salvation Army supposedly recovered £8.7 million (thereby generating a 30 per cent return on their initial investment).

Business fraud

During the late 1990s a number of quality newspapers around the world carried advertisements for loans drafted in a way that sought enquiries from those who may have had difficulties in obtaining them. The company involved – Corporate Advances, based in Brighton – 'assessed' completed applications as eligible (none were in fact rejected), conditional on a £6–7,000 administration fee, after which the application would be passed to Peninsula Holdings for a due diligence report. This company was run by a mortgage broker, George Steen, who was based in Darlington where he had been involved legitimately in second mortgages (which was how he met his co-conspirators) and who also owned property in the Philippines. Peninsula would issue an offer letter but indicate that it would cost applicants between £25–50,000 to undertake the due diligence. Once paid, this triggered off a 'commitment' letter and also another letter stating that, before payment could be made, a further check would have to be undertaken by a third company to see if the applicant satisfied the lender's security conditions. This requirement was referred to in the offer and commitment letters as essential for a loan to be made; the requirement in each case was that the applicant provide an 'assignable collateral bond' as security, to the value of 40 per cent of the loan. This had to be paid within 30 days, otherwise the loan and any previously paid fee would be lost. Essentially the fraud was an advance fee fraud, taking around £30,000 an applicant; Steen had some 400 files in his office when he was arrested.

The four arrests (one of the defendants later died) followed separate complaints in 1997 from Canada – a group of 49 aggrieved investors organised by Jeff White, one of the victims, who took out his own newspaper advertisement to trace fellow victims – and from victims in New Zealand to UK police forces and the SFO. Originally dismissed by the police as a contract dispute, the new complaints triggered inquiries by two forces (Durham and Sussex) and the SFO whose investigations suggested a complex, persistent, carefully orchestrated fraud. Arrests of the four suspects were undertaken in mid-1999. None of the companies or individuals had any evidence of lines of credit that would produce the loans on offer; all claimed an independent, professional relationship; any delays or apparent additional criteria could be passed off as the responsibility of another of the companies in the chain. Clients never went to Brighton or Darlington (where Steen had offices in a former bank but lived in an ex-council house) but were cossetted in the Grand Hotel in Brighton or the Dorchester in London.

The 400 files – including applicants from Chad and Ethiopia, an international aircraft business, and an African government parastatal company – were reduced to 50 potential (and most aggrieved) witnesses; 25 from the USA and Canada and 25 from Australia/New Zealand. These countries were chosen simply on the basis that they are English-speaking (thus saving on translation and other fees) and the relations with the relevant law enforcement agencies should be relatively easy (although the FBI insisted in chaperoning the Durham officers). The SFO introduced electronic scanning to catalogue and present key evidential documents that were put together by a former police officer hired by the SFO to manage disclosure. Some 30–40,000 pages of evidence were thus reduced to a couple of well-indexed, easy-to-search CDs. This meant that the documentation to be used in the overseas trips could be stored on laptops.

The charges were conspiracy to defraud, helped by the fact that the four defendants only dealt with the same set of applications. The SFO counsel, Richard Latham, constructed his opening around a notional loan application, taking the jury on a journey – using PowerPoint displays – from the time a victim first saw a press advertisement to the moment of realisation that they were never going to receive a loan. He used an example of every single document used by the defendants in real client transactions, creating what was, in effect, a 'master' transaction that revealed every twist and turn of the fraud's overall structure (see SFO, 2004).

The trial itself was beset by difficulties: problems were caused by two of the remaining defendants not giving evidence; it was necessary to timetable the appearance of witnesses flying in from abroad; the prosecution counsel was attacked in a pub and required dental treatment; and Steen disappeared after giving evidence when he realised that his denials had not convinced the jury. He took the cross-Channel ferry to France and then a plane to the Philippines, with which the UK had no extradition agreement. He achieved this using the spare passport the police belatedly discovered from the Passport

Office that he still had in his possession. He was extradited when his spare passport was voided at the request of the British Embassy in the Philippines. Steen then immediately became an 'undocumented foreign national' who, according to Philippine law, was eligible for immediate deportation.

According to the Philippines National Bureau of Investigations (NBI), Steen had significant resources in the country and a number of officials were later questioned about their links to him when he allegedly tried to get a complaint of fraud made against him in the Philippines. (The court case for this would take priority over extradition.) In the circumstances, the deportation order was granted and Steen was put on a flight (which he thought was returning to his home in the Philippines) to the UK on which he was greeted by two waiting British police officers.

In June 2003 George Steen, 54, was sentenced to six years' imprisonment. A further six months was added the next month for absconding. His co-conspirators – David Andrews, 39, and Dennis Alexander, 48 – received prison terms of five and two years respectively. In 2004 all three appealed against conviction and sentence but lost. The appeal was notable for one of the grounds being based on the disclosure that in the original trial the female foreman of the jury had sent a telephone number, bottle of champagne and a note to the prosecution counsel saying, 'What does a lady need to do to attract your attention?' All three had substantial confiscation orders made against them by the court in 2005.

Corporate sector fraud

Founded over 40 years ago, Blue Arrow is one of the UK's largest recruitment businesses providing specialist recruitment services in the office, industrial, catering, driving and construction industries. It operates through a network of 150 specialist sector branch locations, on-site staffing operations, and call centres. In January 1991, when it was beginning to grow, three City firms – County NatWest, the securities house, NatWest Investment Bank, its parent, and UBS Phillips & Drew Securities – were acquitted on charges of conspiracy to defraud. This related to a £837 million rights issue in 1987 for Blue Arrow to fund its intended takeover of the US employment firm, Manpower. The following month, suspended prison sentences were imposed on four former advisers from the three firms for conspiring to rig the stock market by not telling the truth about the issue; they worked to give the market the impression that the issue was successful by secretly acquiring the stock. The 1987 stock market crash showed up the deception.

In sentencing them, the judge told the court that the four men had committed the offence under entirely exceptional circumstances: 'It can only be regarded as a one-off offence committed in a situation involving great personal pressure, certainly overenthusiasm. It was not intended anyone would suffer loss, and certainly part of the reason for the decision was to help Blue Arrow and existing shareholders and not just the defendants' own companies and employees', he said. The conspirators took no steps to conceal or disguise their actions and the offence had not been committed for personal gain. Not one of the defendants had made one penny from the transaction (*The Times*, 31 January 1992). The judge said he would not be making any order against the defendants for costs, nor would he disqualify them from being directors in the future, or from running companies.

In July the convictions were overturned on both procedural grounds and because of the complex and detailed nature of the prosecution case. As the Appeal Court observed in relation to the trial (said to be the second longest criminal trial in the UK): 'The awesome time-scale of the trial, the multiplicity of issues, the distance between evidence, speeches and retirement and not least the two prolonged periods of absence by the jury (amounting to 126 days) could be regarded as combining to destroy a basic assumption. This assumption is that a jury determine guilt or innocence upon evidence which they are able as humans both to comprehend and remember, and upon which they have been addressed at a time when the parties can reasonably expect the speeches to make an impression upon the deliberation.'[7]

Blue Arrow is now part of the Corporate Services Group (CSG) Plc. CSG operates multiple specialist recruitment brands in the UK, USA, Australia and New Zealand. In September 2003, two former directors of CSG were convicted after an SFO investigation into the company's financial statements for 1997 which were prepared in such a way as to overstate the true extent of its profitability in the accounts that were published in 1998. In 1997, the overstatement amounted to just over £3 million. In 1998, the accounting irregularities came to light before the statements could be published; the potential overstatement of profit for 1998 was estimated to exceed at least £25 million (see Box 4.6).

The inflation was done by instructing company employees to make false and misleading entries in its books when accounting for PAYE, leasing, loan and other liabilities; to draw up fictitious sales invoices; and to reinstate invoices that had previously been written off. They

Box 4.6 Explaining what happened – the corporate language

(In) 1998, the Group [CSG] underwent a fundamental transformation from being an essentially domestic UK operation, which itself had grown very rapidly, to being an international operation with important market positions in the UK, France and the United States. This transformation came about through the Group making a number of major acquisitions, with the core companies in France and Corestaff in the United States being the most important ... By early 1999 it had become apparent that the Group's UK business systems were struggling to cope with the demands being placed on them. This was evidenced in the significant increase in the number of debtor days outstanding, and in working capital being sharply squeezed – all at a time when sales continued to increase. In addition, in March 1999, the Group announced that its profits for the year ended 31 December 1998 would be materially short of stock market expectations. This led to a loss of investor confidence and radical changes being made to the composition of the Board in early May at the behest of the Company's major institutional shareholders ... [I]t became apparent that in the preparation of the 1998 results, certain of the Group's accounting policies had been applied aggressively and in some cases that there had been material errors. Accordingly, an extensive review of the Group's results for 1997 was undertaken. That review identified a number of material irregularities, principally in the head office records. As previously reported, these errors were corrected in the results for the year ended 31 December 1998, which were announced on 30 June 1999.

Source: CSG 1999 Annual Report

were also responsible for disguising the true nature of a number of the company's acquisition agreements – concealing the debtors figure, allowing the company to boost its profits, and concealing the Training Division sale agreement. In 1998, it was also intended that a substantial amount of the company's UK costs should be charged to the books of a recently acquired American company.

Despite only a tenuous connection between corporate profits and directors' reputations, salaries and bonuses, the courts were less forgiving on this occasion. The two directors were each sentenced to three years and nine months' imprisonment and both disqualified from acting as company directors for eight years for accounting irregularities designed to overstate profits for 1997 and 1998.

Summary: the dynamics of fraud

Fraud, as the more detailed examples suggest, can occur in a City boardroom as well as in the terraced streets of Middlesbrough (one of the ILA fraud hotspots). It can also occur in new or novel contexts but, above all, there is an obvious interdependency between personal and contextual issues and the balance of the gain as opposed to risk, detection and sanction. Additionally, as the last case indicates, what might be seen as marginally criminal in one decade may, as attitudes and the compliance framework change, come to be seen as worthy of more serious sanction.

The examples in this chapter also confirm three points: fraud may occur in relation to any activity, it appears an entrenched and permanent activity, and it may take place deliberately or fortuitously. In other words, those setting out to be deliberately dishonest will find situations where money can be made; others find themselves in situations where the opportunity to take money presents itself. Some undertake fraud where the deception is for ends or purposes other than personal gain. Yet other frauds appear to depend on a balance of opportunity, incentive and risk. This in turn may also depend on necessity or ambition or even just how pleasant life can be with an untaxed additional income, particularly if perpetrators can persuade themselves that, in some way, they are not doing 'wrong', are entitled to the money or are able to justify their actions. The next chapter looks at motive in more detail.

Notes

1   One hypothesis suggested by a senior law enforcement figure is the attraction of being invited on to the *inside*, appearing to be able to profit from operating in a shadow financial world where the lucky invitees share the (legitimate) gains their entrance fee, risk-taking or connections offer them. This certainly would explain the gullibility of some invited to invest in high-yield investments, Prime Bank Instrument (PBI) frauds, 419 frauds and so on.
2   The SFO website also notes the position of Doherty and Kellner.
3   The following cases are drawn from official reports, police reports, law enforcement websites and interviews by the author.

4   Worth up to some £200,000 in potential fraudulent claims on the transfer market between providers.

5   The current major government activity threatened by fraud involves the £7.5 billion miners' compensation scheme set up by the government in 1999, involving 750,000 cases relating to miners who have suffered from chronic lung disease and vibration white finger. The DTI had agreements with hundreds of solicitors' firms who were to handle the claims and claim their costs directly from the scheme; the frauds range from claimant fraud (for example, on behalf of deceased miner's estates) or solicitor fraud, such as inflating fees which are paid retrospectively from the same fund (this latter loophole was closed in February 2006). Of particular concern has been law firms inflating their costs and handing over a proportion of the agreed claims to the miners they represent and retaining the rest. The fraud-related exposure is said to run at over £2 billion and is now subject to several inquiries.

6   In 1994, the *Observer* ran some stories which alleged that some of the money ended up with professional fraudsters and Mafia-linked businessmen.

7   Discussed as part of a 1994 speech by an Australian barrister in relation to complex trials (see www.cdpp.gov.au).

Chapter 5

From need to greed – why is fraud committed?

Is money the root of all fraud?

John Palmer, at the time of his arrest for timeshare fraud, was ranked 105th richest person in the UK according to the *Sunday Times* annual survey. Nick Leeson was a young inexperienced trader at Barings with an uneven financial background whose high-risk investments led to the collapse of Barings bank. Both cases raise a question. It may be understandable why a salaried employee gambles with his supportive employers' money because both they and he want to get rich. But why does an apparently rich man want to lead a timeshare fraud which, according to court estimates, might have made him a further 10 per cent of his existing assets?

And what about Colleen McCabe and Malcolm Bingley? The former was the ex-nun who became headmistress of St John Rigby College, London, a grant-maintained school, outside LEA control and funded directly by the DfES with an annual budget of around £3 million from which she stole up to £500,000 of school funds to pay for a lifestyle of foreign holidays, designer jewellery and expensive clothes. She claimed some of the money was for the pupils – 'I just wanted to make sure they had the best' – while her real problem was that 'I didn't concentrate on the finances perhaps as I should, that is my fault. At the end of the day a lot of it is whether you are liked by the jury.' Malcolm Bingley was the former gentleman's outfitter who had not worked for 17 years and who was later discovered to have £75,000 in a bank account, some of which he had spent on one of Concorde's final commercial flights while claiming £56.20 a week in benefits. He was convicted in 2005 of 10 counts of benefit fraud, after which he said: 'I was under the impression from the DWP that if I had been left the money in a will I could still claim Jobseekers' Allowance. The court's decision is very harsh. I have to pay back the full amount. I think everyone should be entitled to a holiday.' (*Daily Telegraph*, 19 October 2005).

Do any of these cases provide any grounds for commonality or comparison as to why fraud is an increasingly significant and integral issue in both public and private sectors? Did they set out deliberately to commit fraud or did the opportunity or circumstances tip them over? Did they see what they were doing as fraud? In other words, do people or organisations commit fraud for reasons as simple as the finding from a November 2004 KPMG survey of companies in Australia and New Zealand put it: that fraud is committed by 'a greedy 31-year-old man.'

The view from the surveys – who and why?

Fraud and honesty are regular subjects for study and analysis in public opinion surveys. Some of the surveys are undertaken by academic institutions for commercial clients or for research purposes, some by organisations trying to understand their market base or why organisations are the subject of fraud, while many are marketing their prevention and detection services, products and, sometimes, moral panic. The surveys range from one-off surveys, such as a 1995 *Moneywise* magazine survey (that suggested that younger people were likely to be more generally morally ambivalent about honesty), to regular reviews by the big accountancy firms, to more detailed academic research.

Academic research tends to fall into a number of areas: research contracted by commercial concerns trying to understand the nature of fraud (this has been common in relation to insurance fraud); research into areas of policy relevance that therefore attracts official funding (such as benefits fraud or cheque and credit card fraud); research into an area or activity where fraud is an integral feature (such as research into the shadow or informal economy); and research into wider social and cultural issues (such as perceptions of right and wrong). Overall, they suggest a very varied and dynamic landscape in terms of reasons for committing fraud.

Who commits fraud?

1. Practitioner surveys
The common types of practitioner survey are those carried out by

accountancy and management consultancy firms. In the examples below all but the Bank of Scotland are accountancy and management consultancy firms who regularly publish analyses of cases or the results of stratified sample telephone surveys[1] on a range of issues, primarily about the threat of fraud but also about the motivations for fraud.

KPMG: A 2004 KPMG study examined 100 fraud cases and found 'that many of the perpetrators were long serving employees – 32 per cent of them had been working for their companies for between 10 and 25 years. And they were not operating alone – in more than half of all the cases (51 per cent) two to five parties were involved in the fraud. In 72 per cent of cases, the fraudsters were found to be male-only. Female-only fraudsters were identified in 7 per cent of cases and both male and females were involved together in some 13 per cent of cases. In the remainder of cases, no perpetrator was identified. The age of the principal fraudster was typically between 36 and 45 (41 per cent of cases); 29 per cent of cases involved those aged between 46 and 55. Those aged between 18 to 25 made up only one per cent of perpetrators (KPMG press release, 26 April 2004).

PricewaterhouseCoopers: The 2005 telephone survey of 300 UK executive board members noted that 55 per cent of companies had suffered from fraud in the previous year, with an average loss of £1.2 million a case, and half the cases perpetrated by employees. 'The profile of the UK fraudster as male, on average aged between 31 and 40, and holding a position in middle management or below, was broadly consistent with the global results. Essentially there is little to distinguish the fraudsters from the average member of staff. Our own experience is that fraudsters tend to be surprisingly ordinary' (PricewaterhouseCoopers 2005: 4–5). The causes of fraud were lack of internal controls, and an expensive lifestyle; most knew that they were committing fraud.

Bank of Scotland: Losses due to theft or fraud by members of staff were a threat to one in four small businesses. Fraud was primarily carried out by employees and involved a wide range of dishonest practices, many of them in the 'petty' category. The problem grew with the size of the business: almost 20 per cent with fewer than 15 employees said they had suffered from fraud or theft but for companies with more than 36 staff the proportion more than doubled to 48 per cent (reported in the *Daily Telegraph*, 28 July 2003).

BDO Stoy Hayward: From an analysis of 209 cases, the most frequent type of fraud cases involved employees attempting to defraud their own employer (either alone or in collusion with customers or suppliers). Of the frauds reported for the first time in 2003, 84 per cent of the perpetrators were male. Frauds by men were typically for sums averaging three times the amount involved in those perpetrated by women. The median age of fraudsters was 44 years old for men and 41 years old for women (Press release, 14 June 2004).

McIntyre Hudson: A survey of owner-managed businesses reported that 38 per cent of such businesses saw fraud as the single biggest threat to the security of their business, compared to 36 per cent citing burglary. Among those worried about fraud, the biggest concern relates to the possibility of fraud by employees, with 27 per cent of owner-managers seeing a fraud committed by one of their own employees as the biggest threat to their business. Only 39 per cent of owner-managers ever checked for irregularities by undertaking on-the-spot checks. Just 26 per cent required cheques to have double signatories and only 11 per cent ever changed the staff who reconcile their bank accounts. While 82 per cent took up references for new staff, only 39 per cent checked the legitimacy of qualifications and only 34 per cent carried out criminal record checks (www.macintyrehudson.co.uk, August 2004).

The survey results must be seen in terms of sample size, the way fraud is measured and whether or not the information has general applicability as to why fraud is committed. Overall, the material suggests that fraud is a problem and it is more likely to be committed by mid-career, male employees, more probably in larger companies.[2]

2. Practitioner research-based perceptions

Business itself has tended not to study its own problems with fraud, possibly because it does not acknowledge there is a problem, or because senior management are not interested unless fraud demonstrably threatens reputation or profit, although there has been some limited assessment. One industry where this is belatedly changing is the insurance industry. Until the mid-1990s individual insurance companies were coming to grips with changing perceptions on the part of the public. Rather than the 'utmost good faith' mantra that traditionally regulated the relationships between insurance companies and those they insured, insurers found themselves treated as another profitable industry whose products and services were seen as an 'investment' to be drawn upon by legitimate policyholders who then decided, when the opportunity for making a claim occurred, to make a fraudulent or exaggerated claim. In 2003 the ABI noted from one of its surveys of 2,000 people that 7 per cent admitted having made a fraudulent claim, while 47 per cent said they had not done so but were tempted. An ABI spokesman said: 'People who commit insurance fraud tend to be university-educated homeowners, male and aged 35 or more – not the type of people you might perceive to be dishonest.' He added, 'Many people who were caught claimed "Everybody is doing it, why can't I?" They say insurance companies are awash with money and a few hundred pounds will not be missed' (*Daily Telegraph*, 1 November 2003).

Businesses also commit insurance fraud for the same reasons; a 2005 survey of commercial insurance fraud conducted by MORI on behalf of a number of insurers suggested losses of over £500 million to insurance firms, the majority of which came from the exaggeration of genuine incidents, followed by inventing a claim or providing false information on an application for insurance. Other frauds resulted from customers, suppliers and employees making claims against companies which were then passed on to insurers (these included a false personal injury claim from a member of the public or a false compensation claim made by an employee). The reasons for the frauds were: personal gain (18 per cent); companies believed that policies may not cover all the costs involved (34 per cent) and to claw back the money paid in premiums (31 per cent) (ABI 2005).

There has been some analysis of the crime statistics through the 2003 British Crime Survey and the 2003 Offending, Crime and Justice Survey; the former involved random interviews with over 18,000 people about their experience of and concerns about credit card fraud while the latter interviewed some 10,000 people on self-reported offending (see Allen *et al.* 2005). The younger the person, and the less likely they were to have educational qualifications, the greater the likelihood of card fraud (although only involving around 1 per cent of the sample). The second survey found:

Overall falsified work expenses and income tax evasion were the most common types of fraud, followed by false insurance claims. Benefit fraud was the least common. However the pattern changes when controlling for those who had the opportunity to commit these offences. Falsified work expenses is still the most prevalent, but insurance fraud increases to 5.1 per cent. The prevalence of income tax fraud among those eligible increases slightly to 2 per cent. Benefit fraud is still the lowest but the proportion increases from 0.5 per cent to 1.8 per cent. Again it should be noted that as many of the behaviours are rare it is difficult to detect significant differences in the prevalence of these behaviours between different groups (p 7).

Although in percentage terms the actual numbers were low, tax fraud is most likely to be committed by men, and by those with qualifications, with the self-employed more prone to tax fraud than employees. Falsifying work expenses is more likely to be committed by young men within a certain income band and young men on lower incomes are also prone to insurance fraud. More interesting was the link to the propensity to other types of crime such as theft, criminal damage, assaults and robbery, and drug offences:

Those who had committed a fraudulent offence were significantly more likely to have committed mainstream offences than other 18- to 65-year-olds. Fraudulent offending was particularly linked to theft offences, reflected in similar motivations. A sixth (16.1 per cent) of fraudsters also admitted committing a theft offence in the same period, 7.8 per cent violent offences, and 5.5 per cent drug offences. The lowest was for criminal damage at 2.3 per cent. Respective figures for those who had not committed a fraud offence are theft: 3.3 per cent, violence: 2.9 per cent; drug selling: 0.7 per cent; and criminal damage: 0.2 per cent (p 9).

Why do they commit fraud?

In 1997, Department of Social Security-funded research into benefits fraud noted that most claimants interviewed understood that benefit fraud was unlawful but did not see it as criminal. Indeed, working for cash was a consequence of the need for more money for the family, and seen as 'often the lesser of the two evils and that people who were desperate for money might otherwise turn to crime if they could not make extra money "on the side"' (Rowlingson *et al.* 1997: 39). Part of the process of justification also involved an assessment of the nature of the fraud: 'judgments about benefit fraud depended on five factors: the perceived motivation behind the activity in terms of need or greed; the scale of the activity in terms of the amount of money involved; the regularity or persistence of the activity; the degree of premeditation; and the degree to which other people might possibly suffer as a consequence' (Rowlinson *et al.* 1997: 40). More generally, the 2000 Grabiner Report on the informal economy suggested that:

... working in the informal economy brings the individual a real and immediate financial gain. Evading tax or NICs may raise people's take-home earnings, without pricing them out of the labour market: this is especially true for unskilled work. Working while claiming boosts the income of benefit recipients above social security rates. If not detected, people who behave in this way or facilitate this behaviour avoid the administrative burden of reporting earnings and the risk of losing the steady source of money from their benefit payment (Grabiner 2000: 12).

On the other hand, the Small Business Council, a DTI NDPB, issued a report in 2004 that suggested that 'it is not primarily "marginal" populations (e.g. the unemployed, people living in deprived areas) who engage in this work but those already in employment and residing in relatively affluent populations.' It categorised them as:

- The informal work of micro entrepreneurs, such as those starting up fledgling business ventures who use the informal economy as a short-term risk-taking strategy to test-out their enterprise and/or establish themselves (about a quarter of all informal work);

- The informal work of more established small businesses and self-employed people who use this sphere in an on-going and serial manner as a strategy for 'getting by';

- The informal work of 'favour providers' who conduct mostly casual one-off tasks as 'paid favours' for friends, family and acquaintances (about a quarter of all informal work). (Small Business Council 2004)

Levi (1994; see also Duffield and Grabosky 2001) has looked at such perspectives for corporate fraud, suggesting that power, the drive to control their lives and status, lavish lifestyles and the wish for social respectability all have a role, as does the belief that their approach to the world is one played by their rules (and something they cannot relinquish, even beyond the point where they need to). A 2005 report (Gill 2005) for Protiviti interviewed a number of convicted fraudsters which noted:

- Reasons for offending include debt and greed, boredom, a lack of life structure, blackmail and temporary insanity.

- Some interviewees claimed that a corrupt company/industry culture facilitated their offending. Some felt very poorly treated by their employers, either through low pay or inadequate rewards, but also because they felt unsupported.

- Committing offences was easy, there was little evidence of fraud prevention strategies, and there were easy opportunities not least because of weak financial or regulatory systems.

- Offenders abused the position of trust – which is not only associated with seniority – because it was that that gave them the autonomy and the lack of visibility to commit offences, and enabled them to feel they would not be detected.

- Most offenders had acquired all the knowledge and skills they needed via their normal course of employment.

- The audit function was rarely perceived as a threat, although it was responsible for identifying some frauds and contributed to the identification of some offenders.

- Whatever their initial reason for committing the offence, most continued because they enjoyed the benefits of having money.

A 2001 report by the Public Audit Forum (Public Audit Forum 2001) noted 'the presence of an overbearing individual as chief executive or chair of the board, or its equivalent, resulting in a bypassing or ignoring of controls or standards of propriety' (p 18). A later 2005 Audit Commission study (Audit Commission 2005a) more generally highlighted standards and behaviours 'which can be associated with failing services and/or fraudulent and corrupt practices. In most cases there were breaches of the ethical code of conduct by members and protocols by officers. Poor executive and non-executive relations were factors, together with examples of intimidation and bullying' (p 7). Other characteristics of those in authority included: arrogance; full of self importance; autocratic, dominant and dictatorial; unofficial deals to get own way; manipulative; reluctance to delegate; prone to secrecy; driven; engenders blame or fear; intimidates or bullies; workaholic; interferes in low-level operational matters.

Academic and other studies – is there a fraud type?

There is a limited amount of academic research on fraud, but often focusing on seriousness, prevalence and type of business fraud (see, for example, Barnes and Allen 1998; and Levi 1987: 57–75). The Barnes and Allen survey suggests that, while the reasons for fraud may relate primarily to the financial motivation of the fraudster and their ability to manipulate modern technology, the largest group of

87

perpetrators are those working alone within companies and would either be middle managers or non managerial employees. They suggest that 'middle managers have sufficient power to appreciate the full extent of a business transaction. They also know the workings of the checks and controls in the organisation – and their shortcomings! Middle managers also have the necessary personal power, influence and external contacts, if necessary, to effect the fraud' (Barnes and Allen 1998: 26). They also note that external fraudsters present a different picture, and often work with internal colluders, particularly with larger organisations that are more likely to have internal controls that only insiders know how to circumvent.

Two further areas where academic research has been undertaken into the possible reasons for fraud are insurance fraud and benefits fraud. In relation to the former, one survey argued that fraud against travel and household policies was 'commonplace', that people considered it 'permissible to submit inaccurate claims in some circumstances' and that they often did so because there was significant 'resentment against insurance companies on the part of legitimate and fraudulent claimants' and because they 'held a deep sense of grievance against insurance companies for what they viewed as unfair (and expensive) practices' (Gill *et al.* 1994: 80, 81). The benefits research is very much bound up in academic social policy with an emphasis on claimant perspectives. Research was conducted as part of an Economic and Social Research Council (ESRC)-funded project (see Dean and Melrose 1995: 17–18) into citizenship which noted three points from a limited sample:

- Claimants are not particularly knowledgeable about the system they are defrauding, but do so from economic necessity – which in turn maintains the pressure to continue frauds over and above the risk of being caught;

- Claimants do not see their frauds as wrong, in part because others commit similar types of fraud and because they do not see what they are doing as particularly dishonest;

- There is no one type of fraudster.

An extended discussion of the research also noted that, while undisclosed informal earnings was the main type of fraud (working while claiming), the survey respondents did not adhere to one type of fraud. Many did not plan their frauds, and their reasons for becoming involved with fraud revolved around four themes: 'deprivation and hardship; dependency and disempowerment; risk and vulnerability; justified disobedience' (Dean and Melrose 1996: 9). Later analysis of the same body of research argued that 'the predominant reason is that of economic necessity, of not obtaining sufficient income from benefits'; that 'claimants often felt more comfortable about fiddling because they believed it to be widespread'; 'claimants who fiddle will not easily be deterred from doing so ... low income was a bigger worry than the prospect of getting caught'; 'most claimants did not admit that fiddling was dishonest, or else they distinguished between fiddling (which they felt to be harmless) and more serious or organised forms of fraud (which they did not)' (Dean and Melrose 1997: 104, 105).

There is an extensive although (until recently) marginalised academic research on the shadow or informal economy. This has tended to divide into the sociological/anthropological perspectives (begun by Henry, Box, Mars and Ditton and others) which looks at individual and group dynamics in relation to cash economy or low-level occupational crime where the motivation often appears to be related to availability, pervasiveness of similar activities and attitudes, and perceptions of acceptability. For example, Copisarow and Barbour (2004) argued at the launch of their report that it 'challenges the general misconception of people working in the informal economy as "benefits cheats and tax dodgers".' These are 'people who use cash transactions to try to make ends meet and support their families. They want to advance into financial independence from the state, but frequently find the obstacles insuperable ... The informal economy is a highly complex issue without a simple solution.'

Such surveys form part of a wider 'perception' approach that has some interesting insights into dishonesty and potential dishonesty. Of interest has been the British Social Attitudes surveys (www.britsocat. com), with a focus on right and wrong. What is surprising from the surveys is less the variations by gender and age, or even the dynamics of social or occupational group, than the variations in perceptions of what is or is not honest, and the relationship between the person committing the offence and the person or organisation it is committed against.

In other words, what the survey found was that people's attitude to dishonest behaviour, and their willingness to become involved in it, depended on a range of perspectives – whether it was seen as 'right' or acceptable, or not, as opposed to whether or not it was legal (language was important for labelling conduct and what might be known to be illegal but was not seen as 'wrong', such as 'fiddling expenses'); whether the person was a private individual or whether they held a position where such conduct was not expected; and so on.

The nuances are important in building up a picture of what motivates people or how they view the acceptability of their own or others' conduct. For example, lying to avoid paying tax is more acceptable than lying to get benefits (around 70 per cent thought the former wrong or seriously wrong while some 94 per cent thought the same about the latter). It is seen as more wrong for a police officer to ask for a bribe than for a motorist to offer one (81 per cent as opposed to 58 per cent). Seventy-five per cent of respondents disapprove of tax avoidance but only 60 per cent would report it.

Here the British Social Attitudes 1984 survey findings (some of which have been updated) are instructive in pinning down suppositions about differentiated perception. The analysis (Johnston and Wood 1985) suggests that not only age, religion, gender and class but also the nature of the activity (paying cash, and so on) and whether or not it happens in the public or private sector, impact on people's perceptions. These, in turn, were also graded in terms of levels of 'wrongness', the amounts involved, familiarity with the activity involved, and whether the activity is precipitated by the person concerned or offered to him or her. In conclusion, the authors suggest that: 'in looking for explanations of censoriousness or tolerance, we do not find formal props, such as the legality or illegality of the action, very helpful … when laws or rules are known to be at odds with common practice … people in all subgroups tended to come down in favour of practice; or at least they did not judge breaches of the rules very harshly' (p 138).

How individuals move from being inducted to acting illegally may happen in a number of ways, although there is little research into the break points that commit people to act accordingly. Osse in her work with Dutch organised crime police discusses the inception of the possibility of deviant conduct – the free coffee or meal, the insidious development of a 'friendly' relationship with overtones of obligation, followed by the cognitive dissonance issue (see also Punch 1996: 242– 244). Here initial, and subsequent, deviant behaviour is increasingly subject to internal justification or mitigation before dissipating because the 'cognitive reduction process may distort the perceptions of situations in which one has to take the decisions' (Osse 1997). This only tells half the story; Gorta argues that the range of various justifications of dishonest conduct – denial of responsibility, or entitlement, as well as appeals to common practice or expectation, the 'right' to compensation and the tolerance of minor aberrations – has to be set in a context that asks whether the claim precedes the deviant behaviour or is used retrospectively (see Gorta 1995; Gorta and Forell 1998).

Perspectives: why do people and organisations commit fraud?

The simple answer here is that there is no simple answer and, while it would be easy to list a range of examples of fraud and unpick the reasons that that person or company may have committed fraud, for every such example or retrospective explanation, there will be another where fraud has not taken place. This, in terms of trying to explain why fraud is committed, takes us back to the point that Weisburd and Waring raised – 'situation plays a central role in explaining participation in crime for most offenders in the sample' – and those points Levi (and others) have noted about whether criminality is systematic or opportunist, whether those committing fraud 'specialise', and what are the impacts of external drivers and internal changes.

The limited evidence would suggest that there are professional fraudsters (corporate and individual) but there is also a much larger number of others whose activities can be denied or explained away or whose view of fraud is pragmatic (a plumber paying tax on work carried out during the working week but taking cash for weekend work) or subsumed within other justifications (such as need). Here explanations of why fraud is committed may lie in an (immeasurable) assumption that many people may be predisposed to commit fraud but do not do so because they have not the opportunity (the situation), nor the incentive (whether it be to get rich or to fit in with one's peers), or fear the consequences of being caught (from, for example, loss of employment to social stigma, or personal shame). Some may even have an innate sense of honesty, drawn from or sustained by religion, family, education or job satisfaction.

At the same time the issue of risk may change, while people's perceptions of what is accepted may be ahead of or behind the compliance framework which might take a more serious view of the conduct concerned. In other words, propensity may be influenced by the likelihood of investigation, what sanctions may be imposed and how far could their conduct be explained away. To try and look more closely at what is in fact a complex issue it is necessary to look at what may be termed organisational, ideological, cultural and compliance influences.

Organisational Influences

Do dominant organisational cultures shape or socialise their members? Do some cultures mitigate or enhance attitudes or conduct shaped by wider social trends? Do times of change and fragmented cultures impact on the morally ambivalent to act, or do the morally ambivalent feel more able to explain away or justify their actions during times of change? The 1991 Cadbury Committee talked of 'competitive pressures both on companies and on auditors', the Audit Commission warned in 1993 of a local government environment which had been 'rendered more demanding and complex by recent changes' while the Committee on Standards in Public Life said in 1995 that: 'frequently … we heard the expression 'grey area' as a rationalisation of morally dubious behaviour … some no longer seem to be certain of the difference between what is right and wrong … ' (Committee on Standards in Public Life 1995: 16).

In looking at the private sector, Punch discusses a number of contextual possibilities that may trigger corporate deviance. These may be structural in terms of markets (either competition or anti-competition factors); size of organisations (which dilutes both control and responsibility); achieving organisational goals; opportunity; total loyalty to the company; assimilation of existing corporate ideologies and practices; business as war; risk-taking; dominant personalities; necessary dirty hands as part of corporate competition; pressure and rewards. Cumulatively these lead to the development of a 'corporate mind.' The mind is attuned to the 'signals' from the corporate environment (what they are expected to do, or what others are also doing, or what it takes to succeed) that are set by the 'fundamental concerns of senior management … centred on corporate survival, continuity, power, reputation/face, and profits …' (Punch 1996: 239). To fit into and rise up within a company, managers will conform in style and conduct, and collectively will adhere to 'group-think', a reinforcing dynamic that gives managers the rationale for what they are doing and comfort that they are doing what others are doing and which will bring the approval of peers and superiors.

Ideological influences

Slapper and Tombs take it further in arguing that, while it is difficult to pinpoint why a company at a point in time may opt for a deviant approach to business, or to understand why 'normal' rather than pathological organisations should act this way, societal context or culture is crucial: 'For us, a society with a strong competitive *ethos* …, a socially developed fear of failure (which permeates both individuals, and the *esprit de corps* of corporate bodies), an increasing commodification of all human relationships and practices, an ever increasing number and frequency of transactions … which at the same time are less open to public scrutiny, and a capitalist economy constantly pushing people with targets to hit, promotions to seek and emotions to avoid, recessions to try and survive, and so on, can thus be seen as a society likely to engender corporate crime' (Slapper and Tombs 1999: 161–162). Thus, unless one argues that individuals or groups of individuals are entirely susceptible to their working environments, to the exclusion of their upbringing, backgrounds or private lives, then arguing that the work environment by itself, or disproportionally, determines morality may be too simple. Indeed, it can be argued that congruent societal and occupational attitudes and cultures are crucial.

In the private sector, the economic climate engendered by the Conservative government from 1979 in its general promotion of entrepreneurial activity, with the removal of controls from commercial, economic and financial sectors, as well as the endorsement of financial gain and material status as a reward for and an indicator of worth and hard work, certainly put a premium on corporate 'success' as the key driver. In similar circumstances the impact and direction of change in the public sector – from changes in organisational attitudes to devolved management, from privatisation to enterprise cultures – led to a number of well-publicised cases where the effects of dysfunctional change were noted, including: concerns over job security, the potential conflict of interest over privatisation and public position, poor management control, misinterpretation of performance rewards, over-ambitious projects, mismanagement or misappropriation of public funds, and the failure to enforce or police regulations and procedures.

As Jenny Harrow noted about public servants, changes in organisational attitudes to devolved management, from privatisation to enterprise cultures, can have a significant influence on how people interpret how they are expected to behave in their work and how they perceived themselves as a consequence. Thus the development of a management culture within a public service context may have led to a 'misunderstanding among public servants about the quasi-private sector environment ... (and) ... inaccurate perceptions of private sector values and practices' (Harrow and Gillett 1994: 4, 5 – see Box 5.1).

Cultural influences

It is hard to determine, and even harder to identify, how far factors such as class, cultural or social influences shape the way in which people may react to the opportunity to commit fraud. What little work has been done suggests a variety of personal, professional and

Box 5.1 The district auditor's 2005 public interest report on Whalley High School

Whalley Range High School represents an educational success story, having been transformed from being a school in significant difficulty 10 years ago to now being a thriving and successful school. I wish to make it clear that my report makes no adverse comments about the educational effectiveness of the School. Whilst a number of the allegations made to the Audit Commission are not proven or supported by the available evidence, my conclusion is nevertheless that there has been a significant breakdown in appropriate standards of governance and accountability at the School.

In my view, the Governing Body of the School has, until recently, failed to properly perform its role. The Headteacher has made serious errors of judgment in her dealings with a number of staffing matters, particularly in relation to the role and remuneration of her sister. Insufficient consideration has been paid to the high relative cost of school management. The culture within the School has been lacking in openness and accountability and in my view it is not surprising that allegations of nepotism have been made. Payments to staff on termination of employment outlined below are in my view contrary to law. The lack of intervention by the Local Education Authority (LEA) raises questions about the level and effectiveness of LEA support to the Governing Body and the effectiveness of LEA monitoring of expenditure incurred by the School.

Source: Audit Commission (2005b)

social contexts at play whose permutation or propensity towards fraud continues to be hard to define: 'Some do and some do not abide by the law; we cannot say with any accuracy why some decide to stick to the rules and some do not; but we are obliged to take into account the collective circumstances that lead to the deviance because it forces us to acknowledge the seductive power and potent influence of organisational life in general, and corporate existence in particular ...' (Punch 1996: 247). In relation to benefit fraud similar variations in terms of propensity have been noted: ' ... many people do not need deterring. They see benefit fraud as wrong; they already fear sufficiently the risk of getting caught; and, beside, they rarely get the opportunity: bits of casual work paid on the side really are "gold dust". At the other end of the scale are a relatively small group who would be very difficult to deter initially from committing fraud since they will have convinced themselves their fraud is invisible to detection. This leaves another group who might be considered as "waiverers" – those who might break some rules if they were given the chance' (Rowlinson *et al.* 1997: 134).

If there are organisational and ideological drivers to personal and organisational 'success', and there is an increasingly permissive compliance and control environment then, as Maureen Mancuso noted of British MPs, this could lead 'to a progressive legitimisation of behaviour that is more and more removed from the original boundaries of probity ... [where] once exceptional and questionable practices become routine and unremarkable' (Mancuso 1993: 186–187). Punch describes business as criminally minded in arguing that 'the business organisation provides the setting, the means, and the ideology for rule-breaking' and that 'the very nature of business, however, may reinforce organisational duality and moral ambivalence. Business is competitive and even combative; it may accept a measure of "sharp practice" and may skate a fine line on legality ...; and it sometimes produces calculating, manipulative, devious, predatory, and ruthless people ... but it also simply takes ordinary people and asks them to do extraordinary things like bribing, spying, and falsifying data. At some stage these are no longer seen as out of the ordinary but as normal ...' (Punch 1996: 244, 246–247). The National Audit Office's report (NAO 1996) on Yorkshire Regional Health Authority drew attention to the culture driven by senior management and the Board that lay behind the 'poor practice.' It noted the arguments of some of the senior figures involved. One argued that his judgment took precedence over the regulatory framework where 'the new climate in the NHS at the time justified adopting an approach in which the highest priority was to ensure that problems were solved, even if the rules were bent or broken in the process'. Another stated that they were acting 'within the entrepreneurial culture which appeared to be sanctioned by senior NHS management at the time.' The potential for misconduct may thus have been exacerbated by the changes during the 1980s and 1990s, and the perks, bonuses, corporate trappings and so on that were the identifiers of the successful encouragement of entrepreneurial management competition that the ideology promoted, and for which the work environment may have provided the means.

Compliance influences and boundary maintenance

Criticisms of conduct in both sectors came at the end of a decade of change. Various regulators and official inquiries felt the need to step in to reassert the boundaries between conduct that was both legal and acceptable and conduct that was not, once it was becoming obvious that overall changes may have overridden, or rendered ineffectual or irrelevant, existing compliance or control procedures or expectations. In other words, irrelevant or ineffectual rules and controls provided increased opportunity, together with decreased risk for those whose incentive or propensity to fraud had been fuelled by ideological or societal change. Court cases, codes of conduct, and so on, may spell out the boundaries of acceptability but often these follow or lag behind scandals and controversy, and recommendations may not be implemented as quickly or as comprehensively as the wider changes that gave rise to the unacceptable conduct. In any case they are unusually not intended (even if they could) to reverse those changes. Rather, it may be more a case of adapting or realigning the boundaries than a reassertion of past standards.

While regulation of business in general and the financial services in particular was recognised from the 1980s on as a necessity if the UK were to compete internationally and become a major international financial centre, the compliance framework was primarily posited on self-regulation which the major financial institutions were quick to grasp. Lloyds, the insurance market, accepted legislation as preferable to an agency along the lines of the US Securities and Exchange Commission: 'The Lloyd's Act (1982) was devised in the shadow of the fear of more draconian government intervention. Scandals over fraud, threats from American insurance interests, and bad publicity over the management of Lloyd's had made reforms of some kind politically and economically necessary' (Levi 1987: 87). Similarly, the 1986 Financial Services Act had the role of self-regulation at its heart (albeit putting the independent regulator – the Securities and Investment Board (SIB) – on a statutory footing): 'External and statutory investor protection, though important, became less salient, and preserving (or creating) London's pre-eminence as an international financial trading centre became the central concern not only of financial entrepreneurs but also of a government faced with declining world markets and the possibility of creating new jobs' (Levi 1987: 89–90; see also Gunn 1992).

The comfortable corporate–political nexus continued, however, to protect the flexible and somewhat forgiving impact of self-regulation where the line between corporate self-interest, sharp practice and insider profitability became increasingly blurred, so long as the intent was not so obviously and deliberately at the expense of the investor and thus the credibility of the self-regulatory institutions intended to protect them. Where such conduct did provide evidence of criminality – and investor protection from corporate theft *was* an issue – the reform of the law enforcement aspect was equally slow. First there was the creation of a Fraud Investigation Group within the Crown Prosecution Service and then, following the Roskill Committee Report recommendations, an organisational shape to the FIG approach with an allocation of specific powers through a specific agency, the Serious Fraud Office.

The establishment of the SIB and the SFO did not initially have between them a significant impact on corporate conduct. Indeed, some of the early SFO cases, such as Blue Arrow, underlined the reluctance of the courts and the City to attempt to criminalise activities at the margin of corporate acceptability. The recognition that the private sector's own internal responsibilities needed to be addressed was undertaken by the Cadbury Committee which considered that its Code would have led to earlier identification of fraud but believed that it 'must, however, be recognised that no system of control can eliminate the risk of fraud without so shackling companies as to impede their ability to compete in the market place' (Committee on the Financial Aspects of Corporate Governance 1992: para 1.9).

The balance between self-regulation, light-touch compliance and self-interest has shifted back and forth through the 1994 Rutteman Committee and the 1995 Greenbury Report until the 1998 Hampel Report made it plain that profit overrode regulation and compliance. It argued that big business was 'now among the most accountable organisations in society', that 'a board's first responsibility [is] to enhance the prosperity of the business over time', that 'business prosperity cannot be commanded' and that 'it is dangerous to encourage the belief that rules and regulations about structure will deliver success.' (Committee on Corporate Governance 1998: 17). The Combined Code that subsequently emerged required listed companies to subscribe to it, and its core principles indicated how companies *should* conduct themselves. Whether this and its revisions have actually had any impact is debatable. Listed companies continue to be required to confirm how they have applied the Code and that they complied with the Code's provisions throughout the financial year or – where they do not – to provide an explanation. There is no statutory and regulatory provision to ensure enforcement, nor to confirm compliance and explanation other than through shareholders.[2]

In the public sector, the revision of the control environment was similarly slow in evolving. The 1986 Efficiency Unit which was responsible for the disaggregation of civil service departments and the promotion of semi-autonomous agencies had already warned that 'pressure from parliament, the Public Accounts Committee and the media tends to concentrate on alleged impropriety or incompetence, and making political points, rather than on demanding evidence of steadily improving efficiency and effectiveness.' Nevertheless, the Audit Commission in 1993 warned that many of the changes to the delivery of local government services, 'such as the delegation of financial and management responsibilities, while contributing to improved quality of service, have increased the risks of fraud and corruption occurring' (Audit Commission 1993: 2). It argued for the value and relevance of an anti-fraud culture or an ethical environment which, it suggested, had yet to be recognised. Its concerns were echoed in January 1994 when the House of Commons Committee of Public Accounts warned that there had been 'a number of serious failures in administrative and financial systems and controls within departments and other public bodies, which have led to money being wasted or otherwise improperly spent. These failings represent a departure from the standards of public conduct which have mainly been established during the past 140 years' (Committee of Public Accounts 1994a: v). In 1995 the Committee on Standards in Public Life recommended a number of institutional reforms intended to ensure an independent element in the regulatory processes and also common threads – codes of conduct (based on seven principles of public life), independent scrutiny by auditors or independent bodies, guidance and education (induction, guidance and training, monitoring awareness and setting a good example) – to revive the ethical dimension of public life.

Summary

Academics such as Weisburd and Waring, and Croall, see fraud along a greed–need continuum. The Weisburd findings in the USA suggest that, put simply, fraudsters either *have* to or *want* to commit fraud – what Hazel Croall calls the *greed* and *need* drivers: 'Financial crime is related to different levels of constraint or inducement – for those at higher levels, constraints or pressures focus on demands for continuing capital accumulation, whereas, at lower levels, pressures are related to survival where full-time employment is no longer a realistic option' (Croall 2001: 93). The questions – are people predisposed to commit fraud? Did any of them seek out the position that would allow them to commit fraud? Would any of them have committed the fraud they did if they had not been in the situation they were in? Were the links between any of the above about opportunity, incentive and the likely risk of being caught, or were there other reasons? – still do not lend themselves to a simple answer.

Further, Croall notes the Pearce and Tombs distinction between first and second order causes of crime: 'The immediate cause of many white-collar crimes lies in the individual decisions to engage in activities that can be defined as crime, whereas second order causes relate to the structural and economic background within which these choices are made. Individuals' choices must be located in their specific occupational or organisational settings which, in turn, have to be placed in the context of their environment, in their particular market and in a social and economic system that prioritises goals ...' (Croall 2001: 100).

Whatever the reason, fraud is the archetypal acquisitive crime and it should not be considered surprising that it has a self-sustaining dynamic. There are four themes that its pervasiveness might suggest: first, people are prepared to act fraudulently across a spectrum of activity; second, the focus on detection and investigation may become inadequate or ineffective because it lags behind changes in culture and behaviour; third, the drive for acquisition – the greed, the need or the thrill of the inside track – takes advantage of opportunity and incentive; finally, the combination of all of these makes fraud an easier and more rewarding route than more traditional criminal (or even orthodox) means for those involved in criminal activity, as the next chapter discusses.

Notes

1 In other cases, the 'findings' are put out as a press release, with the company responsible reluctant to release the methodology, the data or more detailed findings.
2 On the other hand, following the impact of Enron, World.Com and Tyco, the requirements of the US 2002 Sarbanes-Oxley Act on effective internal controls over financial reporting, and other measures to curtail internal fraud and ensure independent investigation, have encouraged a higher degree of corporate control in those companies operating directly or with subsidiaries in the USA for fear of attracting the far more draconian and criminal-focused approach used by US authorities.

Chapter 6

Overspill – old frauds, new frauds and fraud in other criminal activities

This chapter discusses the growth of fraud in what might be termed 'new' areas or activities and as an increasingly integral feature of criminal activity not normally associated with traditional definitions of fraud. It also emphasises the tenacity of fraudulent activity in lucrative markets, and the ability of fraudsters to exploit changes in technology and market conditions. The first part of this chapter links three areas together – cybercrime, identity 'fraud', and cheque and credit card fraud. The second looks at the links between fraud, corruption and organised crime.

Cybercrime, identity fraud, and cheque and credit card fraud

Cybercrime

There is a media fashion to talk about cybercrime, as though the expansion of the use of information technology has resulted in a range of new fraud-related offences. In practice, computers, the internet and broadband have combined to expand the availability of criminal material or material for criminal purposes, the production of documents to be used for fraudulent purposes, the ease of access and storage, and the jurisdictions in which and from which such offences may be committed, as well as frauds using the internet as the medium (see NCIS Website: Hi-Tech Crime [www.ncis.co.uk]). It might make fraud easier to commit, and more difficult to detect and investigate, but rarely involves 'new' offences. At the same time, the enthusiasm with which financial services and retail industries have embraced on-line delivery has also opened up the opportunity for the internet, and thus PCs, to be used in the commission of fraud, including: 'denial of service' attacks that interfere with company business, buying goods with counterfeit or stolen credit cards (Card-Not-Present or CNP fraud), offering bogus investments schemes (boiler-room scams), 'spoofing' or 'phishing' (sending out bogus bank and building society e-mails to persuade customers to hand over their account and password details because a 'computer fault' requires the need for reconfirmation), and the need to maintain a presence on the internet itself – see Box 6.1.

Most police forces now have hi-tech crime units, in part to deal with cases such as Operation Ore (the on-line paedophile investigations) and also to assist force investigations in seizing and accessing computers, and securing the contents as suitable for use in courts. Here the 1990 Misuse of Computers Act is important not just for its intended purpose – unauthorised use and interference – but also for the implications for investigators who may be caught inadvertently by

Box 6.1 New tools, old frauds adapted

Peter Francis-Macrae, 23, spent a fortune on designer clothes and learning to fly helicopters after allegedly tricking thousands of innocent victims in e-mail and website frauds run from the bedroom of his father's terraced house. Although his business was run from a bedroom, his website had included pictures of Canary Wharf, East London, with the invitation to 'take a tour of our state-of-the-art data centre'. The defendant ran two scams based on the system of internet 'domain names', the individual addresses that every user needs to run a website or receive e-mails, usually with a suffix such as .com or .co.uk. First, he sent unsolicited 'spam' e-mails to thousands of people around the world offering to register them for new '.eu' European domain names. The money rolled in at the rate of £200,000 a fortnight, people thinking that he was a genuine registrar, the court was told. One customer paid £5,780 to register a long list of addresses. The defendant accepted payment for offensive names such as f***theeu although they would never be allowed, it was alleged. The other trick involved posting letters to people whose domain names were due to expire, demanding a renewal fee under threat of service being withdrawn. This brought in nearly £600,000. His entire bogus earnings were calculated at £1.6 million.

Source: *The Times*, 12 October 2005

such provisions. Indeed, most of the various frauds through computers or against information held on computers could be dealt with under conspiracy to defraud, theft, false accounting or obtaining property by deception. Only what is called 'manipulative fraud' – inserting a rogue programme to carry out a fraud in order to, for example, round down accounts to the nearest pound on volume payments and divert the surplus pence – might qualify for prosecution under the 1990 Misuse of Computers Act (see Sommer 2005: 13/4, 13/27).

One particular 'cybercrime' involves e-banking and e-retail where the relationships do not require personal or physical presence for the transaction is based on card details keyed in (Card-Not-Present or CNP). There is significant UK growth in the Net. Total spending through technology-based channels, including e-mail, fax, EDI and automated telephones, grew 15 per cent, from £170.8 billion in 2002 to £195.6 billion in 2003. Web-based sales now represent 17 per cent of all business conducted using IT in the UK, and the value of internet sales to households rose to £11.4 billion in 2003 from £6.4 billion in 2002 (*Computing*, 22 November 2004). This attracts fraud. It has also attracted the label of 'identity' fraud. Despite this attention, CIFAS has noted that identity fraud is still a comparatively rare type of crime, although it is on the increase (it has recorded over 100,000 cases in 2003, up from 20,000 in 1999). Yet the 'cost' estimated by the Cabinet Office in 2002 is £1.38 billion out of a total fraud cost of £13.8 billion in 2002 (Cabinet Office 2002). CIFAS also reported on other agencies claiming to be affected by identity fraud – the Department for Work and Pensions estimated that benefit fraud involving false and stolen identities cost approximately £50 million in 2001/2; plastic card fraud losses totalled £420 million in 2002 with identity fraud accounting for 5 per cent (or £20.6 million) of this figure. CIFAS also reported that there were 'proven' links between identity fraud and organised crime, and involving illegal immigration, drug trafficking, money laundering, vehicle theft and so on.

Identity fraud

'Identity fraud' usually occurs when either someone assumes the outward identifiers of another – the name, and associated details and documentation that provide confirmation that that person is who they say they are through details that provide access to goods, services, and so on without the rightful owner knowing. This is not really identity fraud. Stealing someone's credit card details to pay for goods then delivered to the fraudster's address is not identity fraud nor theft but deception; pretending to be someone else is impersonation. Like the former, the latter is a recognised offence in, for example, election law; the Electoral Fraud (Northern Ireland) Act 2002, for example, requires personal identification information in the form of a person's date of birth, national insurance number and signature to register as a voter and voting requires photographic identification at polling stations.

To understand both the confusion and what impersonation, identity theft and identity fraud actually are, it is important to understand what makes an identity (see also Home Office 2002; 2004b). Of the various person identifiers, one relates to the formally recorded birth details (which define sex and date, and parental details); one is biometric detail – fingerprint, retina, etc.; another is the signature; and the final identifier is the documentation that traces biographical or life event details – passports, marriage certificate, electoral registration, telephone number, car registration, court decisions, divorce, postal address, council tax payments, qualifications, property rental or ownership, financial accounts, etc. (see Jones 2005). These are recorded with various agencies which confirm the person's identity by providing multiple checks, and offer time-line and location checking. This is how a credit history is built up (and is the type of checking done by vetting services for corporate and security services appointments).[1]

Part of the advantage of such checks is that – if a full life event check is made – even a committed fraudster would find it difficult to create and then sustain a wholly fictitious identity or recreate the identity of another, although it can be done – see Box 6.2.

On the other hand, most agencies check only documentation that relates to their purpose (for example, opening a bank account) and usually rely on documentation that is believed to be validated by the issuer after extensive checks on biographical details. The most common of the documents looked at are known as breeder documents (such as passports), because it is assumed that the issuing agency has done the necessary checks and, on the basis that the document validates the person, further document-issuing actions or decisions are taken ('breeding' further documents such as bank account or credit card details).

Identity theft – becoming the other person or company – is rare. The likelihood of detection increases with use and, in any case, it is difficult to get legal title in a way that precludes the rightful owner reasserting their ownership (which is why account takeover or changes to company registration are a means to an end – for immediate fraudulent purposes – rather than long-term control). Identity fraud

Box 6.2 Identity creation

A bogus doctor who made more than £1.5 million by treating patients and helping hundreds of asylum seekers remain in Britain was jailed for 10 years yesterday. Barian Baluchi, a 43-year-old former minicab driver, convinced lawyers, charities, Government departments, High Court judges and other doctors that he was an eminent psychiatrist and a respected professor. Baluchi, of Hampton, south-west London, admitted 30 specimen charges including perjury, perverting the course of public justice, possessing a class A drug, causing actual bodily harm and deception between December 1998 and August 2003.

Judge Henry Blacksell told Baluchi at Middlesex Crown Court in London: 'You are a practised and out-and-out fraudster and deceiver. The Charity Commission was deceived, charitable organisations were deceived, the Department of Health was deceived, Barking council was deceived, the courts were deceived and the people who went to your clinic and were supposedly treated by you were deceived.'

Iranian-born Baluchi arrived in Britain as a student in 1979, then claimed asylum. He married his first wife in 1983 to avoid deportation and made a living driving minicabs, waiting tables and working for a dry cleaning firm. But in the late 1990s he set about reinventing himself as 'Professor Barian Samuel Baluchi, MB, ChB, MSc, PhD, consultant psychiatrist and neuropsychiatrist'. He bought a PhD from America for £12,000 and qualified for it using 'credits' accumulated from such tasks as playing golf, watching television, reading newspapers, keeping tropical fish and serving on a jury, Louise Kamill, prosecuting said. Baluchi established what started out as a counselling clinic in September 1998 but after realising that clients also needed medical attention, he set about becoming recognised by the medical profession to make more money.

He assumed the identity of a former trainee doctor and told the GMC he had changed his name to Baluchi. He then used a Spanish psychiatrist's name to get full registration. His false CV claimed he had trained at Harvard, Columbia, Newcastle and Sussex universities, went to Leeds Medical School, and lectured on both sides of the Atlantic. He duped a string of charities, including the King's Fund and The Baring Foundation, and Government departments out of £440,000. He registered with the Expert Witness Institute and the Law Society's Directory of

Expert Witnesses and prepared hundreds of reports for asylum seekers trying to avoid deportation.

'We can see at least £1.5 million going through his accounts,' said Miss Kamill. 'He took in people from all walks of life, from the newly arrived asylum seeker to senior officials at the Department of Health, local authorities and established charities, from people practised in detecting dishonesty such as judges sitting at the Old Bailey, the Immigration Appeals Tribunal, solicitors, to his own personal acquaintances, including his English first wife.' Baluchi, said Miss Kamill, made huge sums by 'bleeding the public purse'. His intricate deception forced the NHS to write to more than 2,000 people on his clinic files warning them of the situation.

Baluchi's downfall began when an immigration appeals presentation officer noticed his reports were so similar that they had 'clearly come from the same template with just a change of name added'. He alerted the Home Office, which in turn informed the NHS and police.

Source: *The Daily Telegraph*, 27 January 2005

is deception, using details to obtain goods and services for which those details, so long as the fraud remains unreported, would confirm entitlement (see Jones 2005; Hamadi 2004). In the case of CNP fraud the only details are those on the card, which is the only link with, or identifier of, the person and thus this type of fraud is termed identity fraud.

Just as press reports about mugging focused attention on street robberies, what makes the use of identity fraud and theft more sexy is the rise in media stories less about the loss than the disruption and the efforts to resolve the issue – see Box 6.3. The onus is increasingly on the victim, as well as the card issuer, retailer and credit agencies, to deal with this matter because the volume of cards issued and used creates a greater likelihood of fraud occurring, with a consequent drop in police interest.

Cheque and credit card fraud

Cheque and credit card fraud appeared as an issue in the 1980s and into the 1990s, with mid-1980s losses assessed at some £75 million. This rose proportionally less than transaction turnover (causing some card issuers to talk of a drop in fraud) and involved relatively small

Box 6.3 Identity fraud – a journalist's tale

The first [fraud] was when the boyfriend of a tenant of mine opened some direct mail with all my bank details that had been mistakenly sent to my rented property's address. The fraudster's surname was Brown – similar to mine though without the 'e' – and, pretending to be me, he opened a storecard account at Next, the high-street clothing retailer. The first I knew of the scam was when a debt recovery firm said I owed almost £400 on the card. As I've only ever bought one item, a woolly scarf, from Next I was instantly suspicious. I contacted the retailer's head office and explained my position. Several weeks of police statements and identity-checking later I was able to prove my innocence and revert back to the real me.

Having your identity duped is bad enough. The side-effects can be disastrous. The debt was logged on my credit file at Experian, the data-reference agency, which would have meant instant refusal for any credit, mortgage or loan I may have applied for. To get it removed I had to send the agency a Notice of Dissociation, a signed statement that I was not the debtor. I also made my own inquiries; I found the other Mr Brown, a former market trader who lived in the same town, had been interviewed by police for many other debts and frauds.

Source: *The Observer*, 19 June 2005

amounts. While the police showed little interest, the industry was making attempts to tighten up basic procedures on issuing cards, and introducing features on cards (such as holograms) and various computer-based controls and techniques to monitor transactions between cardholder and stores (such as floating floor authorisation limits).

Nevertheless, a 1991 Home Office report noted that, with losses running at over £150 million, cheque and credit card fraud was comparable to the other costs of crime: 'During 1989 – the most recent year for which data are available – thefts from the person cost £22.2 million; robbery, £31.4 million; thefts from vehicles, £138.4 million; recorded theft from shops, £16.2 million; burglary other than in a dwelling, £218.6 million; and burglary in a dwelling, £271.8 million' (Levi *et al.* 1991: 3–4). The report, accompanied by political support, underlined the importance of a concerted response through industry preventative measures, including information-sharing to the point where the police felt that their involvement was worthwhile (Levi *et al.* 1991: 45–46).

In consequence of this report, and acceptance within the industry's representative bodies to act collectively, an ACPO Report was produced in 1992. This showed that half of respondent forces did not have a cheque and credit card unit. Those that did, located the unit in the fraud squad (although there was no force policy on such work). Overall the units had over 140 staff (although not all squads had handwriting analysts) and relied heavily on 'on the job' training. The report noted a number of issues: that banks and retailers were unaware of police policy; people did not know who to contact; there was no consistency; and a lack of understanding between the banks, retailers and police. In addition, the police were concerned about the cost-effectiveness of investigations, the role of organised crime, the need for prevention and the use of smart card technology. The report contained six core decisions: all forces should have a cheque and credit card squad, including an intelligence officer and handwriting analyst; there should be informal regional intelligence meetings; greater emphasis should be put on prevention; cheque and credit card squads should have appropriate technology; handwriting analysis should be standardised; cheque and credit card fraud should be addressed by a partnership approach for which the police 'should actively seek sponsorship' from these (financial) agencies to fund these recommendations.

The lack of central direction over the priorities of individual Chief Constables has meant that the implementation of ACPO recommendations has not been comprehensive. The 1998 Home Office review of the 1991 report noted that handwriting analysis and training on basic investigation was being delivered, but that outside sponsorship only occurred occasionally (and then only in relation to specific expenditure such as cars, and equipment). It noted that few forces had set up designated cheque and/or credit card squads which, in any case, 'like many headquarters services under "devolved policing", are under threat where divisional police "fund-holders" are not prepared to pay for their assistance' (Levi 1998a: 9–11; see also Levi 1998b). The Levi and Doig 2000 survey also reported that less than half of English, Welsh and Northern Ireland forces had dedicated squads. Research elsewhere confirmed this, also noting that less than half of fraud squads had cheque and credit card units and, of those that did, only half were operational while the remainder provided guidance and support to other officers. The same research also noted that, in the growing area of fraudulent use of cards over the internet, or payments made by cards for goods that were not delivered, the units neither had training, nor expertise nor the interest in investigating what would be, usually, a low-value crime without a scene of crime, without an identifiable perpetrator, and often involving a cross-border or international dimension.

The 1998 review also warned that, despite a number of measures, losses would rise and that the industry would have to take on the bulk of the responsibility for doing something about it. Indeed APACS (which had already established a Plastic Fraud Prevention Forum) had also taken action at the same time, setting up a small Fraud Investigation Bureau as a rapid response unit of fraud risk managers to co-ordinate information on skimming, counterfeiting and cross-border frauds, and to feed into both commercial prevention and policing operations in response to the 'organised criminals' involved, at home and overseas. This latter aspect of cheque and credit card fraud – that of organised crime – came to the forefront shortly afterwards when cloning pushed losses steeply upwards.

A 2000 review again visited the changes in card fraud, noting that card losses were running at over 100,000 annually and that, although overall losses had doubled since their mid-1990s low, and had now exceeded the losses at the start of the decade, the pattern of losses was changing, with a rise in CNP fraud and cloning. One-third of losses come from abuse of cards overseas, thus bypassing many of the controls introduced in the 1990s (Levi 2000). The review made a number of proposals, including: the introduction of chip cards, the use of PIN at the point of sale, focus on card 'hot spots' and more effective policing either by the police or through an enhanced role for the APACS Fraud Investigation Bureau. Here, since it was obvious that the police had not delivered the 1991 ACPO agenda, it suggested an industry- and/or government-funded central agency.

The view from law enforcement was that, while closing down counterfeiting factories was a police matter, dealing with the losses from their use still lay with the industry (some industry members argued that the police had a perception that staff and executive fraud should be investigated – since it may involve breach of trust etc. – but that product-related fraud is a commercial hazard). On the other hand, the misuse of cards and cheques was not only becoming organised but that some organised crime was becoming increasingly involved. Subsequent informal discussions centred on setting up a dedicated unit. This was proposed in business plans submitted through the City of London Police, together with lobbying of the industry and the Home Office.

After 18 months, in April 2002, a two-year pilot was begun with the Dedicated Cheque and Plastic Card Unit (DCPCU). It was to be a £5 million investment shared 25 per cent/75 per cent between the Home Office and the industry through its representative organisation, APACS. Originally intended to be staffed jointly between the City of London Police and the Metropolitan Police (who never fulfilled their commitment but still provided some staff) to 23, it reached a total of 11 staff plus two support and three investigators from the industry. Operating semi-independently and dealing only with organised card and cheque fraud (Level 2/3 crime in the terms of the NIM – see p 192) within the M25 area, it fell within the City of London Police for operational purposes, with links to it and the Metropolitan Police. Its work was directed by a Steering Group whose membership included the Home Office, APACS, the two police forces, and the BBA. Its key performance targets related to recovered compromised (counterfeited) cards and numbers with a target range of between 2,200 to 8,800, whose value was calculated at an average of £1,800 a card or number. At the end of two years it recovered 32,000 cards and numbers (although one case involved 22,000 compromised numbers) at a value of £65 million – see Box 6.4 for an example.

At the end of the pilot, a review was undertaken which endorsed its work and recommended its continuation. At this point the Home Office decided to withdraw its funding (at the same time it was being asked to find extra funds for the City of London/SFO development – see below, p 132) when the industry was hoping for shared funding. The DCPCU is thus now wholly industry-funded (the APACS trawl for industry funds gave the unit £1.7 million and invested £1.3 million in its own Financial Intelligence Bureau) although both the City and the Met underwrite costs in terms of location, and other logistic and operational support.[2]

The Unit now has 19 staff (with another two secondments from the industry to deal with intelligence and exhibits) working in three teams to develop card and cheque specialisms. It runs its own referrals criteria for cases that come from APACS and BBA members or the police, with a Management Group overseeing the decision-making process. The performance measures still include counterfeiting but the remit has widened to cover disruption of organised crime networks (one measure judges the level of crime figure arrested), proactive work and use of informants, particularly to respond to the rapid dynamics of, for example, the technology for ATM fraud (currently running at £6 million a month) and the differentiation in crime groups specialisms.

Box 6.4 DCPCU card fraud

Dan Mazar, 33, whose uncle, Yitzhak Ben-Zvi, was Israel's second president, used 300 credit cards in an array of bogus identities to pay for holidays, hotel rooms and shopping sprees. Martin Hicks, prosecuting, told Southwark Crown Court, in south London: 'He was involved both as prime mover and principal beneficiary. It was a meticulously planned, carefully executed conspiracy to defraud credit card companies on an unprecedented scale.'

Mazar, of Hendon, north London, admitted one count of conspiracy to defraud, reflecting £286,903, the UK element of the scam. His two-year 10-month crime spree – interrupted by a seven-month prison sentence for the Israeli end of the scam – ended when his 'luck ran out' in a central London branch of Superdrug in April. As a taxi paid for with one of the many credit cards waited outside, Mazar tried to embark on yet another shopping expedition. But staff became suspicious and called the police, who arrested him as he tried to escape in the cab. Police found 15 credit cards in different names, and an extensive 'aide memoir' with identification details.

Mr Hicks said Mazar, the only one to be arrested in connection with the scam in this country, used cards obtained from various American issuers, including American Express, either based on a variation of his own name or using other people's identities. He had a string of credit card telephone numbers to check that the cards issued in the names of others had not been cancelled, and to make sure he did not exceed credit limits. Judge Stephen Robbins said: 'This type of offending is rife in this country and it causes massive losses. The annual loss to the banks in Britain is said to be £700 million each year.' As well as ordering him to pay £40,000 of prosecution costs, the judge made a £286,902 confiscation order.

Source: The Guardian; December 14 2002. See also: www.dcpcu. org.uk

Organised crime

The DCPCU deals with organised cheque and credit card fraud – the ATM scams are very much a Romanian expertise – and takes the lead on new types of card-related fraud, such as account-takeover or the suborning of bank employees, because the industry response is not geared to sophisticated criminal activity and neither the National Crime Squad (NCS) nor the National Criminal Intelligence Service (NCIS) appeared particularly interested in fraud despite the fact that it involves organised criminal enterprise (and the international dimensions of that enterprise).

An organised crime enterprise (OCE) within the revised and much shortened NCIS definition is an enterprise which contains at least three people and where:

- criminal activity is prolonged or indefinite;
- criminals are motivated by profit or power;
- serious criminal offences are being committed.

The term 'enterprise' recognises the business of crime – an organised crime group makes decisions that 'involve a balancing of anticipated profit and risk, but also rely on identifying an opportunity and having the capability to exploit it' – and the business dynamics that shape the organisational structure, partnerships and networks. These are often, in practice, 'loose networks, the members of which coalesce around one or more prominent criminals to undertake particular criminal ventures of varying complexity, structure and length'. They also work with 'people outside their immediate circle, not least with the criminals that they buy from and sell to, and those that provide them with a service, such as money laundering or transport' (NCIS 2003: 16).

It is thus the organisational context that defines the response, rather than the activity in which organised crime is engaged. Any activity that allows the organisation to make money – and that is what sustains the organisation like any other business – offers the means to embed and stabilise the organised crime enterprise as an enduring business structure with potential for expansion or diversification. Income is earned through a range of activities that either 'tax' an existing activity or supply legal or illegal products and services where there is demand and which are provided at below market rates. As such, there are a range of backroom services required – from sales venues to money laundering, running front businesses, using firearms, and so on. Fraud is a constant underlying theme, on unpaid tax, claiming benefits, laundering income, using forged and counterfeit documents, and so on, but is often seen as a side consequence of the enterprise that is the focus of the law enforcement agencies concerned.

The point about organised crime is that it is assumed that they are continuing businesses, structured or working on a federated basis in relation to acquisitive crime on a flexible basis to maximise the financial returns, often in commodities that the public will buy irrespective of its legality and provenance. The focus of the law enforcement agencies is on the disruption of the business, asset confiscation and occasional prosecution of the members of the groups and their associates.

In particular, tracking and then seizing the profits from organised crime has become an increasingly influential alternative to the difficulties of securing evidence for prosecutions. The relevant legislation – the 2000 Proceeds of Crime Act (POCA; see below, p 215) – had its genesis in the 1986 Drug Trafficking Offences Act. This latter established the crime of money laundering which, between 1988 and 2002, was extended by other laws to cover suspicions of laundering the proceeds of any crime including the 1994 Drug Trafficking Act requirements making it an offence not to report if there is 'suspicion or belief.' The responsibility for reporting fell primarily on the private sector which was overseen firstly as a self-regulating industry initiative and then as a responsibility of the FSA. All suspicious transactions (SAR) are reported to NCIS as part of its role in gathering and disseminating intelligence to law enforcement. Until the FSA arrived, NCIS received around 12,000 SARs annually, most of which were not used by local forces or by NCIS itself (see Levi 1994b and 1995). FSA undertook to energise the SAR regime with an unequivocal stance on effective reporting and institutional arrangements by financial institutions, even though the SAR regime was known to be one-way, badly managed and poorly used (KPMG 2003) to the point that the role of NCIS ground to a halt.

Organisational dysfunctionality and overlap, as well as the failure to develop intelligence-led law enforcement, was one reason why the Labour government decided to merge NCIS, the National Hi Tech Crime Unit and the NCS with part of the Immigration and Nationality Department and a large part of what had been the National Investigation Service of HM Customs and Excise before its merger with Inland Revenue to form HM Revenue and Customs, together with some former Inland Revenue staff from the same agency, to create the Serious and Organised Crime Agency (SOCA).[3] From April 2006 SOCA will concentrate primarily on drugs and organised immigration with an overall objective of reducing 'harm' to society by disrupting and dismantling the OCEs involved (and seizing the profits from their activities), as well as attacking their business infrastructure. Fraud remains a low priority, after such issues as: the role of professionals (such as solicitors – see Middleton and Levi 2004 – and accountants), the growth of OCE partnerships and inter-organisation coordination, and the corruption of law enforcement and public officials. In its 2003 UK Threat Assessment, NCIS warned of the threat of corruption posed by organised crime enterprises using 'corruption to secure help from people with access to information, influence or access they want or need' (NCIS 2003: 20; see Box 6.5).

Box 6.5 Liverpool connections

A star of the television programme *Gladiators* and a senior police officer were jailed last night after they were found guilty of corruption and trying to pervert the course of justice.

Michael Ahearne, 37, who had played Warrior in the popular ITV series, was sentenced to 15 months' imprisonment. He acted as a 'runner' between Detective Chief Inspector Elmore Davies, of Merseyside Police, and a powerful gang run by Curtis Warren, a convicted drugs baron. Davies, who was only weeks away from retirement, used Ahearne as a go-between in a ploy to help Warren's brother-in-law to evade prosecution for attempted murder. Davies was sentenced to five years' imprisonment. He passed on sensitive information about a fellow officer that included information about his home, his car and the location of his children's nursery. Ahearne, Tony Bray, 37, a businessman, and Davies, 50, all of Wirral, each denied conspiring to undermine the prosecution of a man later convicted of firearms offences.

The court heard that Davies had 'changed sides for money' and agreed to pass on information about the case of Philip Glennon junior, a member of an organised crime gang who was, at the time, facing attempted murder charges. Glennon had been accused of firing at PC Gary Titherington and a doorman at a Liverpool nightclub in July 1996. He was later sentenced to six years on lesser charges. Details of the conspiracy emerged when the Chief Constable of Merseyside, Sir James Sharples, authorised the electronic bugging of Davies's living room in December 1996. Ahearne was living as Davies's guest. The prosecution claimed that Davies was later heard discussing a payment of £10,000 with Ahearne. The jury of eight men and four women at Nottingham Crown Court spent seven hours and 37 minutes deliberating before reaching unanimous guilty verdicts. Bray was jailed for three years.

Mr Justice Curtis told Ahearne: 'I have not the least doubt that you were led into these crimes by Elmore Davies.' He accepted that Ahearne had not been involved for as long as his co-defendants. The judge told Davies that his motives for corruption were 'sheer greed' and anger at being passed over for promotion. His sentence reflected his betrayal of public trust. The judge said: 'No legal system can possibly tolerate the corruption of a senior detective in the very force responsible for the prosecution of the case.' The jury was told that Davies was the police end of a chain which led, via Ahearne and his associate, Tony Bray, to the Curtis Warren gang. Davies was recruited to supply inside information about the police prosecution. Peter Joyce, QC, for the prosecution, said that between July 1996 and March 1997 Davies did his best to 'undermine the prosecution of a man who had been charged with the attempted murder of a policeman from his own station – and he did it for money'.

Source: *The Times;* 25 September 1998

Corruption

While fraud has its roots firmly in the protection of property, the offence of corruption – and the current legislation – arose from the wish of Victorian reformers to develop a public interest dimension to holding public office and then to protect the interests of employers and others. There are three Acts dealing with corruption – 1889, 1906 and 1916[4] – while the 1925 Honours (Prevention of Abuse) Act made it a criminal offence to deal in honours, either as a broker or a purchaser (see Committee on Standards in Public Life 1998: 184–193).[5] Although there is no offence termed 'corruption' in the three laws, the adverb 'corruptly' is the term that implies motive to decisions or actions (or the failure to make a decision or to act) of an officeholder in both public and private sectors where the decision or action (or absence of either) is to the advantage of a person or entity which is providing the reward, fee or other item of value to the officeholder.[6] This may be either in advance or retrospectively (although case law states that the decision or action need not be followed through for a charge of corruption to be brought). Indeed, there is a common law offence of misconduct in public office which is concerned with doing or not doing what would be expected or required of the officeholder (and does not need to involve a third party – see Box 6.6) in relation to their official capacity.

Corruption and fraud are often linked together, in part because contracts won through bribery invariably involve fraud (the bribed officials often allow over-payments on the invoices or sign off work

Box 6.6 Misconduct in public office

The Conservative leader of a county council who re-drew the route of a £25 million road scheme to boost the value of his land was jailed for 18 months yesterday. Jim Speechley, 67, the former head of Lincolnshire County Council, persuaded engineers to move the route so it no longer passed through a field he owned. The change left his 4.21 acre plot untouched and inside the line of the projected A1073 Spalding to Eye bypass, vastly increasing its value as prime development land. A jury took over 10 hours to convict him of a charge of misconduct in public office after an eight-week trial at Sheffield Crown Court. Judge Simon Lawler, QC, told him: 'When such conduct is found proved the court is bound to take a serious view. It strikes at the very roots of our democracy. The public must have confidence in our public servants.'

Speechley, a farmer and landowner, from Crowland, near Peterborough, south Lincs, was also ordered to pay £25,000 costs. He bought the field at Barbers Drove on the outskirts of Crowland in 1971 and at today's prices it would be worth up to £17,000 as agricultural land if compulsorily purchased. But sandwiched between the bypass and the village, the plot could fetch £190,000 if developed for light industry and £375,000 if used for housing. Speechley, who spent 38 years in local government, had told the jury that it 'never crossed his mind' that he could benefit from its development potential. The court heard that while talking to a council engineer Speechley took out a red pen and drew a line on the plan to illustrate his preferred route.

Source: *The Daily Telegraph*, 3 April 2004

that is not completed) and in part because the recipient is seeking to obtain some form of covert financial advantage. Michael Allcock, for example, was a senior tax inspector in the then Special Office who was convicted and sentenced to five years' imprisonment for receiving some £148,000 in cash and kind – holidays, a prostitute, a cruise, etc. – from various foreign businessmen to vary or ignore their tax liability when he visited them, sometimes abroad, to negotiate tax settlements. Other inspectors were also disciplined for accepting hospitality and gifts (NAO 1998).

Corruption, like fraud, has been dealt with by police fraud squads or economic crime units. Most police forces (and now a number of public sector agencies) also have professional standards units that deal with internal corruption. In the case of the police this has come about because of officers' involvement with organised criminals, misuse of informant relationships, involvement in robberies and in the drugs trade (see Cox *et al.* 1977; Jennings *et al.* 1991; McLagan 2004). The Metropolitan Police unit is known as the Anti-Corruption Group and currently has 180 police officers and 32 civilian support staff and a budget of over £11 million.

Like fraud, corruption relates to the abuse or misuse of a 'normal' relationship, whether genuine or contrived, by either or both parties. Further, the decision or action (or absence of either) by one in favour of the other also requires deception of others and collusion between the two parties involved. It is not, on the other hand, noted for a significant number of reported cases. In 1999 it was argued that the cases of police corruption were not seen as numerically significant: as at 31 December 1998, 153 officers were suspended for alleged corruption and similar matters but 'this figure represents only 0.1 per cent of the 136,285 police officers serving in England, Wales and Northern Ireland. There were 28 officers convicted of corruption-related offences during 1998, which represents 0.02 per cent of serving officers, (HM Inspectorate of Constabulary 1999: 7).

Equally those in both public and private sectors under investigation by the various UK police forces in recent years has not been numerically significant – see Table 6.1. In fact, not all of the cases reported here actually relate to offences under the three Corruption Acts. Thus of the 2001 allegations six involved failure to disclose financial interests during council business, two involved theft, and one involved voter impersonation.

Table 6.1 Public sector corruption enquiries (1995–2001)

1995	1996	1997	1998	1999	2000	2001	2002 [part year]
83	95	99	64	69	36	67	20

The Committee on Standards in Public Life, like the 1976 Royal Commission wants a new corruption law (which would also include bringing MPs, currently exempt from the provisions of any criminal law in any parliamentary proceedings, within the ambit of that law). The Law Commission in a 1997 report had proposed that such a law should not be linked to fraud:

1.28 We provisionally conclude that corruption is not in essence, and should not be treated as, an offence of dishonesty or fraud. Dishonesty and fraud involve the unlawful infliction of loss, or the risk of loss; corruption is conduct conducive to breach of duty, and may or may not involve dishonesty or fraud.

1.30 ... Our view of corruption as a crime in its own right, independent of the law of fraud, has led us to the conclusion that it would be misguided to try to make it conform to the structure or conventions of that law. We have, for example, provisionally rejected the possibility of including a requirement that the defendant act 'dishonestly', either instead of or as well as a requirement that his or her conduct be 'corrupt'. We have instead tried to devise proposals which can be justified in terms of what we regard as the *essence* of corruption, rather than a feature which, though often present in corruption cases, is essentially incidental. (Law Commission 1997)

The Commission proposed a consolidation of the existing law and the introduction of a single bribery offence (in four Sections) around the agent–principal relationship which is still waiting for legislative time (see Parkinson 2005: 5/25–27). In the meantime, in response to the OECD Convention on Combating Bribery of Foreign Public Officials in International Business Transactions which sought to encourage developed countries to agree to try in their own countries company officials and others who pay bribes overseas, the government extended the territorial jurisdiction of the existing legislation. It hurriedly added clauses to an Act of Parliament which mainly addressed anti-terrorism matters brought about by the terrorist attacks of 11 September 2001.

The implications of extra-territorial investigations have been treated with concern by UK police forces because, despite the attempt to distinguish corruption from fraud, both are seen as economic or financial crimes and, as such, are investigated by fraud squads whose resources for any such investigation have been reduced in recent years (see Sharp 2005). Indeed, it is the SFO, set up primarily to deal with corporate fraud, that includes in its criteria for referral, corruption and which is currently looking into allegations of bribery by British Aerospace of MOD officials and Saudi princes and middlemen as part of the multi-billion-pound Al Yamamah arms contract. It now has a small group coordinating inquiries into the 20 or so allegations of corruption by UK companies overseas being reported by embassies and other sources.[7]

Summary

Whether the Law Commission likes it or not, the distinction between corruption and fraud, as with organised crime and fraud, is narrow. In addition, there is an increasing international dimension for both, whether involving arms contracts or people trafficking. While corruption involves a specific act and is criminalised as such, its inter-relation with other criminal activity raises questions of how agencies may work together to investigate fraud which crosses into many other areas. One of the other issues this chapter has drawn attention to, is that fraud is no longer (if it ever was) a white-collar crime or a specific area of criminal activity. Yet, as the next chapters will discuss, the various approaches to the investigation of fraud, and the agencies involved in it, often focus on a particular aspect of fraud in, or affecting the work of, their organisation or business. As has been seen from organised crime, therefore, it is often the objective of the organisation that determines the response for the prevention, detection, investigation and prosecution of fraud. The next three chapters discuss these agencies, what they do, how they do it and why.

Notes

1   The Office of the e-Envoy produced a document in 2003 indicating the minimum requirements for the verification of the identity of individuals (firstly to validate – does the claimed identity exist – and then to verify – is the person who they claim they are). The documentary evidence includes birth certificate, passport, driving licence, and so on; community-based evidence (that is, verifiable by the issuer) includes tax bill, mortgage statement, etc. Corroboration would come from a range of public and private sector agencies.

2   A number of police forces have received industry funding for specific types of crime such as frauds involving cars (the Finance and Leasing Association fund five police in the Metropolitan Police Vehicle Fraud Unit). Following a successful experiment in Greenwich, there is a current initiative to second an officer to each of the London borough, to be half-funded by the borough). Section 93 of the 1996 Police Act states that 'a police authority may, in connection with the discharge of any of its functions, accept gifts of money, and gifts or loans of other property, on such terms as appear to the authority to be appropriate' and that 'the terms on which gifts or loans are accepted … may include terms providing for the commercial sponsorship of any activity of the police authority or of the police force maintained by it.' A 2005 appeal case, *R. v. Hounsham* and

others, has raised the question of whether soliciting funds from corporate victims 'may compromise the essential independence and objectivity of the police when carrying out a criminal investigation.'

3   The trend towards organisational merger is also being pursued with police forces, in part to merger specialist squads that will deal with terrorism, organised crime and fraud that occurs at the inter-force or the National Intelligence Model Level 2 levels.

4   The 1916 Act transfers the presumption of guilt in cases involving public sector contracts when it has been proved money or any other advantage has changed hands but is avoided in England and Wales because it is assumed to breach defendants' human rights. The 1889 Act includes the power to forfeit or confiscate 'the amount or value of any gift, loan, fee or reward ...'.

5   The 1922 report of a Royal Commission which proposed the 1925 Act also led to the setting up of a committee concerned with checking the background and circumstances of those who were put forward for political honours (usually for having made contributions to party funds) and with 'deciding whether the nominees were "fit and proper" persons'. The recommendations are advisory and are not directly related to the Act. The Act makes it an offence to deal in honours, either as broker or purchaser, activities that have in the past (and currently) sparked off controversy in relation to possible breaches of the law.

6   This concept is applied elsewhere, but rarely known about. Thus the 1994 Medicines (Advertising) Regulations, a Statutory Instrument (or secondary legislation) approved under the 1972 European Communities Act and 1968 Medicines Act, made it a criminal offence punishable with up to two years' imprisonment for medical sales representatives to offer payments, excessive hospitality, sponsorships or gifts to any person 'qualified to prescribe or supply relevant medicinal products.' Hospitality includes invitations to and attendance at conferences where the social side has to be 'subordinate to the main scientific purpose of the meeting.'

7   As part of the Prime Minister's enthusiasm to tackle corruption in developing countries, a task force to deal with international corruption is to be set up, with the Department for International Development (DFID) minister as the 'ministerial champion for international corruption'. As part of this initiative DFID, the UK overseas development agency, has taken on the financial responsibility of funding 10 police posts within the City of London police Economic Crime Unit to focus on investigating allegations of corruption involving UK companies which the SFO decide to take on. A government action plan is to follow, as is a proposed enhanced role for the Metropolitan Police's Economic and Specialist Crime Unit in relation to overseas government politicians and officials laundering corruption proceeds in the UK.

Chapter 7

How fraud is dealt with – investigations

If the landscape of fraud is complex and varied, then so are the agencies and processes that govern its prevention, detection, investigation and prosecution. In order to bring some shape to the landscape, the next three chapters profile a range of approaches as follows:

- This chapter looks at what might be termed the more traditional law enforcement agencies whose remit in whole or in part relates to the investigation of fraud, but where resources are becoming limited and thus focused on more serious frauds.

- Chapter 8 looks at agencies which might have a range of statutory functions, including compliance and investigative, as well as anti-fraud responsibilities. This chapter looks at the specific powers the agencies have to deliver those functions. These powers explain in part why they, and not law enforcement, deal with fraud in their own areas but the other reason is because they can combine both investigative and compliance functions.

- Chapter 9 looks at fraud prevention, detection and investigation in both public and private sectors, primarily from the perspective of how individual institutions approach the question of fraud within their own organisations, either from their own remit or from that dictated by regulators and others.

General law enforcement: overview

By the end of the 1990s, most police forces acknowledged a decline in resourcing and prioritisation, such that the two surveys that established this (Doig, Levi and Johnson 1998 and Doig, Levi and Flanary 2000) noted that:

- Only one police force (City of London) identified fraud in their Local Policing Plan (although some have now included fraud in their Force Control Strategy);
- Most fraud squads had fewer than 10 officers, with only three having more than 40;
- Most had lost experienced senior officers and were now often led by middle-rank officers and experienced junior officers.

In work terms the surveys reported that police fraud squads were out of step with the rest of their forces; around 600 officers dealt with some 2,000 cases, averaging fewer than four cases a year, most of which took over a year to conclude. Yet, when assigned a value, the lowest value was £46,000 and the highest £2.3 million a case, with the average around £100,000 a case. The cases did not fall into an identifiable pattern (see p 56 above for the list of categories) and involved both professional criminals and corporate offenders. Fraud squads tended to become the repository of any case that had links to economic crime; thus they included cheque and credit squads, computer crime units, financial investigation units.[1] More than half of the cases involved work across force boundaries and a substantial minority had an overseas dimension.

The emphasis on serious crimes is complemented by a view that fraud may not be a police function and, if it is, should not be undertaken by each and every force. A report by the MHB consultancy (Morgan et al. 1996) into central specialist squads for the Home Office Police Research Group considered that:

- because of the high number of cross-boundary cases and the small size of fraud squads in some provincial forces, there was an argument that fraud squads should become regional, with smaller cases handled directly by BCUs.[2]

- due to pressure on resources, it could be argued that the police should stop investigating frauds which do not directly harm the general public; larger frauds, where big businesses were the victims, should be dealt with by those businesses.

Interestingly, both suggestions have, in different ways, occurred. The first attempt at the regionalisation of fraud squads has come with the formal arrangements between the City of London Police fraud squad and the SFO, see below, p 129) while the second suggestion is addressed in the private sector funding of policing (see the DCPCU, above, p 109).

The police fraud squad or economic crime unit

The criminal investigation of serious fraud still falls within the responsibility of the police. In the late 1990s only one did not have a fraud squad. Today an increasing number have either abolished them or merged them into a general serious crimes unit. The armed forces have a police force and each service has a specialist (detective equivalent) police unit (which often deals with travel and subsistence fraud). The Ministry of Defence has a police force responsible for armed forces bases and MoD activities; this includes a fraud squad. While the numbers of fraud officers are now around 600 for the whole of the UK, the volume and complexity of the work has not altered, as is illustrated by the work of one provincial force – South Yorkshire.

In the mid-1990s the South Yorkshire Police Commercial Branch had 12 staff – six Detective Constables (DC), four Detective Sergeants (DS), a Detective Inspector (DI) and a Detective Chief Inspector (DCI). The Squad began 1996 with a range of cases, but only one major case – a joint investigation with the SFO into a financial adviser. In the next two years, its resources were almost entirely taken up by two new cases; Facia and Doncaster Council.

Facia was the corporate vehicle used by Stephen Hinchcliffe to create one of the fastest-growing private retail empires in commercial history. In July 1994 he bought the Salisbury luggage chain and used it as a springboard to do a series of deals with major retailers to buy their unwanted chains. At its height Facia controlled more than 800 stores and 8,000 employees, including the Freeman Hardy Willis and Saxone shoe shops, Sock Shop, Oakland menswear, Contessa lingerie and the Red or Dead fashion brand. Hinchcliffe also bought Bata Shoes, the German footwear chain in 1996 but Facia collapsed soon after with debts of more than £30 million. Facia's main backer was the United Mizrahi Bank (UMB), which is based in Israel, but it pulled the plug after Sears sought an administrative order against the shoe division of Facia. In the same year, UMB asked a new manager to look through some of its loans after it found itself the owner of a cruise liner after the default on an unrelated loan. He found loans to Facia, unsupported by relevant documentation, which were reported to the police. Separately, a firm of accountants had looked through the books of Facia prior to taking up the external audit contract and had reported its findings to the SFO.

South Yorkshire police then found itself with a seven-year investigation into corporate theft, corruption, false accounting and conspiracy to defraud. Nine officers and six SFO staff had to unpick a complex and ramshackle business empire to see what Hinchcliffe had been doing. This resulted in two trials; one involving corruption and conspiracy and the other the theft and false accounting charges. The Branch also collected approximately 250,000 documents in the course of the investigation and utilised scanning technology in the prosecution of the case at the Old Bailey. The investigations costs were approximately £2.5 million.

In 2001 Stephen Hinchcliffe was sentenced to five years in prison (reduced to four on appeal) for bribing a UMB bank manager in return for some £8 million in unsecured loans to keep afloat the company (and fund his lifestyle, including a £3.5 million house, four cottages, Steve Davies's World Championship snooker table, a helicopter and a number of classic cars). He was declared bankrupt in the same year, with accountants PwC tasked by the DTI to trace any assets ('likely to be a complex task, given the nature of Mr. Hinchcliffe's business dealings', said PwC). In 2003, after he had left prison Hinchcliffe was back in court on charges of conspiracy to defraud (the charges involved sums in excess of £3.6 milliom) only to be awarded a suspended sentence of 15 months. Judge Jeremy Roberts had said it was 'entirely appropriate' for the defence team to ask what his sentence would be if Hinchcliffe pleaded guilty. This they did and Judge Roberts indicated that he would pass a suspended sentence of around 15 months, prompting Hinchcliffe to admit to the conspiracy charge. The judge argued that a new trial would involve 'an enormous expense', estimated at £6 million, involving three teams of lawyers and IT equipment (Hinchcliffe's co-defendant on the conspiracy charge was his Finance Director) and, because both men were bankrupt, the cost would fall on the public. 'The expense of the trial will be disproportionate to the benefit of the public from what will be achieved if they were convicted on all counts,' said Judge Roberts. The SFO was having none of it, having spent with South Yorkshire police some £4 million investigating Hinchcliffe, and appealed on grounds of 'undue leniency.' Three months later, in July, Hinchcliffe received an 18-month sentence (the Finance Director got a six-month suspended sentence).

Meanwhile, in 1997, after recording his concerns in an official report, the District Auditor was outlining to the Commercial Branch what was to become Operation Danum, the investigation into Doncaster Council. The final trial – a case involving regeneration projects – was held in 2004. The case was handled by a Corporate Investigations team which started with 20 officers and ended with five; two of those came from the Branch. In what turned out to be the largest ever local government corruption case, there were five related sets of investigations and trials – involving expenses, planning corruption, perverting the course of justice, contracts and regeneration. The District Auditor's full range of concerns in fact covered the following areas: members and officers' expenses, allowances and benefits; tendering procedures (including the identification of instances where contracts had been awarded without the tendering process having taken place) and private partnerships with local companies; open associations between elected members and prominent business people within the local community, which included gifts and hospitality; a general lack of financial control; and an absence of leadership at senior management and political levels within the Council.

These allegations swiftly appeared in the local (and subsequently national) press. After some random sampling to see whether or not the allegations had substance (they did) South Yorkshire police set up a dedicated team, including detectives from elsewhere in the force to offset the existing fraud squad commitments. A number of people came forward to help the police in their inquiries, including council employees, former councillors, members of the public, all of whom contributed further allegations including: planning and contracts corruption; nepotism; theft; deception; blackmail, and political bullying. As a result of this initial assessment, the police decided to concentrate on four specific areas of investigation: expenses/subsistence claim payments; tendering and contracts; planning (land deals and planning permission/bribery and corruption); council partnerships with large building developers.

The offences related to use of the corporate credit cards, official cars and mobile phones for personal use (leading to the arrest of a number of councillors); excessive hospitality and influence-peddling by development and building firms; bribes for contracts and planning permission (in one case, the cost of bribes were about 10 per cent of the £2 million a property dealer netted from the sale of land turned from being a protected countryside area to land approved for residential building). Over 60 councillors, officers, contractors and land developers were arrested. There were over 30 convictions for corruption, false accounting, theft and perverting the course of justice. The successful outcome of the investigations resulted from a large pool of police investigators at the outset, together with the use of a council internal inquiry team, access to all departments and personnel within the council (although often in spite of rather than with the cooperation of senior figures), contact with the District Auditor, specialised case management software, financial investigation, intelligence and other policing skills with appropriate staff. There was also early collaboration with the Crown Prosecution Service (CPS), who supplied special case workers to provide specialist advice and guidance (especially useful in analysing tendering and contracts, as well as planning enquiries).

The Commercial Branch of the South Yorkshire Police has since evolved into an Economic Crime Unit with the addition of a proactive money laundering team following the 'Payback Time' Report from HMIC in 2004 (a review of progress on asset recovery by police forces). That has led to abstraction of staff from the Unit towards an emphasis on money laundering rather than fraud investigation. Major fraud investigation still sits outside the Force Control strategy although the money laundering capability is catered for. Currently the Unit has nine staff, two of whom are employed under the 2002 Police Reform Act which allows for civilian appointments. It had 120 cases referred to it in 2003; one involves an alleged insurance fraud where the exposure of the uninsured companies through the theft of premiums runs to billions of pounds; a long firm fraud; an advanced fee fraud and the aftermath of the ILA fiasco (see above, p 66) A further 100 plus cases were referred to it in 2004, from which an invoice discounting fraud has been taken on together with inquiries into allegations regarding miners' health compensation claims (see above, p 78).

The criminal prosecution

When the Royal Commission on Criminal Procedures was set up in 1978 the then Labour Attorney General was also keen to address the delays and costs (largely associated with hiring accountants) associated with fraud trials. He agreed an interdepartmental committee to set up streamlined procedures but, when they didn't appear to be working, his Conservative successor agreed to a smaller group that was the genesis of the Fraud Investigation Group (FIG) within the Crown Prosecution Service (the 1981 Royal Commission report proposed that the police should no longer decide on who was to be prosecuted, and recommended an independent prosecution agency. This – the Crown Prosecution Service (CPS) – was introduced through the 1985 Prosecution of Offences Act). FIG was intended to bring together agencies dealing with fraud and to provide specialist prosecutors. Continuing concerns over the length of time to get cases to court from first inquiry (which was not always by a police fraud squad but often, for example, by the DTI), the availability or otherwise of specialist help (such as accountants), problems in accessing evidence, and delays in case preparation between lawyers and investigators (see Kirk and Woodcock 2003, Levi 1993, Widlake 1996) were then addressed by the Roskill Committee. Primarily known for its wish to do away with jury trials for fraud, its intended purpose was to review 'the conduct of criminal proceedings ... arising from fraud' (Roskill 1986: 5) and its major legacy was the recommendation for an organisational shape to the FIG approach and the allocation of specific powers. This was achieved through the 1987 Act which established the SFO (see also p 97).

With the establishment of the SFO (whose lawyer-led investigative teams operate in exactly the opposite way to the Phillips recommendation that led to the creation of the CPS), the FIG approach, based in London but with offices in the regions, continued. It dealt with more cases than the SFO, each involving substantial losses (see Levi 1993: 12–14 for a range of cases undertaken by FIG in 1992). This did raise the question of the boundary between the FIG and the SFO, reviewed in 1994 and 1995. At that time the balance between the two was that the FIG was dealing with 439 cases totalling £2,057 million and the SFO 51 cases totalling £4,429 million. FIG and SFO cases were of a similar type although the former worked on far more cases of corruption (51 in 1993 as opposed to four with the SFO) and mortgage fraud.

The 1994 Graham Report then recommended an expanded SFO take on the bigger cases being dealt with by the FIG (the Report recommended that a 'merged organisation comprising all the current caseload of the SFO and all the serious and complex cases being dealt with at FIG offers the best solution'). The revamped SFO would then operate a differentiated approach to cases depending on their complexity and what resources would be needed to investigate. The report declined to recommend whether the new body should remain as an independent agency or be established within the CPS where FIG was already renamed as the Fraud Divisions (and later Central Casework). This decision was given to another working party, the Davie Committee, which recommended in 1995 that no merger was necessary, subject to clearer implementation of acceptance criteria, possible sharing of staff and resources, and more formal arrangements between the police and the SFO. All this was lost by the time of the next review of the CPS – the 1998 Glidewell Review. It noted that the CPS internal organisational changes had prioritised devolution and front-line prosecution at the expense of the more serious or sensitive longer-term work (terrorism, police corruption, official secrets, cases from the Criminal Cases Review Commission, asset confiscation, etc.), as well as changing work practices and office arrangements. Within CPS serious fraud (overall the CPS presented 4,650 defendants for 'fraud and forgery' offences during 2004–05) has become part of the 'general work of Central Casework', or of specialist crime lawyers – Special Casework Lawyers. These have operated in two centres, dealing with fraud regionally, with the number of lawyers dealing with serious fraud limited, as have their relations with police fraud squads, although this is changing, along with other reforms currently underway (including a Fraud Prosecution Service within CPS).

Fraud cases which go to Central Casework should involve: losses over £750,000, corruption, an international dimension, specialist knowledge (relating to the regulators, shipping, currency, art, for example), or liquidations. Such cases follow the guidance laid down in the mid-1990s. This proposed involving the CPS early on: the choice of charges, file preparation and briefing reports, case planning and management, accountancy advice, witness statements and exhibits. Cases to go to court are assessed against the CPS Code for Prosecutors – a two-part test that looks at, the evidential criteria (can the evidence be used in court, is it reliable, the likelihood of conviction and appropriate punishment etc.?) and the public interest test (relating to the seriousness of the offence, the victim, the age of the allegations, etc.). Cases are then considered in terms of whether they should be dealt with at magistrates' or Crown Court as an indictable offence (see p 41). The decision to investigate fraud continues to lie with the police but, under statutory charging (a strand of the Criminal Case Management Programme, see p204), the CPS now decide who is charged, when and for what (see Fraud Review 2006: Chapter 9). This encourages their early involvement in cases and the 2004 Home Office circular 47/2004 indicates the criteria that may be used:

Priorities
- Frauds involving substantial sums of money. (NB: cases meeting the acceptance criteria of the SFO may be referred directly to the SFO, either by the victim or the police.)
- Frauds having a significant impact on the victim(s). A negligible loss to a large company, for example, could be catastrophic for a private individual or small business.

- Frauds affecting particularly vulnerable victims (e.g. the elderly, people with disabilities, businesses providing key services in difficult circumstances) or in distinct communities.
- Frauds giving rise to significant public concern (possibly highlighted by a high degree of press interest).
- Frauds committed by, or knowingly facilitated by, professional advisers (e.g. lawyers, accountants, merchant bankers).
- Frauds likely to undermine confidence in leading UK institutions or otherwise undermine the economy.
- Frauds committed by members of boards or other senior managers.
- Frauds where law enforcement action could have a material deterrent effect.
- Frauds which indicate a risk of more substantial/extensive fraud occurring.
- Cases where the victim has devoted significant resources to fraud prevention or has been willing to participate in appropriate crime prevention partnerships or otherwise assist the police.
- Frauds which it has been agreed should be a current law enforcement priority.

Cases where a more cautious approach might be appropriate

- Cases where the victim's motive for making the complaint appears to be malicious, primarily focused on recovering monies owed, or designed to distract attention from the complainant's own involvement in the fraud. (Such cases might nevertheless merit investigation, particularly where there are other victims involved.)
- Cases where victims are not prepared to cooperate fully with investigation and prosecution, although the police will always consider carefully how to assist victims and witnesses who have concerns about safety.
- Frauds more suitable for investigation by another enforcement or regulatory agency.
- Cases where another police force has decided not to investigate other than for geographical reasons.
- Frauds that have already been investigated by the police or other enforcement agency or that have been the subject of regulatory proceedings, unless significant new evidence has come to light or the previous investigation had a narrow remit that did not address all the relevant issues.

- Cases where the existence of other proceedings might have a detrimental effect on a criminal investigation and subsequent prosecution.
- Frauds where the victim's conduct has contributed to the loss, in particular where the police have previously given guidance or warnings to victims about fraud risks that have not been acted upon.
- Frauds which took place a long time ago (probably more that two years) unless there are exceptional circumstances.
- Frauds where the likely eventual outcome, in terms of length of sentence and/or financial penalty, is not sufficient to justify the likely cost and effort of the investigation.

Police and prosecutors – the SFO and the City of London Police

The SFO was set up with a permanent staff that included accountants (including some from DTI and Inland Revenue, plus seconded staff from City firms, which the Treasury funded, unasked) and lawyers (some of whom lead the investigations as 'case controllers'). It is a department of central government under the supervision of the Attorney General, rather than a law enforcement or police agency. Most of the police it used were drawn from the City of London and Metropolitan services who were seconded to, but who cannot be part of the staff complement of, the SFO. The case controllers directed the investigations but could not give orders to the police officers (although the SFO went on to employ some ex-police officers among its investigators). Outside London, officers were seconded to cases in their area, with the SFO paying for the non police investigation costs (such as contract accountants, IT forensics, SFO investigators and prosecutors) although there was still some resistance over officer abstraction.

The criteria for cases which both public and private sector institutions were expected (but not required) to send to the SFO were: a value of £1 million or more (it was raised for a time to £5 million but returned to the original figure after the Davie review – see above, p 126); public concern; the need for specialist financial knowledge; complexity; an international dimension; the need for the joint use of accountants and investigators; and the use of its particular powers. These include an ability to share information and the Section 2 requirement. This seeks to overcome confidentiality by requiring witnesses and suspects to attend for interview, answer questions,

129

provide explanations and produce documents believed relevant to an investigation at the request of a designated SFO official (a definition which excludes a police officer). The purpose of the SFO's structure was to use teams for cases, with the lawyer determining the lines of inquiry, to focus means in order to produce and present evidence, as the Act says, 'in a form ... to be likely to aid comprehension by the jury', and to expedite a multi-disciplinary investigative approach to a range of innovative, complex or serious frauds.

Today, operating under unchanged criteria and to the same business plan, the SFO comprises a number of divisions: policy, corporate services, accountancy (including forensic computing and graphics work for presentation of evidence), and four investigation and prosecution divisions (each with approximately 50 to 70 staff, including lawyers and SFO-employed investigators) which have geographical responsibilities. There is an ad hoc team staffed by contractors – outside staff – and funded by a specific allocation to deal with the NHS pharmaceuticals case. There are 300 staff in total; approximately half are investigators, recruited from other agencies like the HMRC, the private sector and, increasingly, ex-fraud squad officers.

There is a formal vetting process which considers whether or not the allegation meets the SFO criteria, whether prosecution is in the public interest, and whether there is a realistic prospect of conviction. This generates a paper up to the Director for him or her to agree a (Section 1) decision to take on the case. There is also a Joint Vetting Committee, set up after the 1994 Graham Report on the handling of serious fraud to improve inter-agency contact between the SFO and the CPS. It comprises, among others, the DTI, ARA, the FSA and the City of London police, to consider cases referred to each of them in case of mutual interest or, occasionally, to transfer cases between them (but, despite its title, the Committee does not vet cases).

This process allows the SFO to take on approximately 20 to 30 new cases a year. Annually the SFO, which costs some £42–45 million annually to run, has about 80 cases under investigation or going through the courts. The SFO publishes its acceptance criteria, its investigative approach (its website includes a number of files oultining the approach), lists of completed and on-going cases (where appropriate). While the majority of cases continue to come from the usual routes (the police, followed by the DTI) the SFO now has an on-line reporting facility. During 2003 the SFO worked on a total of 84 cases (excluding appeals) and by the end of the year had 71 on-going cases with an aggregate value of £1.84 billion. During the year, 14 trials were concluded involving 39 defendants; 19 were acquitted either by jury or on direction of the judge. 10 involved guilty pleas and 10 were found guilty in court cases. Nineteen of the convicted defendants received custodial sentences, four of which were suspended. There was one community service order. The longest term of imprisonment was six years. Seven other cases at trial were part completed with six defendants waiting to be sentenced, three defendants acquitted and verdicts on 17 still to be determined. Confiscation orders, amounting to £2.9 million, were made against eight defendants in five cases. The largest confiscation sum ordered against a single defendant was £1.29 million. Over the past decade, its rate of successful conviction completion has run at over 60 per cent.

The SFO considers that its focus and approach – regular conferences, task management, early involvement of counsel, multi-disciplinary team work on each case, graphical and electronic presentation of evidence, and so on – works. It has funding for big cases and can deliver complex cases relatively quickly. The issue has been staffing over and above its own in-house investigative capability. At the same time, Ross Wright had, as head of the SFO, written to the Attorney General in her letter accompanying the 1999/2000 Annual Report that: 'I continue also to be concerned about the ever increasing attrition in the police resources both in terms of numbers and experience available for our cases. As I wrote to you, in the letter prefacing last year's annual report, it is essential in every SFO case that we are able to rely on the active involvement of the police, working closely with and as part of the SFO case team. My fear then was that this involvement was diminishing. In the past year, the situation has, if anything, deteriorated further. In addition, it is no secret that there is a body of fraud being committed that is outside our criteria which is not being investigated or prosecuted by any agency.'[3]

Efforts by the SFO to be certain of sufficient officers in provincial forces or to secure the long-term secondment of Metropolitan or City Police officers, have not been successful. A Cabinet Office working group – Improving the Response to Fraud and comprising representatives from a range of organisations, including ACPO, the DTI, the CPS, the FSA, HM Treasury and the Home Office – was set up with Wright as the chair to agree the investigative capability for the SFO. While initial thoughts were around more police officers and more money, the concept of a National Fraud Squad, with regional teams, along the lines of the National Crime Squad, emerged. This would comprise some 1,200 officers (the existing 600 among the various fraud squads and a further 600) and include the SFO; the costing put the price at £85 million. While the Cabinet Office was in favour and HM Treasury did not object to the costs, ACPO (and the Home Office taking its lead from ACPO) did demur, on the grounds of loss of staff and the anticipated top-slice of funds to the forces to pay for the new Squad.

The secondary position proposed by the Working Group was for larger forces to link to the SFO as 'lead' forces in their area to take responsibility for all SFO-accepted cases nationally. This led to an amended proposal for this to occur in the first instance in the south-east with the City of London Police fraud squad as the lead force. The decision was not followed through when the SFO's budget went up but was revived after the Attorney General put pressure on the Home Office to make a decision on the proposal. Following a costing exercise by the City of London police (which asked for £5.3 million and 63 more staff) the decision finally went ahead for some extra 26 officers to be recruited by the City of London Police fraud squad. The additional funding was found by the Home Office by switching its funding from the DCPCU (see above, p 109), topped up with an annual £1 million from the City of London Corporation. A set of performance measures for the initiative was drawn up, based on the City of London fraud squad taking a number of cases annually that were neither SFO nor City cases but occurred in the south-east region.

The current City of London Police fraud squad structure was introduced in April 2004. It covers the Home counties whose forces may or may not retain their own fraud squad and has some 130 officers (12 in the Cheque and Credit Card Unit, 17 in the Financial Investigation Unit and 90 in the Fraud Squad; the DCPCU is attached for organisational purposes). The force collaborates with the SFO but is not part of it (indeed, the officers are not located at Elm Street although co-location is planned) and the work is allocated on the basis of: the normal City of London Police fraud squad work, all SFO cases from London, any Home Counties case that is not taken on the existing fraud squads. The distribution of cases from these three sources is: 100 to 120 cases relating to normal work; 4 to 9 SFO cases; 12 to 30 Home Counties cases.

The relationship is new in that the SFO is lawyer-driven, working on the basis of the pivotal role of the case controller. It is reluctant either to let the lead force take the lead or to allow anyone other than SFO staff to exercise its statutory Section 2 powers. On the other hand, continuous team-working, proposed shared premises (by 2007), shared IT and an evidence management system (Docman) are all intended to promote common practice and culture. It may beg the question of other possible changes. The 2006 Fraud Review looked at a number of options, such as reversing the decline of staffing in existing police forces, regionalisation, a bigger role for SOCA and a national Fraud Squad. Apart from suggesting that existing force fraud staffing be ring fenced (or even increased; it did suggest another 306 officers) and that BCUs have the capacity to undertake Level 1 fraud investigations, the main proposal, modelled on the Special Branch approach, was for the City of London to develop its 'Lead' force role to act as a Centre of Excellence to advise, support and even provide leadership to other forces' investigations, as well as disseminate good practice, coordinate training, and offer fraud prevention advice. It would also house a National Fraud Reporting Centre which would take in all crime reports of fraud (to 'relieve police of the burden of accepting reports of fraud') and reports from other areas, using them to ensure accurate crime reporting and to develop analyses of trends and so on, to inform a more NIM-led approach, before sending packages relating to Level 2 and Level 3 frauds to the police and other law enforcement agencies on a pre-agreed basis. This would be underpinned with eight regional support centres to provide surveillance and other technical support to fraud investigations, new performance measures to make the investigation of fraud worthwhile for forces, and access to specialist fraud CPS lawyers (outside the Fraud Investigation Service within CPS), as well as experiments in increasing the civilian staff component within fraud squads or using more external accredited investigators (see p234).

Summary

While the SFO has begun to address the resourcing of the investigation of serious and complex fraud, the Fraud Review Final Report (2006) has also noted what has been known for a long time: that, in general, 'police investigative resources are small and declining and often diverted to other "high priority" tasks and that, within police "Economic Crime" departments, which is where many fraud squads are located, the allocation of resources is being prioritized towards financial intelligence and money laundering and away from fraud' (2006: 131). This is clearly a consequence of the wider public order, public safety and financial confiscation agendas pursued by successive governments. Investigating and prosecuting fraud does not count in terms of measuring the delivery of those agendas or league tables of performance, and so is not seen as a priority by politically attuned

Chief Constables. The SFO, which was concerned about the resourcing of investigations, now has an enhanced lead force to draw on, and may consider the regionalization of its activities – a variation on a proposal raised in the Fraud Review in terms of the regionalisation of existing fraud squads. That there has been no public, political or corporate outcry about the decline in police resources devoted to fraud is itself noted by the Final Report which states that:

> ... by comparison, investigations into frauds committed against some areas of the public sector ... are well resourced; other public sector bodies investigate some frauds against business and the personal sector ... but have limited scope and powers; most large financial institutions have internal investigative capacity which is largely directed at disciplining staff who commit fraud and seeking civil redress where this is worthwhile. (2006: 132)

The comparison is, however, not so simple. If investigative capacity is at one end of the spectrum, then audit, compliance and regulation is at the other, with various permutations in between. The next chapter addresses these latter areas.

Notes

1   The 2006 Fraud Review Team Interim Report reported that, currently, England and Wales's police Economic Crime Units comprise 416 fraud officers, 118 dealing with cheque and credit card fraud, 495 in financial investigation units and 143 dealing with money laundering. In total they represent less than 0.3 per cent of the 143,510 police officers in England and Wales.
2   BCU: Basic Command Unit, the basic management unit in a police force.
3   In July 2006 the current head of the SFO repeated the concerns in the annual report: 'There remains a gap between the incidence of fraud and the number of investigations, let alone prosecutions. Some way needs to be found to ensure that there is adequate resourcing for the investigation of crimes which unjustly enrich some while impoverishing others. I am not suggesting that the justice gap can be closed – merely narrowed.' (see *Times* 25 July 2006).

Chapter 8

Regulation, compliance and audit

This chapter looks at the role of audit, compliance and regulation to deal with fraud. There are a number of areas where the state has provided regulators with statutory powers to regulate specific areas or activity. The powers usually include the right to control entry to, and take part in, the activity, as well as to monitor the conduct associated with that activity and sanction offenders. Some, like the FSA and the Law Society, discussed here, are funded entirely by their members; others, like the Charity Commission, are funded by the state.

Financial investigations

Revenue

Today, the bulk of HM Customs and Excise (including VAT and frontier protection) remains with Inland Revenue to form the new HM Revenue and Customs Agency (HMRC) which will focus on intelligence, detection (including contraband and drugs), serious civil investigations (including dealing with Hansard) and criminal investigations. The powers, co-location, staff integration, common terms and conditions of service, etc., of the new agency have not yet been completed. The core difference between the new HMRC and any other enforcement agency has been that its business is about maximisation of revenue to the state which means that compliance and settlement are more important than investigation and prosecution. At nearly 50 per cent of the £214 billion annual revenue, income tax is the largest source (followed by National Insurance contributions at 31 per cent and Corporation tax at 15 per cent). Nearly 75 per cent of tax paid on income is individual PAYE. There is (see above) a common law offence of cheating the revenue and, since 2001, a criminal offence of fraudulently evading income tax. Most of the work of the 86,000 HMRC staff is concentrated on the collection of taxes – from National Insurance (when it took over the Contributions Agency) to the repayment of student loans – but it is now also involved in making payments through tax credits.[1]

The investigations into failure to pay tax centre on error, negligence and evasion; of the latter two, negligence is concerned with a failure to take reasonable care on providing information and documentation while evasion adds deliberate intent. In relation to business, the potential areas of fraud cover manipulating profits and expenditure (and associated invoice, stock recording and other documentation) to reduce the tax liability, not registering for tax purposes, entering into leasing and other deals with the primary purpose to avoid tax liability, and falsifying (with or without collusion with employees) NI and PAYE returns.

The general level of revenue fraud work is based on compliance. This now includes random checks (full or partial), risk profiles, benchmarking and data mining (introduced in 1997 with the introduction of self-assessment; previously there had to be 'good reason' to initiate inquiries). This work suggests that around 30 per cent of returns are non-compliant which, at local office level, will yield around another £1.3 billion. Most non-compliant taxpayers will have the opportunity to settle and be subject to appropriate payments and associated financial penalties.

Specialist revenue work, with a particular focus on fraud, is undertaken by the Special Compliance Office (SCO). The SCO was set up in 1994 through the merger of the Board's Investigation Office (which dealt with internal fraud, and construction industry prosecutions and PAYE fraud), the Special Office (dealing with the more complex avoidance cases, such as celebrities or foreign taxpayers resident here and liable to UK tax – known as 'ghosts' – and so on), and the Enquiry Branch (which dealt with frauds working towards civil settlements, using the Hansard approach, and prosecution of accounts-based fraud). The SCO is divided into 10 regional offices, most of whom have three main investigative groups – evasion (undertaking the former Enquiry Branch work, with about 80 staff), avoidance (complex cases where serious fraud may not be suspected but where the individual or company have arranged their tax affairs to minimise tax liability,[2] with over 70 staff) and criminal investigations which deals with complex fraud investigations and volume-fraud investigations (tax credits and Grabiner informal economy cases) that may be prosecutable.

There are further units within each group (such as the Insolvency and Confiscation Group which deals with confiscation associated with criminal cases or abuse under the Insolvency Act) although the old specialist units such as those dealing with entertainers or sports personalities have gone. The SCO handles some 400 fraud cases and 400 avoidance cases a year, with the main sources coming from internal referrals and the use of its own intelligence. The civil side undertakes 'Hansard' inquiries where those suspected of non-compliance have the opportunity to respond to the 'Hansard' questions – see Box 8.1 – in full and make appropriate restitution. Failing to respond would lead to a full investigation and possible prosecution.

Box 8.1   The five questions which are asked in conjunction with the Hansard extract (in Code of Practice 9)

QUESTION 1

Have any transactions been omitted from or incorrectly recorded in the books of any business with which you are or have been concerned whether as a director, partner or sole proprietor?

QUESTION 2

Are the accounts sent to the Inland Revenue for any business with which you are or have been concerned whether as a director, partner or sole proprietor, correct and complete to the best of your knowledge and belief?

QUESTION 3

Are all the tax returns of any business with which you are or have been concerned whether as a director, partner or sole proprietor correct and complete to the best of your knowledge and belief?

QUESTION 4

Are all your personal tax returns correct and complete to the best of your knowledge and belief?

QUESTION 5

Will you allow an examination of all business books, business and private bank statements and any other business and private records in order that the Revenue may be satisfied that your answers to the first four questions are correct?

Source: www.hmrc.gov.uk

With the emphasis on collection, HMRC has tended not to rely too much on prosecutions; current cases taken to court are some 60 involving complex fraud (and associated with the construction industry), 500 involving tax credits, and 70 involving Grabiner cases. On the other hand, professionals, such as accountants, will be prosecuted in the hope of a deterrence effect and will include recovery by tax assessment or confiscation. The SCO has an intelligence unit, as well as seconding staff to NCIS. It has a number of legal gateways to share intelligence and operates a number of formal joint working arrangements such as being part of the Northern Ireland Organised Crime Task Force. The decision on whether to prosecute is based on whether or not there is a fraud against the revenue, or falls within certain criteria (including that of the CPS Code for Prosecutors) and whether evidence is available. Investigators work to police standards; although staff have no power of arrest, they do have search and production powers (including production of original documents that could be used as evidence in court) which come from the 1970 Taxes Management Act (which remains in place pending harmonisation of powers and legislation for the new agency).

While there are local investigations, and for which there are powers to access records, the SCO is normally informed following compliance work of any cases where: false accounts have been deliberately compiled; there has been alteration or falsification of documents supporting accounts or tax liability; there are grounds for suspecting the honesty of a solicitor, accountant or any tax adviser; the taxpayer or directors have conspired with a third party to defraud the revenue; a Certificate of Disclosure or Statement of Assets signed during a current or earlier investigation turns out to be false; the potentially fraudulent taxpayer is a member of either House of Parliament or has a special status in the administration of justice or tax; there is suspected fraud or evasion using the vehicle of an offshore company or other foreign entity; informers have valuable information about a suspected fraud or substantial evasion; the case involves case 'phoenixism' (bankrupting a company but then setting up a new company with the assets of the old company); there is a failure to notify chargeability or very late filing; there are serious PAYE irregularities.

More specialist areas include: shadow economy working; money laundering and serious and complex non-compliance, including fraud. Post-Grabiner work was developed with HM Customs and Excise and DWP, initially allocating 40 staff for civil recovery (in 2001 HM Treasury provided funding within SCO for seven teams, each with seven staff to deal with the new criminal tax evasion offence as part of the Grabiner work). Neither the additional tax yield or cases being taken to prosecution are significant in relation to Grabiner work. More recently, the Inland Revenue established an Anti-Money Laundering Unit (AMLU) in the SCO. AMLU has a remit to undertake criminal investigations into acts of money laundering predicated on tax offences.

Regulation

The Department for Trade and Industry (DTI)

The DTI's work covers everything to do with business from the promotion of SMEs to support for exports with credit facilities (through the Export Credit Guarantee Department, one of several executive agencies that work on a semi-detached basis to the DTI). Its work is divided into 'Groups' (General Innovation Group, General Energy Group, etc.), including the Fair Markets Group. This Group includes the Corporate Law and Governance Directorate. One of the core DTI objectives is ensuring a fair market – to support confidence in the capital market through effective company reporting, promoting a system of governance, ensuring a supportive legal framework, and enforcing the framework to support enterprise, ensure compliance and deter wrongdoing. The Directorate has a division dealing with law and corporate governance (a policy function responsible for changes to company laws, negotiating the harmonisation of UK and EC requirements on laws and governance, liaising with the accountancy bodies and the CBI on corporate governance). There is a much larger division – Companies Investigations Branch (CIB) – dealing with company investigations.

CIB was set up in 1998 and is responsible to the Secretary of State for considering complaints about the conduct of companies and carrying out investigations and inspections under the Companies Acts and the Financial Services Act 1986. It covers investigations into possible fraud, insider dealing and offences arising from insolvency and initiating appropriate follow up action and disclosure of information to other regulators. The differences in focus and implementation for the main triggers within the Companies Act are:

- Section 431 is an inquiry at the request of the company or its shareholders;
- Section 432 is where the Secretary of State him/herself suspects fraud, misconduct or information concealed from the shareholders;

- Section 442 is concerned with who owns a company;
- Section 446 relates to share dealings by directors, families or associates directly or through companies the directors control.

Inspections may be undertaken by CIB officers or by appointed private sector lawyers or accountants. CIB may also investigate under the 1989 Companies Act (Section 82 – investigation to assist overseas regulator), the 1982 Insurance Companies Act (Section 44 – examine records of insurance business), the 2000 FSMA (Section 168 – insider dealing), and the 1973 Fair Trading Act (Section 29 – investigate money circulation schemes and illegal lotteries).

The CIB has around 100 staff and running costs are around £5 million a year. The CIB essentially has two activities: the vetting of complaints (pre-vetting and full vetting) and the investigation of complaints. About 25 staff members are assigned to the former activity, dealing with (on average) over 4,700 annual complaints primarily from the public (nearly 60 per cent) and from within the DTI (20 per cent, often from existing inquiries). Many do not fall within the CIB remit (either the wrong department, or involving individuals, sole traders or partnerships). Nearly 900 are fully vetted. Where there is evidence of misconduct or fraud and where the case falls within the responsibility of the Department, and after various checks with Companies House, other regulators, and sometimes the complainant, about 200 of these are accepted. The basis for acceptance – the legislation governing DTI investigations requires 'good reason' – includes: evidence of the public interest being served; the 'amenability' of an inquiry (whether or not there is corporate entity to investigate, or whether it trades in the UK); the amount of money at risk (usually over £50,000), the 'freshness' of the complaint; the reasonable possibility of a 'positive outcome'; and so on. Most of the complaints concern fraudulent trading (92 per cent of accepted investigations in 2003/04 and 84 per cent the next year).

Many of the cases concern smaller, often unlisted businesses, although investigations also involve major companies, such as Versailles and British-American Tobacco.[3] Most of the offences involve: deliberate investment fraud (such as wine investment, property-to-let frauds); failure to provide services; fraudulent trading; and money circulation schemes. Some of the frauds follow a fashion (such as holiday clubs). CIB's principal function is to stop the activity and protect the public. Much of its approach is thus away from the large formal Section 432 inquiries led by outside appointments towards the shorter and quicker Section 447 inquiries – see Box 8.2. The Section 432 inquiries were expensive and could last for years – Guinness ran from 1986 to 1997 and cost £2.8 million; the *Mirror* inquiry ran from 1992 to 2001 and cost £8 million; Atlantic Computers lasted from 1990 to 1994 and cost £6 million. A serious concern related to the possibility of a prosecution after such a long time.

Box 8.2 a Section 447 inquiry

A company which lured aspiring publicans to part with substantial fees in return for training and a placement in a pub of their choice has been wound up following a DTI investigation. Tudor Inns Ltd, based in West Yorkshire, took fees of around £4,000 to £5,000, claiming that clients would be trained in how to run a pub. Around 60 people from across the UK parted with money after being told they could put their name down for a pub of their choice. They were often shown lists of pubs that were expected to become available, and were able to specify what type of pub they would like to run. In reality, the training was poor and the promised pub often failed to materialise. Those who were given pubs to run often found that they were far below the standard they had requested; some had even been closed down following drugs busts.

DTI investigators found that the company:

- made misleading statements in their training contracts by promising a public house placement after trainees completed their training;
- failed to maintain and/or preserve adequate accounting records;
- failed to file accounts and annual returns; and
- had been abandoned by their officers on ceasing to trade.

Tudor Inns Limited was wound up in the public interest on 18 April 2005. The Official Receiver was appointed liquidator of the company, and a forerunner, Britannia Inns, which was already in liquidation.

The petition to wind up the company in the public interest was presented on 4 March 2005 under the provisions of Section 124A of The Insolvency Act 1986 following enquiries conducted under Section 447 of the Companies Act 1985 by the DTI's Companies Investigation Branch.

Source: DTI website – filed 28 April 2005

Section 447 inquiries are quicker, fact-finding inquiries (taking on average three months and costing on average £25,000) undertaken by CIB's 48 staff in Branches B, C and D to an average target of 90 days to complete. The inquiries are not criminal investigations but seen as 'pathfinder' inquiries for other action. The inquiries are confidential. The DTI does not announce investigations, or respond to questions as to whether or not a particular company is under investigation, to preclude reputational or trading damage. Officials have formal 'authorisation' to serve a notice of the start of a s.447 inquiry (necessary to later access bank records of the business) and then to obtain records and to require past or present directors or employees or relevant advisers to give explanations (although as this is a civil inquiry, PACE considerations do not apply) on any aspects of their contents. It is an offence to fail to do so, to give a false or misleading answer, as it is to falsify, hide or destroy documents. No statements are taken – the investigation is all about production of documents and explanations of them – and nor is a transcript of the explanations required, although notebooks are used to keep a record.

While CIB investigators do not have a right of access, they do have the powers to obtain warrants for entry and document seizure. The new Companies (Audits, Investigations and Community Enterprise) Act is introducing wider powers – the right of access, to move around in and remain on 'relevant' premises (including private residences if believed to be used for the company's business purpose), to specify the handing over of information (the term 'records' in the previous legislation becoming any information relevant to the inquiry in whatever form), the ability to require explanations from anybody 'reasonably' believed to be able to assist the inquiry, and the ability to offer protection from any legal liability for a breach of confidence by anyone – including complainants – making a 'relevant disclosure.' It is also an offence to 'intentionally' obstruct an investigator and a possible contempt of court for failing to produce documents, or refusing to allow an investigator to enter and remain on premises.

Information obtained in these inquiries is generally confidential and it is usually a criminal offence to reveal such information without agreement. There is however a list of exceptions (s.449) which allows information to be passed on, for example, in cases of suspected crime or to enable regulatory and professional authorities to take action. Indeed, as a pathfinder inquiry, the CIB has the decision during, but more usually at the end of, an inquiry to ask another agency to take on the case (as with Versailles) or progress it internally.

An s.447 investigation has a number of possible outcomes – winding up the company; prosecuting offenders or passing information to another prosecuting agency, regulator or disciplinary body; publishing a report; seeking the disqualification of the directors. In 2003/04, there were around 100 disclosures to other bodies, two convictions, 19 disqualifications and 370 companies wound up. When the public is at risk, the Secretary of State may ask the court to stop a company trading at once by appointing an Official Receiver (see below) as provisional liquidator to safeguard any assets and records until such time as the company is wound up. Where there is evidence of misconduct by a company's directors, DTI can also ask the courts to disqualify them as directors of any company for a specified period up to 15 years.

Within the Legal Services Group the Legal Services Directorate has a small office (D1) that can give advice during the vetting process or during or after an s.447 inquiry. If the CIB considers that there is evidence of criminality then it may send it to another agency or refer the report to the DTI prosecution lawyers (termed D2, and which has 19 staff). D2 vets the allegations and decide that, if there is evidence of criminality (primarily under companies legislation or the Theft Acts), then the actual inquiry is handed to Legal Services investigators (of whom there are 50 in seven offices in England and Wales) to undertake inquiries and interviews to a criminal standard (although they have no special powers). Sometimes DTI will pass information to other regulatory bodies, and ask them to consider whether offences have been committed in their areas or if other action is necessary. In the same way DTI sends information to professional bodies (for example, the ICAEW) for them to take disciplinary action. In less serious cases, DTI may simply give companies or directors a warning, and tell them to rectify the faults found.

The Insolvency Service (IS)

Most of D2's work comes from the Insolvency Service for insolvency offences – failure to disclose assets, disposing of assets, failure to cooperate, providing false information, or acting as company director when disqualified. The Insolvency Service (IS) became an Executive Agency of the DTI in March 1990. The Service operates mainly under the 2000 Insolvency Act, the 1986 Insolvency Act (which gives the IS the power to investigate the cause of business failure), the 1986 Company Directors Disqualification Act and the 1985 Companies Act. It deals with insolvency matters in England and Wales and some limited insolvency matters in Scotland. The Insolvency Service has 39 Official Receiver (OR) offices at 33 sites throughout England

and Wales together with 15 Headquarters Sections based in London, Birmingham, Manchester and Edinburgh. The ORs have a statutory duty to investigate the causes of failures of debtors and company directors; they are responsible for all bankruptcies and for companies wound up by the courts. They:

- undertake the initial administration of the estates of bankrupts and companies in compulsory liquidation;
- act as trustee/liquidator where no private sector insolvency practitioner is appointed;
- investigate the circumstances and causes of failure of companies wound up by the court and of individuals subject to bankruptcy orders;
- report any misconduct on the part of directors or bankrupts;
- deal with the disqualification of directors in corporate failures;
- provide banking and investment services for bankruptcy and liquidation estate funds.

Its work is largely concerned with the compulsory bankruptcy or winding-up of partnerships and limited liability companies by the courts 'to ensure that financial failure is dealt with fairly and effectively and that fraud and financial misconduct is detected and deterred.' The Insolvency Service acts as trustee for the former, liquidator for the latter and covers the causes or circumstances of failure, misconduct by directors or bankrupts and reports from liquidators alleging criminality. The OR heads the Insolvency Service offices around the country, overseeing teams of examiners to interview directors with the intention of ascertaining what went wrong, who is owed money and what assets exist. If there are assets then a meeting of creditors is called and a private sector insolvency practitioner appointed as trustee or liquidator (although who will take on such work depends on the level of assets).

The OR also deals with investigations into the conduct of directors with a view either to disqualification (a D report to the DTI's Disqualification Unit) or reporting to the DTI's prosecutions office if there is evidence of wrongful or fraudulent trading, etc. Disqualification is dealt with primarily through the 1986 Company Directors Disqualification Act and the 2000 Insolvency Act (which cover 'persistent' breaches of companies' legislation, fraud in winding up, etc.). The Disqualification Unit acts on OR or insolvency practitioner reports, taking into account the size of the failure, the nature of the alleged misconduct and any mitigating factors. In 2003, over 1500 people were disqualified – nearly two-thirds for up to five years.

The Insolvency Service has extensive powers relevant to its work – requiring cooperation for the public examination of officers or managers of companies or requiring banks to produce bank statements, or accountants to produce records on, for example, information relating to the recovery of assets or misconduct. The Insolvency Service caseload is over 25,000 bankruptcies and over 6000 compulsory liquidations a year. The main fraud-related offences are: fraud while the company was being wound up; failure to keep accounting records; fraudulent trading.

From 2004, as a result of the 2002 Act, there are five new regional units to deal with complex or lengthy asset realisation work and also new post-bankruptcy individual voluntary arrangement cases which were previously only dealt with by insolvency practitioners. The 2002 Act changes the impact of bankruptcy on the basis that 'honest failure' should not be treated as harshly as dishonesty. This would allow discharge to take place more quickly in some cases. Where dishonesty has been demonstrated, however, those involved would be subject to a bankruptcy restriction order that bans certain types of employment and requires disclosure to a third party if seeking, for example, credit over £500. A breach may incur imprisonment or a fine (known by some as the corporate ASBO). It is suggested that the DTI's CIB will be absorbed into IS in the next few years on the grounds that its work better fits with that of the IS.

The Law Society

The Law Society is currently overseen by a Council of over 100 solicitors and lay members who determine general rules (subject to the approval of the Master of the Rolls) that govern admission as a solicitor to the Roll, how an admitted solicitor may practise and how they maintain their accounts and records, as well as rules as and when required on specific areas (most are in the Guide to Professional Conduct of Solicitors). The Law Society had an extensive range of functions and powers, from determining when solicitors may supervise their own practice to its members accepting the right of the Society to review their affairs. The Law Society undertakes five functions typical of regulated professions – deciding entry (standards to be achieved to satisfy entry, training to be undertaken as a member, and so on); formulation of the rules by which members are expected to work; enforcement of those rules; dealing with complaints; disciplining members for breaches of the rules. The role of the Law Society means that solicitors belong to a professional association which provides two functions. One is representative that provides services and support for members. The other is regulatory which provides the parameters within which solicitors and their employees work and ensures compliance. This has a number of advantages and disadvantages. Included in the advantages are the detailed rules (the Solicitors' Account Rules and the Solicitors' Practice Rules among others) governing solicitors' conduct, such as the safeguards for client money, or billing procedures. All trainee and admitted solicitors are subject to the regulation function.

The Law Society, however, has had to balance the representative and the regulatory functions, especially in the eyes of the public, given the amounts of monies held by solicitors and the solicitors' access to specific funding – see Box 8.3 – and monopoly of certain functions.

In the early 1980s, the Law Society was the subject of substantial criticism over Glanville Davies, a solicitor who at that time had been a member of the Council of the Law Society of England and Wales. He had seriously overcharged a client; the bill was reduced after 'taxation' (review) by court officers from £197,000 to less than £68,000. The Law Society Council refused to pursue any disciplinary action and the client had to go to the courts who found that Glanville Davies had been guilty of 'gross and persistent misconduct', and ordered he be struck off the Roll (Law Reform Commission, 1993). A subsequent report by external consultants led to the establishment of the Solicitors Complaints Bureau (SCB) and the start of proper self-regulation.

The regulatory function rested first with the SCB and then the Office for the Supervision of Solicitors (OSS) followed by the Regulation Directorate of the Law Society. The Directorate was then split into Consumer Complaints Service (CCS) and Compliance Directorate (CD). CCS deal with client complaints, for example, Improper Professional Service (IPS) such as speed or quality of service. CD deal with Regulation. Any conduct element of IPS is passed to CD, which deals with information concerning loss of funds, money laundering, and so on. Further governance reforms were implemented in 2006.[4]

Currently an initial review of complaints – the Law Society receives around 16,000 a year – is made by CCS. Those complaints made by clients of solicitors that can be quickly conciliated are dealt with directly by CCS; all other client complaints are referred by the CCS to one of three complaints centres (referred to as Customer Contact Centres) for more involved case working. All complaints made by non clients of solicitors are referred to the Conduct and Assessment Unit (CAI), part of the Compliance Directorate. The Law Society will suggest that those clients with negligence claims take action via the courts. Service or conduct elements of any negligence claims that are not dealt with by the courts may be considered again once the court action is concluded. Caseworkers in CCS and CAI are trained to identify and raise issues in relation to financial irregularity, dishonesty or the involvement of solicitors in criminality directly with the Fraud Intelligence Unit (FIU) and in some cases directly with Forensic Investigations (FI). FIU is a central point of contact and collates internal reports with reports from a number of external sources (e.g. police, financial institutions, other regulatory bodies and other solicitors). It refers them to a Risk Management Group (RMG) for general consideration of the firm's activities or directly to FI as a recommendation for an investigation.

Box 8.3 Solicitor fraud

Solicitor Timothy Robinson, now 60, was convicted in 2001 of conspiring to systematically defraud the legal aid system of huge sums of cash over a period of almost six years. As well as being sentenced to seven years in jail, he was ordered to pay more than £1 million in compensation and costs. Details of the case were only allowed to be published today after the conclusion of a related case resulted in the lifting of reporting restrictions. Robinson, who lived in the exclusive village of Badgeworth, near Cheltenham, was found guilty of conspiracy to defraud at Bristol Crown Court in January 2001 following an eight-month trial. He was released on parole in July after serving half his sentence.

A further 21 former employees at his Gloucestershire-based practice, Robinson's, either pleaded guilty or were found guilty of the conspiracy in a total of five trials. Five were acquitted and charges against two lie on the file. The investigation into the firm's activities began more than 10 years ago in April 1993 and is thought to have cost several million pounds. The Serious Fraud Office and three police forces took more than 3,000 witness statements and seized 21 tonnes of documents from the firm's offices as they investigated the scam. The conspiracy involved employees at the firm, once regarded as one of the largest criminal defence practices in the country, claiming legal aid for millions of pounds' worth of work they did not do.

Reporting restrictions were lifted after the charges against the remaining defendant, Archibald Ross, were ordered to lie on the file after medical evidence showed that the trial was unlikely ever to go ahead. It is not known exactly how much was defrauded from the Legal Aid Board, but estimates suggest it could have been as much as half the £17 million claimed by the firm during the period investigated. At Robinson's trial, the court heard that the scam centred on the green forms which were used by law firms to claim for certain types of legal aid work. One of the solicitor's former employees said that up to 90 per cent of the green forms submitted by the firm's Cheltenham office were fraudulent. The jury was told time spent with clients was exaggerated, prison visits were claimed twice, clerks billed for cases which had never existed and crimes that clients may have mentioned in passing, but never wanted advice on, were put down in claims forms.

When police searched the offices, they found 197 forms that had been signed by clients but were not filled in. Some employees were claiming for work totalling more than 24 hours a day, the court heard. Many forms submitted were claims for things such as 'perusal and consideration' which 'was often the code for not actually doing any work', the jury at Robinson's trial was told. The firm's clerks, who were earning a basic salary of £10,000 a year, were paid up to £4,500 a month overtime and were given Mercedes cars with personalised number plates such as 4LAW or 7LAW. But the court heard that one fee-earning clerk, former bookmaker Richard Hill, became reckless and started to forge clients' signatures. The Law Society became suspicious and Hill eventually resigned and blew the whistle. He was later jailed for 14 months for his part in the conspiracy.

Ian Glen QC, prosecuting, said Robinson was described by one of his clerks as 'a mini-Maxwell, obsessed with power and money'. He added: 'Mr Robinson himself was very careful not to dirty his own hands. He got others to commit the frauds with those green forms ... It was his fee-earning clerks who did the dirty work.' Robinson, a well-known figure in the south-west where he had practised since the early 1970s, was in the headlines in 1997 when he represented Tracie Andrews – the woman who was eventually found guilty of murdering her 25-year-old fiancé Lee Harvey on a roadside near their home in Alvechurch, near Redditch. He always denied knowing the fraud was going on at his firm, denied ever filling in green forms dishonestly and denied asking anyone in his office to do so. After Robinson was found guilty, his barrister, David Etherington QC, asked the judge to consider 'the utter ruin and devastation that this defendant now faces'.

Judge David Smith heard the SFO had traced assets belonging to Robinson or his wife totalling £1.6 million and that the lawyer had taken about £3 million from his firm in the period 1991 to 1999. The court was told the trial had cost around £3 million. The judge imposed a confiscation order on Robinson of £532,275 which he ordered to be paid as compensation to what is now called the Legal Services Commission. He also decided he should pay £500,000 in prosecution costs. Robinson appealed against his conviction and then his sentence in October 2002, but lost both appeals.

Source: *The Guardian*, 29 October 2004

RMG identify 'risk' firms and may refer firms to the Practice Standards Unit (PSU) who assist firms in improving their internal controls and the way they work, or to FI who carry out detailed forensic investigations for regulatory purposes. All referrals made to FI are further risk-assessed prior to a decision to investigate. Investigations (471 in 2005), of solicitors' practices are made based on this assessment and a report detailing non compliance with the Law Society's Rules is produced and considered by the Head of Investigations and Enforcement (I&E). Explanations for non compliance are sought from firms by either the Regulation Unit or the Investigation Casework Team (ICT), which deals with reports of serious misconduct, including fraud and money laundering. If it is appropriate, the contents of a report may be disclosed through a variety of legal gateways to various other bodies including the police. Their investigation into any criminality will run alongside any regulatory measures taken by the Law Society and may even ensure a more effective response through:

- prompt incapacitation (which could also be seen as a form of disruption);
- the imposition ... of financial penalties, such as fines or the loss of the solicitor's business;
- establishing that the solicitor had acted wrongfully; and
- providing a public shaming ritual. (Middleton 2005: 831)

Caseworkers in the Regulation Unit and ICT can take the matter to a single adjudicator (simpler cases), or refer it to an adjudication panel who might reprimand or fine the solicitor or impose conditions on the solicitor's practising certificate, such as a condition preventing a solicitor from dealing with clients' money in the future. The adjudicators may also recommend that the solicitor be called to answer for his actions before the Solicitors Disciplinary Tribunal (SDT). The SDT has the power to strike off – deregister – a solicitor (and about 70 a year are struck off). If there have been serious breaches of the accounts rules or reason to suspect dishonesty on the part of a solicitor as a result of an investigation, a request to intervene in the practice may be referred to an adjudication panel. The process of intervention by which a firm is taken over and closed down by a solicitor acting as an agent of the Law Society (involving about 60 practices a year) is dealt with by the Intervention and Disciplinary Unit (IDU). The Law Society also pays out compensation up to £1 million a case, with a current annual total of around £18 million.

The main practice frauds relate to the misuse of client funds, and the misuse of knowledge, for example, in cases of conflicting interest. The main frauds in which solicitors engage are money laundering, immigration fraud, high-yield investment schemes, probate fraud and property fraud (see Middleton and Levi 2004; Middleton 2005). The regulatory powers of the Law Society are based on the premise that the powers relate to the investigation into whether or not solicitors are in compliance with Law Society rules (and thus have implications for the investigative procedures that may be followed). They include: a requirement to cooperate (which falls short of the right of access to a practice); the right to examine solicitors client files; access to documents; the right to require the verification of information with clients, banks or other financial institutions (for which authority has to be given by the solicitor under investigation); the right to inspect material subject to client/solicitor privilege; the right to share information with a range of authorities (including the DPP, the CPS, the SFO and the Solicitors' Disciplinary Tribunal (SDT)). Apart from the ability to 'strike off' a solicitor at the SDT, the strongest power that the Law Society can exercise is that of intervention – taking over a solicitor's practice, which not only puts them out of business but also means the solicitor's practising certificate is immediately suspended. Intervention can follow suspected dishonesty, non-compliance with the Solicitors' Accounts and/or Practice Rules, bankruptcy or imprisonment (the Guide notes a number of examples where intervention powers may be exercised, such as where there is reason to suspect dishonesty on the part of a solicitor or a member of his or her staff or the personal representative of a deceased solicitor; where there is failure to comply with the Solicitors' Account Rules; where a solicitor is practising uncertificated; and where a sole practitioner is incapacitated by, for example, illness, accident or age).

The Charity Commission

Charities are independent organisations with a traditional image of cash collections and crisis appeals, with the emphasis on minimising the amount spent on the charity itself and its costs, and maximising the amount spent on its causes. This image belies an area of activity that ranges from multi-million pound businesses to cat rescue sanctuaries. There are nearly 8000 applications a year for charitable status. Charities employ some 500,000 paid workers. Their £75 billion worth of assets range from land to capital funds. Some charities, such as the RSPB, are major landowners; the RSPB also has significant administrative costs for marketing because its ageing membership base dies off at about one-third a year. Others have moved from collection to delivering public services (now accounting for some 37 per cent of charities' income), commercial activities (such as Great Ormond Street Children's Hospital's ownership of the play Peter Pan), and the production of goods and services.

Section 96 of the 1993 Charities Act defines what a charity is: an organisation established for charitable purposes such as the relief of poverty, advancement of education and religion, and actions that benefit the community. Charitable status comes only with the agreement of and registration with the Charity Commissioners, the statutory regulator. Registration offers a self-governing status, as well as access to tax and council tax relief, and grants and donations. All charities have to comply with legal requirements for the running of the charity, the responsibility for which lies with the trustees. Trustees have a legal duty of responsibility for its 'general control and management'. They also have unlimited personal liability for the activities of the charity and its assets (unless they can demonstrate they had taken reasonable steps to safeguard them), and its organisational shape (which can range from management committees to full corporate boards). Charities are vulnerable to fraud because of the funds and assets they hold, the ambiguity of what goes to the charitable purpose and what goes on administrative costs (particularly when professional fundraisers are involved), the freedom to dispense funds as the trustees see fit, the problems associated with high-volume, low-cost activity such as cash collections, and the right to move funds abroad, often to countries where equivalent supervision is weak or absent.

The Charity Commission's role and powers are set out within the 1993 Act with the following responsibilities:

- to ensure that charities meet the legal requirements for being a charity, and are equipped to operate properly and within the law;
- to check that charities are run for public benefit, and not for private advantage;
- to ensure that charities are independent and that their trustees take their decisions free of control or undue influence from outside; and
- to detect and remedy serious mismanagement or deliberate abuse by or within charities.

This it does by: securing compliance with charity law, and dealing with abuse and poor practice; enabling charities to work better within an effective legal, accounting and governance framework; keeping pace with developments in society, the economy and the law; and promoting sound governance and accountability.

The Commission itself has a staff of over 500 and a budget of over £29 million, with four centres around England and Wales. The Commission is currently undertaking a review of its structure and the way it deploys its resources but its current compliance and enforcement activity comprise: an information and a compliance team (30 staff), a monitoring team of 12 and an evaluation and intelligence team (36 staff); an investigation team (45 staff). These do due diligence work on registrations, check annual charity returns, assess what might be cause for concern, and investigate possible breaches of the Act. Some 20,000 charities are monitored a year. A risk matrix is used, which includes assessments of risks to the charity's beneficiaries, risks to its reputation, and the proportionate response. Although the public is the single biggest source of concerns about the activities of charities, the Commission itself is the second biggest source and the first three teams in the group produce reports where, of the 25 per cent of cases not resolved on initial assessment, 25 per cent of these are passed to other regulators, 25 per cent are given 'advice and guidance' and 25 per cent are investigated.

In 2004/05, 325 investigations were undertaken; these resulted in the Commission safeguarding or recovering over £34 million of charitable funds. The Commission uses modern technology tools to profile trustees and types of charities, as well as checking its internal databases of active charities and failed applications, and checking on external databases. Its risk matrix includes triggers on its databases, such as use of professional fundraisers, cost/income ratios; associated trading companies. Its intelligence function provides the single point of contact for other agencies, particularly those working in terrorist finance or in HMRC, which administers tax relief on charitable donations. The Commission has substantial powers to freeze assets. It can also restrict fundraising, appoint, suspend, remove and replace trustees, appoint receivers and managers. Under Section 8 of the Charities Act, its inquiry powers, it can order and direct trustees and others to attend interviews (where there is an obligation to answer questions and it is an offence to provide misleading information) and obtain documents. Its proposed new powers under a Bill held up by the 2005 General Election will include right of entry to charity premises and the ability to require repayment of misused funds.

Overall, the charity sector is not in itself seen as fraud-prone, although the main areas of concern relate to personal interests of trustees, misuse of fundraising, and the failure to comply with the legal requirements, essentially the areas of corporate governance that the National Audit Office was keen to have the Charity Commission develop (NAO 2001). Nevertheless the charities field is, given its intrinsic purpose and work, vulnerable to infiltration by those seeking to take control of assets, set up fake charities, create fictitious recipients, use charities to move money around the world, and claim tax relief. HMRC has over 100 staff to oversee the tax relief claimed by charities and by those using charities as a tax shelter or claiming relief on donations. The Inland Revenue repays some £1 billion a year in relation to donations (mainly Giftaid) and half of that goes back to charities. Giftaid has no specific form or signature, which makes application fraud and inflated claims a major source of fraud (one case that ended in 2002 allegedly involved a multi-million-pound fraud that resulted in 43 search warrants, 65,000 documents, 5,000 potential witnesses and over 100 Inland Revenue investigators looking at real and false charities).

The Financial Services Authority (FSA)

In 1997 the incoming Labour government announced that banking supervision and investment services regulation were to be merged. Banking supervision – which, as a statutory activity, could be legislated for relatively quickly – was taken on by the existing SIB. In 1998 the SIB was renamed the Financial Services Authority (FSA). Through the 2000 Financial Services and Markets Act, the FSA then took over from 2001 the existing patchwork of the other self-regulating organisations. Under the Act, the FSA now regulates[5] the activities of banks, building societies, the Exchanges (such as the London Stock Exchange), insurance, and so on. While it is accountable to Treasury ministers and thus to parliament, it is solely funded from a levy on the businesses it regulates.

At a cost of over £250 million and with some 2,300 staff and supervising over 25,000 businesses (and around 200,000 'approved persons'), the FSA is a part-decentralised organisaton with three Business Units (Wholesale, Retail and Regulatory Services) and a number of central services. The Wholesale Business Unit deals with market activity, the Stock Exchange, stockbrokers, wholesale banks, etc. The Retail Business Unit deals with major retail business (such as banks and insurance companies) as well as Independent Financial Advisers (IFA), and mortgage and General Insurance intermediaries. The Regulatory Services Business Unit deals with a number of services for the FSA, such as IT or payroll; it also deals with external work such as authorisation, variations in authorisation, and CRIM (contact, revenue, and information management) contact centres for business and the public, collecting fees, etc. The Regulatory Services Business Unit also has a financial crimes policy unit – which deals with the delivery of the financial crime statutory objective – within the Policy and Intelligence Department which also contains an intelligence team. This works to support risk-based regulation and to work closely with NCIS (two members of staff are seconded there). It also has some 10 staff – analysts and a whistleblowing expert – and five support staff. It acts as the information gateway, deals with overseas requests, and focuses on particular projects such as terrorist finance and dubious investment schemes. The Business Units also have a number of directors who are, in addition to their Unit work, responsible for eight crosscutting sector teams – including retail intermediaries, insurance, asset management, financial crime, and so on – whose responsibilities cover, for example, risk identification and mitigation; internal expertise (skills training); and external communication. The teams are small – two to six people in each – but draw on network meetings to develop issues and approaches.

The FSA's four statutory objectives are:

- maintaining confidence in the UK financial system;
- promoting public understanding of the financial system;
- securing the degree of protection for consumers;
- helping to reduce financial crime.

These are expanded in a general statement of regulatory requirement – the set of high-level principles expected of regulated business which is included in the Handbook. More detailed requirements are laid down on risk in the Prudential Sourcebooks (which include addressing various risks) and other parts of the Handbook, including the roles and responsibilities of boards and senior management, the use of the Combined Code for corporate governance principles, addressing different types of risk, the need for a risk assessment function, the role of internal audit and so on, and the responsibilities of 'approved persons.' Approved persons are those in relation to whom the FSA has given its approval under Section 59 of the Act for the performance of a controlled function. These are listed by the FSA and include 'governance' functions such as those of a director or chief executive; 'required' functions such as compliance oversight or money laundering reporting and 'systems and controls' functions, including finance, risk assessment and internal audit. The appointment and subsequent conduct of approved persons are monitored by, and may be sanctioned for breaches by, the FSA in relation to the principles governing the position (including the requirement that they disclose appropriately any information of which the FSA would reasonably expect notice).

The FSA has a risk-based approach which is laid out in the Handbook and backed up by FSA visits as well as by self-reporting by the institutions. There are four key areas: risk identification and assessment; risk mitigation; risk monitoring; and documentation (having policies and procedures that cover the above and deliver effective accountability from the board and senior management down). Compliance is delivered through: monitoring, authorisation (who may undertake regulated business), supervision (compliance) and enforcement (taking action to promote compliance). The FSA has a range of formal investigative powers, including the ability to require the provision of specific information, to order a report on a firm by a person it designates, to investigate the ownership of a firm and any breaches of the legislation or FSA rules. The offences cover a range of activities – such as carrying on a regulated business without authorisation, carrying on such a business when banned, insider trading (an offence under the 1993 Criminal Justice Act), failing to cooperate with the FSA, etc. (Gentle and Hodges 2005: 11/42–43).

The Handbook lays down in general terms what the FSA requires, when and how (and the FSA more generally makes it plain how businesses may breach the statutory objectives *and* high level principles).

Compliance responses are assessed against probability factors – such as the firm's strategy or the firm's business risk (those risks – such as credit, market and operational risk – which are inherent in the business); the size of the firm (in respect of any impact in delivering the statutory objectives); the financial soundness of the firm; the nature of the firm's customers and the products and services it offers; the countries in which it does business, the internal systems and controls and the compliance culture of the firm; the organisation of the firm and the role played by its governing body, management and staff in effectively mitigating risk. The risk assessment will determine how the FSA will approach the business when it undertakes its supervision and enforcement work.

Combating financial crime is one of the four statutory objectives. This is seen as 'reducing the extent to which it is possible for a business carried on by a regulated person to be used for a purpose connected with financial crime.' Under the Act, this covers (in Section 6) fraud and dishonesty, financial misconduct (such as account manipulation and misusing market information) and laundering the proceeds of crime. The FSA has said that it has the following aims in respect of financial crime:

- To make crime more costly for criminals (not honest consumers or firms) and deter abuse of the financial system.
- To achieve an industry perception of money well spent.
- To raise consumer awareness of financial crime issues
- To contribute to an effective wider UK Plc fight against crime.
- To have a balanced, joined-up approach to anti-money laundering and fraud:
  - tactically: e.g. with better use of the FSA's risk assessment process;
  - nationally: e.g. with better coordination with UK partner agencies;
  - internationally: by addressing risks to the UK financial system from abroad.

There are three expectations: that businesses are aware of the risk, have appropriate measures to prevent, detect and monitor financial crime, and provide adequate resources to do so. In terms of assessing financial crime the FSA has a small financial crime sector team whose role is to coordinate and support the work of the whole organisation as part of the FSA's financial crime objective. Internally, this involves discussing with the Units the identification of trends and figures, financial crime risks and how supervision should integrate and prioritise the assessment of financial crime (Unit supervisors also have access to specialist staff within the Risk Review Department of the Wholesale Business Unit for supervision visits for a range of areas across the Units) and how it can be mitigated.

The FSA links money laundering and financial crime by stating that 'one aspect of the reduction of financial crime objective is the risk of the businesses of relevant firms being used in connection with offences which involve handling the proceeds of crime. It follows that an effective and proportionate regulatory regime is important in reducing the extent to which it is possible for the businesses carried on by relevant firms to be used for money laundering.' This means that the FSA has driven home money laundering compliance because it is responsible for a reduction of financial crime, including money laundering which had not been given the highest priority by previous regulators and others who had, in any case, dealt with money laundering in different ways. As an integrated regulator, it intended to formulate more effective ways of dealing with it.

Thus the FSA has focused on money laundering since its establishment through its published guidance (known as DP22). Financial institutions have been criticised for not fully implementing Know-Your-Customer (and their activities) checks, or due diligence checks, and failing to make appropriate SARs to NCIS. The FSA has taken a strong stance on what might be termed the preventative framework, fining companies – six to date (see Box 8.4) – heavily for not getting the basic compliance procedures in place.

In relation to fraud, to which it started to pay more attention from 2004, the FSA is encouraging trade associations to work together closely and provide leadership over fraud management. It wants managers to accept that fraud is a significant threat that needs managing strategically and effectively, more work on the risks and scale of fraud, and better ways of tackling it, and improved organisational cultures and information sharing. This means that, using its reporting and risk-based approach, it will be looking for information on:

- whether a firm has a strong anti-fraud culture, with the lead being given from the top;
- whether there is a clear allocation of responsibility for the day-to-day management of the risk;
- staff training;
- firms' Know Your Customer procedures – how they keep an eye out for potentially criminal behaviour; and

Box 8.4 Abbey fines

Abbey National was yesterday fined a total of £2.3 million by the Financial Services Authority for breaching money laundering and fund management regulations. The bank was fined a record £2 million for breaking money laundering rules, while its Asset Managers funds arm, which manages £30 billion of assets, was fined £320,000 ... The FSA described the offences as 'extremely serious failings'. It said both fines reflected 'wider control failings' including 'inadequate monitoring of key regulatory risks' over 'a prolonged period'. No evidence has been found of money laundering taking place through Abbey's accounts. Weaknesses in money laundering controls were found across Abbey's retail banking division from December 2001 until April this year. Abbey's branches certified their own compliance with the regulator's requirements about the proofs of identity customers must produce to open accounts. An internal review, begun after Luqman Arnold became chief executive in November 2002, found 32 per cent of these reports were not correct.

An FSA spokesman said: 'They didn't know who one in three of their new customers were.' There was no central compliance monitoring and a failure to provide 'key management information' to a money laundering reporting officer. The FSA also found that Abbey failed to ensure that suspicious activity reports were promptly considered and reported to the National Criminal Intelligence Service between February 2002 and October this year. Some took more than four months to be reported, while 58 per cent took more than 30 days. Mr Procter said: 'The size of the fine demonstrates that failure by firms to put in place these fundamental systems and controls will be dealt with severely by the FSA.'

Source: *The Daily Telegraph*, 11 December 2003

- what management information on fraud is captured and how it is used.

The FSA will be looking for firms to demonstrate that they are taking steps to be aware of, and to tackle, fraud risks by being able to identify and report on the headings outlined in its 2003 discussion paper – DP26 – on fraud and dishonesty:

- Who is responsible for managing fraud risks?
- How do you identify key fraud risks?
- What are they?
- What are the key systems and controls for managing your fraud risks?
- How many frauds has your institution suffered recently?
- What are fraud losses?
- What whistle-blowing arrangements are in place and how successful are they?
- How much is spent on preventing and detecting fraud?
- How is the effectiveness of fraud systems and controls monitored?
- What information on fraud goes to the board or senior management?

Anti-fraud delivery will partly come from prevention – acting as gatekeeper on those working in regulated businesses, monitoring firms (who are required to 'manage' risks, and report frauds) – and also from the requirement that businesses will have in place the systems and controls to deliver various legislative responsibilities. These will include looking at IT and manual systems, separation of duties, the role of internal audit, risk assessment, mitigation and monitoring programmes, documented policies and procedures, organisational cultures, collection and use of internal information, reforms following frauds, and responses to DP26 (see FSA 2006, for findings on corporate responses to fraud). On the other hand, the FSA does not see its focus on actual fraud but 'on the defences that industry has in place.' Dealing with those who 'penetrate industry's defences is a matter primarily for law enforcement and prosecutors.' It is also the responsibility of the government 'to lead on the production, with the industry and law enforcement, of a thorough assessment of what really needs to be done on fraud, and then to act on those findings' (Robinson 2004).

Enforcement comprises some 200 staff and takes its cases from within the FSA on behalf of the various Business Units. It has a range of powers – production of documents, attendance at interviews, and so on – and sanctions, with the opportunity to deal with breaches as disciplinary, civil or, for some offences, criminal prosecution (see Box 8.5). It is divided into three areas: retail, wholesale and policy. Breaches of the regulatory regime are dealt with through a number of sanctions, including: financial penalties, removal of authorisation, restitution orders and injunctions against unauthorised businesses, insolvency orders, prohibition of individuals from carrying on a regulated activity, fines, and criminal prosecutions (for breaches of a

Box 8.5 FSA's first criminal case[6]

Carl Rigby and Gareth Bailey, former directors of the software company AIT, were jailed yesterday in a move intended to send a warning to the City over the potential consequences of breaching listing rules.

Rigby, the former chairman and chief executive of AIT, was sentenced to three and a half years at Brixton prison, and banned from taking on a role as company director for six years. Bailey, AIT's former finance director, was jailed for two years and banned from being a director for four years.

In August, Rigby and Bailey were convicted of 'recklessly' misleading the market through the release of an inaccurate stock exchange announcement three years ago, which said the company's profits were set to be in line with expectations. But AIT had not sealed several contracts at the time of the announcement, which were key to the company making its targets. When the contracts fell through, the group was forced to issue two profits warnings in quick succession, decimating the company's share price and market value.

Judge Elwen told them: 'Neither of you cared whether [the information] was true or false and were heedless of the consequences in the madcap hope that all would be right on the night. It wasn't. Conduct such as this cannot be treated lightly by the courts, particularly in view of the message that needs to be sent out ... Every member of the public, having savings by direct investment on the stock market or by and through products themselves tied to stock markets, is injured if the integrity of the market is damaged by misleading information of this kind being announced to the market. If investors, large and small, come to the view that they cannot trust the information companies announce to the market, they will avoid the market when making investment decisions. The health of the financial services industry, which is a major contributor to the UK economy, will suffer.'

Source: *The Independent*, 8 October 2005

general prohibition, misleading statements (that persuade others to enter into an agreement), market manipulation and insider dealing.

All sanctions apart from criminal prosecution, including the size of any fine, are proposed by Enforcement to the Regulatory Decisions

Committee (all but the chair are independent part-time appointments) which decides what if any action is appropriate in a case. There is an independent Tribunal that adjudicates on any contested FSA regulatory decision. Any appeal beyond the Tribunal is to the High Court.

Audit

The Audit Commission

The public sector is subject to statutory external audit which pays close attention to fraud as part of its mandatory functions. In addition to their UK statutory responsibilities for reporting on arrangements to deal with fraud, public sector auditors are also subject to external standards (such as the International Standard on Auditing No. 240 – ISA 240). The National Audit Office also has the distinction of reporting its findings to the Public Accounts Committee of the House of Commons which takes evidence from the audited departments or agencies. Local government and the National Health Service have externally appointed auditors, formerly known as the District Audit Service (DA), an independent public agency, and FB4 (which covered the NHS). The Audit Commission was set up in 1984 to cover local government and absorbed DA. In 1990 its remit was extended to the NHS and it took on FB4. The Audit Commission is tasked with the statutory responsibility of appointing external auditors; promoting economy, efficiency and effectiveness in the expenditure and performance of local authorities and the various primary care and hospital trusts and special health authorities; reporting on the impact of central government actions on local authorities' ability to operate effectively. The Audit Commission chooses auditors from both the public and private sectors – part of the attempts by the first Thatcher government to open up provision of public services by the private sector – but also sets the fees rates for itself and the private sector firms who also provide external audit services. In addition, the Audit Commission sets the audit standard, controls price and monitors quality and market shares, and decides on the firms in the market. Over the years they have considered overall allocations and experimented with many different ways of allocating audits including various types of direct competition.

The driver for fraud work by Audit Commission-appointed auditors lies in the long-established codes of public sector audit practice, first published in 1984. The current iteration (the latest NHS and local government Codes of Audit Practice were published in March 2005) is a legal requirement under the 1998 Audit Commission Act. It is specific about the roles of those responsible for public business, which should be conducted in accordance with the law and proper standards, about proper arrangements for the governance of their affairs and the stewardship of the resources at their disposal, and about public funds being safeguarded and properly accounted for. Thus bodies audited under the Act by the Audit Commission have a statutory duty to manage their affairs 'in accordance with proper standards of financial conduct and to prevent and detect fraud and corruption.' The Code specifies what these arrangements should be in terms of compliance with 'appropriate standards' of corporate governance, promoting values and standards, codes of conduct, standing orders, contract-handling instructions, and strategies to prevent and detect fraud and corruption, including receiving and investigating allegations. The role of the external auditor in reviewing and reporting on this includes a specific requirement to comment on such arrangements.

In the early 1990s, the Audit Commission decided to undertake an assessment of whether 'adequate arrangements' were in place in relation to fraud. This included study teams to look at fraud and corruption in local government in 1993 and the NHS in 1995 (from which practitioner audit manuals were produced) and shortly afterwards it set up a dedicated unit (within Audit Practices and Appointments) to produce audit anti-fraud manuals, to encourage anti-fraud initiatives and awareness and to provide a central point for statistics and warnings. The function changed, evolving with good governance and counter fraud work built into new CPA and NHS assessments and underpinned through the development of a fraud network and National Fraud Initiative (NFI).

The NFI came from seeing how data-matching worked in Canada (although a data-matching exercise had been undertaken by London boroughs through the London Team Against Fraud). This began in 1998. It now involves a bi-annual match of housing benefits, local government, failed asylum seekers, occupational pension schemes in both the public and the private sectors, local government and NHS payrolls (from, overall, 1,150 bodies). It seeks to identify potentially mutually exclusive information (pensions paid after the death of the holder, payments to care homes for deceased residents, housing benefits claimed by owner-occupiers, benefits claimed by employees, double working (prevalent in bank nurse work in the NHS), etc.). The matching does not identify fraud – the data protection legislation does not allow random fishing expeditions – but does point to situations where participants (local councils get CD-ROMs of matches) may want to carry out further checks. The value of detected fraud or overpayments by the participating authorities reached £83 million from the 2002/03 exercise, and (apart from a number of bogus asylum seekers holding doctor and nurse appointments) included 2,000 occupational pensions being paid out after the death of the recipient, 263 NHS employees, 430 students and 1,379 local government officials involved in housing benefit fraud, and 364 cases of NHS staff on pensions returning to work full-time.

District Audit runs a fraud network among auditors – the Good Conduct and Counter Fraud Network. This involves two to four lead auditors in each region feeding down to representatives on each audit team across the country. It is intended to promote awareness, address emerging issues (for example, money laundering reporting of cash purchases of council houses), standardise monitoring arrangements and take a collective approach to selected topics for inquiry (such as the increasing use of agency staff). It provides training for auditors, analyses Public Interest Reports, and shares information on risk areas (such as 419 letters). It also encourages the use of controls assurance workshops – workshops for officials that developed from work in Lambeth designed to test organisational cultures and fraud awareness. The work on controls assurance is linked to the promotion of ethical environments or counter-fraud cultures that combines awareness testing with risk assessments as part of its wider strategic intervention approach, which is part of its Comprehensive Performance Assessment (CPA) work. This could rank bodies for management and governance arrangements (which would include the auditor's score judgments on risk, fraud and corruption arrangements, whistle-blowing and responding to the NFI output). The awareness approach was particularly singled out in the 10th report of the Committee on Standards in Public Life: 'We were particularly impressed with the innovative experience based learning techniques pioneered by the Audit Commission which help organisations reach their own determinations of their strengths and weaknesses and allow the solutions to come from within rather than imposed from outside. The tools have the added benefit of allowing benchmarking against similar organisations and, if widely used, will provide useful aggregate data on ethical culture across the public sector' (2005: 12).

In relation to the investigation of allegations of fraud and corruption, the District Auditor (formally termed the Appointed Auditor) has had two major means to draw attention to or seek to punish alleged abuse. The first was surcharging for financial misconduct. This was voided by the 2000 Local Government Act which now places responsibility for sanctioning councillors who breach the Code of Conduct with the Standards Board for England. However, the surcharge allowed the District Auditor to fine councillors and officers for unlawful or reckless expenditure. This happened in Lambeth and Liverpool but the big case was that of Dame Shirley Porter.

Porter, heiress to the founder of the Tesco supermarket chain, was elected to Westminster Council in central London in 1974 and became leader of the controlling Conservative Group in 1983. After narrowly retaining control in 1986 the Group devised a policy that designated areas of council housing for privatisation rather than for let under council control (an early Conservative government theme on home ownership was achieved through the 1980 Housing Act's 'Right to Buy' policy which allowed tenants and others to buy the property at discounted rates). This was a controversial policy, firstly because inner London had only a limited amount of affordable public housing. Secondly, the policy (called 'Building Stable Communities') was targeted on areas of marginal Conservative support and based on an assumption that new owners were likely to be more predisposed to the council and more conservative in their voting habits. As a policy, it was successful in that it secured a clear majority in the 1990 elections. Porter gave up the leadership the following year and left the council in 1993 to live in Israel.

Three years later, following complaints from the Labour opposition and the public, the District Auditor decided that the policy was partisan, that political motives overrode financial stewardship and that the council had lost up to £21 million as a consequence (in terms of the cost to move tenants out, discounts on sales and, in another scheme, relocating the homeless with other councils). He named those to repay the money which, following various court hearings and appeals, the last of which was to the House of Lords, was upheld. The Law Lords described the policy as 'a deliberate, blatant and dishonest misuse of public power' but by this time – 2001 – the only defendants were Porter, who claimed she did not have the funds, and one other councillor. It was clear that Porter held her funds offshore in a range of trusts and accounts, but new money laundering legislation allowed the council to apply to the courts in 2003 for the order to freeze her assets, including any trusts and companies that she set up to manage her funds. She was also ordered to disclose these and any other assets that she had power directly, or indirectly, to dispose of. The council then obtained third party disclosure orders against companies and individuals in the UK which produced the forensic evidence from deleted files that identified the location of some of the money. In

2004 the council and the Audit Commission agreed to accept some £12 million from Porter as the final settlement (see Hosken 2006).

The second and still extant power is the right to issue a Public Interest Report which often, as in the cases of Lambeth and Doncaster, warns of possible wrongdoing. Further, since the letter is privileged, it provides information to other agencies. Issuing a Public Interest Report allows the District Auditor to investigate and comment on a range of activities or individuals where he or she considers that public funds were at risk or that misconduct may have taken place, where there may be issues to be addressed that do not necessarily involve criminal intent, or where the District Auditor provides information that may encourage councils to initiate their own inquiries.

Summary

Regulation and compliance allows variations in approaches to fraud, in part because a number of the agencies above control entry to the activity and in part because legislation gives them particular powers to prevent and investigate fraud. This may mean the use of dedicated powers and procedures that are not subject to the restraints imposed on the law enforcement approach. It also allows for a range of sanctions that does not require the involvement of the criminal justice system. Overall, regulation and compliance offers the opportunity for the deployment of specific and targeted powers, often at those whose membership is controlled by the agency, and where the bulk of the relevant information is held by the agency or the members. It allows negotiated settlements at any time during the inquiry process where the process of inquiry itself, the burden of proof and the sanctions are more flexible, accessible and cheaper. In particular a number of agencies, such as the Law Society, have the means to deny service – revoke membership – or attach conditions to membership that may be a more effective sanction than a sole reliance on the law enforcement route. Indeed, regulation, audit and compliance is as much a part of the work of those who undertake investigations as in the law enforcement approach, as will be discussed in the next chapter.

Notes

1   This is a significant area of fraud, caused in part by the HMRC allowing a degree of self-assessment and the use of on-line applications which was

not supported by robust anti-fraud measures. The main reliance on a valid National Insurance number (NINO) led to wholesale theft of valid numbers from staff from the DWP and Network Rail, after acceptance of which the fraudsters amended details relating to employment, address and children to secure increased payments. After, apparently, over 60 claims were re-routed to a single address the service was suspended. Some 30,000 cases have been identified so far, with initial multi-million pound losses. The potential for abuse was under-estimated on predicted conduct of the client group and tackling abuse has been hindered by the omission from the Tax Credit Act 2002 of a criminal offence (as opposed to a penalty fine) of failing to declare a change in circumstances. Such an omission ignores the experience of fraud and abuse of means tested welfare benefits where the claim may often be correct on first application but where there is a failure to declare relevant changes in circumstances.

2   Possible fraud arises where the actual arrangements are at variance with the artificial arrangements offered as purporting to be the true position for tax assessment, and this is done with intent primarily to avoid liability.

3   In October 2000, the DTI raided BAT's London offices and launched an investigation into BAT's alleged role in cigarette smuggling. In 2004 the DTI minister announced that no further action was being taken.

4   Following the 2004 Clementi Review, and from 2006, the Regulatory Board is responsible for dealing with all regulatory policy with as much independence from the Central Law Society as is possible within one legal entity. It will advise the Law Society on the funding that need to be collected through the practising certificate to ensure that regulation is effective. The Consumer Complaints Board will oversee continued improvement of consumer complaints handling by the Society's Consumer Complaints Service and prepare for its expected transition to be part of the Office for Legal Complaints recommended by Clementi. The funds to run the Law Society – about £97 million – come from the annual practising certificate fee.

5   The Act defines a regulated activity as 'activity by way of business relating to investment and property' (see Trollope *et al.* 2005b: 4/7). The FSA does not regulate money services, businesses or consumer credit licences; these have been the responsibility of HMCE and the OFT respectively.

6   In December 2005, the two former directors had their jail terms more than halved on appeal in part because they had not been convicted on the more serious charge, brought by the Financial Services Authority, of knowingly misleading investors and in part because sentencing had not taken full account of the directors' attempts to resurrect the firm after the scandal.

Chapter 9

In-house approaches

One reason why the decline of police resources for fraud investigation has not been challenged is that much of the responsibility for investigation (and, often, prosecution) in the public sector has rested with the agency or department itself. In this chapter it will be noticeable that public sector departments tend to dedicate more resources to this, in part because of the nature of the work, in part because of declining police resources and in part because of an expectation that the public sector should make significant efforts to safeguard public funds. The private sector has a much more cost-conscious approach to such issues, as well as the need to balance resources spent on fraud and the increasing pressure from the FSA to improve fraud prevention and detection. Part of the private sector response to this is the use of external agencies to provide anti-fraud resources as and when required (although the public sector also uses such agencies). This chapter looks at a large bank and a smaller building society to consider how each approaches fraud, before looking at how the private sector and how three public sector institutions address fraud. This chapter also illustrates how the law enforcement and other approaches are drawn up to address fraud in various contexts.

The private sector in-house approach

The bank

Bank A is a UK-based bank operating globally with some 30,000 employees with pre-tax profits over $2 billion on assets of over $100 billion. Fraud is dealt with through 'Finance Crime Risk' (FCR), part of the Legal and Compliance Department which reports to the board's Risk Committee. FCR reflects the FSA focus on the minimisation of the risk of financial crime and covers: investigations; fraud (internal and external); money laundering and terrorist finance; and market abuse. Most of the work is on prevention and risk management, with policy devised at the centre, responsibility lying with the various business lines (who are expected to work to appropriate risk methodologies to minimise any loss, including that from fraud), and compliance lying with operational risk groups at regional and country levels.

Thus, although the Bank itself may not be significantly involved in mergers and corporate finance, there is potential for market abuse through the use of insider information on loans for mergers and acquisitions. This is addressed by institutionalised Chinese walls and strict rules on share dealings differentiated by position and access to information. All information on authorised share dealings and areas of work is recorded within the bank, with sophisticated software that can be used to track share purchases and sales against staff work activity.

Fraud falls into three types. First, the threat of credit card fraud is a function of the quality of the customer base – the bigger the base and the wider the access, the greater the potential for fraud. The controls are largely based on scorecard and other technological solutions (for which the bank also has a specialist unit). Second is financial fraud such as forged instructions, bogus loan applications and, to a much lesser extent, internal staff fraud. Here the trend is for organised criminals or their agents to obtain bank employment for access to customer information and to facilitate collusion externally. Finally, money laundering primarily concerns the overseas banking operations which operate to the requirements in specific countries but the SAR and Know Your Customer policies are developed and monitored centrally, as are the staff recruitment, training and reporting procedures.

All financial crime is dealt with regionally or nationally but overseen centrally. All investigations are premised on: stopping the losses; determining how the loss occurred before identifying control weaknesses to be resolved at the point of loss and across the network (and later reviewed); lessons to be learnt on fraud techniques and then disseminated; identifying the perpetrator(s) and removing them, with the option of seeking recovery. Prosecution is instituted in a limited number of cases. The response is escalated on the basis of the size of the loss and the potential reputational damage. Each operation in a country will have between 0.5 and three FTE investigation managers and there are regional FCR heads. The bank also operates a 'speaking up policy' with provisions for e-mail, letters and hotline reporting as well as promoting a visible corporate ethics approach on anti-corruption, exposed persons,[1] and country risk policies.

The building society

The Newcastle Building Society (NBS), on the other hand, is a medium-sized mutual business with an asset size of £3.4 billion. Its core business is mortgages, endowment policy loans and various investment and savings products. It has 850 staff, 33 branches and no overseas subsidiaries. It does not operate a chequebook system and does not operate any ATMs. Any Internet transactions relate only to movements within NBS accounts and to nominated bank accounts. An organised approach to the business has meant a number of reinforcing benefits. First, the absence of shareholders and a share price means the NBS can pursue a policy of profit sufficiency rather than profit maximisation, and therefore, not have to move into areas of competitive products and thus greater risk. Second, a decision in the early 1990s, in part prompted by levels of mortgage fraud in London, meant a strategic decision not to expand its branch network into a national presence but focus on a strong regional presence. As a smaller organisation NBS can thus be more conservative about its client base which is, in any case, stable, have a greater hands-on overview of its activities (there are independent management checks on all new accounts), and more input into the development of new business.

The types of fraud, apart from multiple mortgage application fraud, are thefts from tills or dormant accounts, use of accounts for other frauds and financial transactions reported as suspicious. In fraud threat terms the NBS's approach has meant that, from 1996 when there were suspect fraud cases of £6.5 million against a total lending of £250 million (2.6 per cent), the current (2004) position is that suspect fraud cases are worth £1 million against total lending of £630 million (0.16 per cent). None has resulted in any loss to the NBS. In money laundering terms the NBS MLRO receives all staff concerns over transactions. Each is vetted within NBS and assessed against its various databases: most do not relate to organised crime or terrorism but to attempts to avoid tax. Some 200 SARs are submitted annually.

The fraud and money laundering function rests with an investigation manager who is also the MLRO, with one staff member dealing with fraud and 2.5 FTE staff dealing with money laundering issues. The procedural framework is, as with other financial firms, shaped by data protection, the FSA, the SAR regime and insurance regulations. The external links on fraud prevention and control lie with the CML, the HUNTER Users Group, the North East Fraud Forum, the Building Society Association and the Institute of Money Laundering Prevention Officers. The manager reports to the Head of Compliance and the NBS Audit Committee, as well as submitting a quarterly report and an annual report to the FSA.

The NBS response to fraud is to seek to design out the opportunity at counter level (allowing staff to identify passbook misuse), structured questioning over the telephone, low thresholds for third party withdrawals (and passbook retention after any third party withdrawal). This is supported by relevant staff training, the use of HUNTER software[2] and other computer checks using IDEA software and including footprint transaction controls. Further customer identification software, integrating public domain information, is being installed to diminish the reliance on paper-based documentation. Part of this work is reinforced by FSA requirements (see above).

The forensic accountant: PwC

PricewaterhouseCoopers is an amalgam of Price Waterhouse and Coopers and Lybrand, both large international accountancy partnerships also offering management consultancy services. Today, the UK branch has over 13,000 employees, offering a full range of management services: assurance and regulatory reporting; tax; transaction services (bids, due diligence, etc.); corporate finance; business recovery; human resources and actuarial services (mergers, valuation, financial reporting arrangements, etc.); and forensic accounting services. PwC's main business is audit and 'advisory' work (better known as management consultancy). Forensic Accounting includes: disputes and claims (expert witness in commercial or contractual disputes; accounting evidence); accounting irregularities and breakdowns (regulatory compliance and regulatory investigations); licencing management (intellectual property licences); insurance claims; anti-money laundering compliance; forensic technology and cybercrime (technical and computer evidence; data mining and data matching, data recovery); forensic risk management (fraud policies and procedures); and investigations.

Forensic Accounting is borne out of the need for an investigative capability relating to audit work; the original name of the department was Disputes Analysis and Investigations where the former covered the accounting costs and liabilities, as well as possible expert witness work, associated with company disputes, while the latter dealt with both investigations related to the disputes and to internal referrals from general audit work. The 150 staff include: accountants, insolvency practitioners, construction experts and technical staff. The work continues to be dominated by internal referrals, both from audit work (where clients have a tendency to rely on advice based on the perceived expertise of their external auditor) and non-audit work (such as human resources or change management where the client also wants advice on a matter requiring investigations). PwC operates cross-line teams to identify and promote utilisation of different parts of the business with a client. Thus FA has worked for Lambeth Council as a result of internal audit links, on the Independent Insurance cases as a result of the firm being appointed liquidators, for SFI (the owners of the Slug and Lettuce pubs) on the discovery of an accounts black hole, and for the SFO on the Versailles case.

All proposed Forensic Accounting work goes through a project acceptance committee which assesses reputational and other risks on the basis of identification of the customer (Know Your Client), the available skills resource and the profitability. The international structure means that there are forensic accounting staff both in-house and in-country, with appropriate specialisms (including local knowledge), which has useful control, resourcing and pricing implications for investigations across several jurisdictions. The Forensic Accounting work is based in the existing specialisms, such as the construction industry, intellectual property rights, etc., and focuses on an investigative framework that seeks to identify losses and any third-party liability, the potential for recovery, the root causes, dealing with regulators and the police, and proposals to resolve the problems. The core investigative capability relies on the capacity to build up a case on which to base any questioning; for this, the only technical expertise may lie with data mining and matching (using high-speed scanning and analysis) to produce the evidence on which to challenge answers. The other main investigative requirement is a full understanding of all procedures and regulations which must be adhered to, to avoid losing any case in any jurisdiction or arbitration or other venue on grounds of failure of due process.

One major project entailed investigations into the Millennium Dome – a New Labour initiative that failed to attract both the sponsors and visitors to justify what was an 'ambitious and inherently risky' project. This was compounded because 'the task of managing the project has been complicated by the complex organisational arrangements put in place from the outset, and by the failure to put in sufficiently robust financial management' (NAO 2000a: 3). In the latter half of 2000 the managing company, NMEC, received allegations of fraud and corruption in relation to suppliers and contractors; PwC's Forensic Accounting undertook the independent investigation. The investigation 'focused on the specific issues raised by the allegations and 'a wider review of procurement fraud risk at the Company.' The review team 'focused on the period up to the opening of the Dome and concluded that there was no evidence of systematic fraud, but they did identify several instances of poor or ineffective compliance with the Company's procurement controls; for example, a lack of transparency on appointments, especially on certain single tenders. Given these lapses, the review team doubted whether the Company in all cases fully achieved the objective of realising value for money for the goods and services it procured' (NAO 2002c: 4).

The Forensic Accounting work in relation to the allegations consisted of interviews with staff and a review of documentation, including: manuals, board minutes, employee data, contracts, supplier data, purchase transaction history data and invoices. It found difficulties in locating supporting papers, especially where the responsible member of staff no longer worked for the Company and more problems locating papers to support the tender process, tender evaluation and the necessary contract or single tender action form for the procurement of goods or services. For the 'wider review' the Forensic Accounting work covered 'some 163 of the Company's contractual relationships out of a total of about 4,250 supplier accounts active between October 1998 and September 2000. These 163 relationships were targeted by applying fraud tests on supplier and employee information using data matching exercises, and by using information gained from investigation of the fraud allegations referred to above. In targeting relationships, the review team also considered a number of wider factors, including weaknesses in the Company's procurement procedures and concerns raised by the quantity surveyors about certain contractors. They concluded that there was no evidence of systematic fraud and did not uncover any additional cases of suspected fraud where the weight of evidence would justify further investigation' (NAO 2002c: 17).

On the other hand, the work did suggest that, 'although the Company had in place a comprehensive framework of procurement processes and approval procedures, basic controls such as invoice authorisation procedures were not always applied, and the financial systems did not readily provide senior management with information to enable them to monitor contract spend' (NAO 2002c: 17). Additionally 'there was often a lack of transparency in contracting suppliers, allied to poor record keeping in general. For example, the review team was often unable to locate the evaluations to support the award of work to a particular supplier. In many cases the review team was unable to find a legally binding contractual relationship with the supplier. They identified 129 suppliers, each of which between October 1998 and September 2000 had rendered invoices totalling £50,000 or more, for which they could not find either a contract or, where appropriate, a Single Tender Action form' (NAO 2002c: 17).

The corporate investigator: Control Risks

Control Risks is one of several corporate investigation companies, and, along with Kroll and The Risk Advisory Group (TRAG), one of the longest-standing companies in the UK. Corporate investigation companies provide specialist staff and services to business, from country risk assessments, to providing advice on staff safety, vetting potential employees and carrying out fraud investigations. Control Risks was set up in 1975 as a subsidiary of the then Hogg Robinson insurance and travel group, primarily dealing with advice to business clients involved in kidnap situations, as well as country risk profiles. In 1980/81 there was a management buy-out of the company, establishing Control Risks as an independent, employee majority-owned private company whose core business has continued to be security, kidnap, business interruption planning and risk analysis. There was a corporate decision not to move into investigations because it was the one activity Control Risks felt was more outside its control than the other activities – would investigations produce answers that would satisfy a client and, if not, how far would this reflect on Control Risks' credibility in other areas? In 1994 there were three investigators but there was an acknowledgement of the balance that investigations could bring to the corporate business and during the 1990s, staffing increased. Currently Control Risks has 450 employees, with offices in 17 countries worldwide, offering services in such areas as bomb threats, personal security, guarding, kidnap, extortion; money laundering compliance, asset tracing; crisis planning, business intelligence, business continuity; technical and computer-based work; and fraud work (including counterfeiting, employee screening, corruption inquiries, etc.).

In 2000, Control Risks bought Network Security to develop its computer forensics capability and in 2005 expanded into forensic accounting. It has 100 investigative staff around the world (with 30 in the UK) and another 90 staff who carry out pre-employment screening (it screens about 20,000 applications for companies a year, helped by the FSA's insistence that the regulated sector improve its recruitment policies). The staff mix includes former bankers, lawyers, police officers, Customs officers, and journalists. The common themes that inform recruitment are tenacity, the ability to collect and collate information and to carry out interviews. The investigative environment is now much clearer (or tighter) on what is or is not acceptable practice. All potential cases are vetted; Control Risks has an appropriate mission statement and standards, as well as an ethics committee, to indicate the conduct required of staff in investigations.

The investigation work is split approximately 50-50 between fraud and due diligence checks on companies. The latter involves looking at risk, preventative measures and governance structures in companies. For mergers, especially with partners in more risky countries such as China, Russia or Brazil, lawyers deal with compliance issues, accountants deal with the balance sheets, and companies such as Control Risks will assess the management. Fraud work comes from a range of sources, from inquiries by word of mouth to company legal advisers, and is very much focused on the 'unreported frauds', where a company has lost money internally or to external suppliers (procurement continues to be a main source of cases) and wants the money back, the identities of those involved and the loopholes closed. Cases have included an alleged invoice fraud on IKEA (overcharging by suppliers to IKEA during 1998 to 2000 when over £1.4 million was alleged to have been paid in bribes to facilitate and disguise the fraud – allegedly involving undelivered goods which were invoiced for, or they were supplied but double-invoiced). This case arose out of an internal investigation conducted by the Control Risks Group on behalf of IKEA UK Ltd. Another case was the investment company fraud involving the youngest brother of Sultan Hassanal Bolkiah, the absolute ruler of the small but oil-rich kingdom of Brunei. Control Risks formed part of the team tracing the $10 billion which disappeared, siphoned off on grandiose projects by middlemen, contractors and others.

As civilian investigators, their cases revolve around what the client may want and what the available material will reasonably produce by way of admissible evidence to invoke more formal procedures (from disciplinary procedures to asset freezing). The civilian investigator needs the ability to put together circumstantial evidence and to develop a critical rapport with suspects and witnesses; again, much of the focus is on the use of computer forensics to break down available information as part of this process.

Overall, the corporate investigator offers focus and confidentiality, and in particular the use of asset protection and recovery procedures. In other words, restitution is often more important than retribution and the focus is on the other party rather than the offence itself. The private sector often has an overseas network that means that associate staff can work freely in another country, unlike law enforcement who cannot operate abroad as flexibly, and have to follow elaborate protocols to access information and witnesses. Where the case is dealt with in the civil courts, this can be achieved without the activities that surround the criminal offence (defendants suitably charged, witnesses, documents, etc.), and a much lower burden of proof (on the balance of probabilities rather than beyond all reasonable doubt) is required. The civil courts also allow for much more flexible pre-trial negotiation as they are attuned to actions, such as recovery of assets, that seek to assuage the injured party.

The public sector in-house approach

The Defence Fraud Analysis Unit (DFAU)

The MOD is a mix of separate business groups and executive agencies, differentiated by budget line (Top Level Budgets, High Level Budgets, etc.). It operates both an internal market as well as dealing with private sector suppliers, and facility management companies. It has nearly 200,000 military and 100,000 civilian staff within some 40 budget units or agencies. The total defence budget is nearly £32 billion; the largest element of the defence budget is expenditure on equipment and spares. As an organisation with such a breadth of activity, MOD has been the subject of fraud, internally and externally, from grass-cutting works services contracts to multi-billion pound arms procurement contracts both home and overseas (see, for example, NAO 1995b), including:

- the 1980s case of Gordon Foxley, the MOD director of ammunition procurement who was charged with taking £1.3 million in bribes between 1979 until his retirement in 1984 from European suppliers for contracts for mortar bomb fuses, rockets, tracer rounds and NATO standard ammunition (during investigations, other amounts were identified as having passed through accounts held by another family member. He bought several properties for himself and his family (and five top range cars). His activities were said to have cost jobs at UK factories (NAO 1995b). He received four years' imprisonment and was ordered to repay £1.5 million (it was alleged he was able to retain over £1 million held in Swiss banks because no offence had been committed against or with a Swiss company);

- allegations that during the 1990s millions of pounds were paid out in commissions on the £20 billion Al-Yamamah contract through which British Aerospace re-equipped the Saudi Arabia air force with hundreds of fighter planes. An alleged £60 million in cash, travel, entertainment, and so on went to middlemen and Saudi princes involved in procurement. Considered too sensitive to be seen by the full PAC when the deal was first signed (the Comptroller and Auditor General confirmed that he approved the contract arrangements), initial inquiries by the MOD and by the SFO were rebuffed at both Whitehall and government levels until stories to the *The Guardian* forced the current, continuing, inquiry.

The MOD's expenditure is audited by the National Audit Office (NAO), the public body which audits government departments and reports to the House of Commons Committee on Public Accounts (PAC). For both the NAO and PAC, appropriate anti-fraud arrangements are essential and both will return in future audits and hearings of the Committee to assess whether or not the proposals to deal with previous frauds were in place and working.

The 1988 Committee of Public Accounts, for example, noted the rise of procurement abuse, ranging from forced refunds of £30 million 'additional profit' (or 'improperly gained profit') from 10 per cent of some 1000 contracts valued at over a £1 billion, to contract corruption (Committee of Public Accounts 1988) while its response to the 1991 NAO report (NAO 1991) was to warn of weak controls over stores and expenses claims. In 1991 Committee of Public Accounts described the scale and level of some of the frauds as 'extremely serious and disturbing' and the failure of some of the controls 'completely unacceptable.' In 2000 the NAO reported that 'the risk of fraud and corruption (fraud) in property management is intrinsically high. The Department have made broad estimates suggesting that property management expenditure of up to £180 million a year. 20 per cent of the total may be at risk of fraud, although there is no evidence of actual losses on this scale' (NAO 2000b). Following notice of this draft report, DFAU was established in 1999 within Defence Internal Audit from two existing units (the Defence Fraud Unit and PolC4 – procurement fraud monitoring) to act as the central contact point for fraud. Originally staffed by three people, this has increased to a staff of 11 who have a broad range of expertise (accountancy, contracts,

IT systems, etc.). Its work includes developing fraud deterrence and detection strategies; fraud awareness training (approximately 120 presentations per year); some investigations; proactive work – involving data-mining,[3] spot checks and other sources of information (such as a hotline from which it gets about 120 cases a year, access to procurement data and all MOD information systems).

DFAU works closely with the MOD Fraud Squad which has 32 officers and seven civilian support staff and works from three sites, one of which is in Scotland (MOD operates across two distinct legal jurisdictions). The Squad's core staff are split into financial investigation work, education and awareness training, investigations and proactive inquiries (which covers intake work, running informants and intelligence). Much of its work is concerned with procurement fraud and corruption.

The DFAU's current caseload is 400 cases per year, approximately 10 per cent of which is overseas (including Cyprus, Brunei, the USA, Australia, Bosnia, Kosovo, Germany and Gibraltar). There are usually around 12 spot checks per year, and they arise when there are suspicions of numerous frauds in one locale. Approximately 40 per cent of cases have been passed over to the police, 20 per cent have been closed after an initial inquiry, and 40 per cent are on-going civil disciplinary actions. DFAU has a number of working relations with other agencies, as well as developing Fraud Focal Points with Top Level Budgets to promote fraud awareness and a culture of prevention.

DFAU has identified a number of trends in fraud investigations since it was established. These now include: internal fraud following the devolution of managerial responsibility and the removal of many front-line checks (e.g. counter-signatures from line managers are no longer needed on travel and subsistence claims); a rise in fraud reporting – by approximately 400 per cent – which is probably due to the huge increases in fraud awareness training (the corresponding number of frauds reported by line managers has dropped); and fraud and corruption relating to prime contracting or facilities management where major contractors self-certify work.[4]

The Department for Work and Pensions (DWP)

The DWP is the largest spending department in the public sector – £100 billion and rising. Its various sub-departments and agencies include Jobcentre Plus, the Child Support Agency and the Pensions Service. Over two million people receive Income Support at an average of £88 a week, and over two million claim Incapacity Benefit at an average of £84 a week. Nearly four million claim Housing Benefit at an average cost of £61 a week. Over 11 million claim state pensions; one million of these live abroad, and the number of people eligible for pensions has increased by one million since 1995. In other words, the DWP is involved in high volume, low cost payments where numbers of claimants are constantly changing. In addition, other factors impact on what is paid, how much and to whom. When, for example, the private rented housing market was deregulated in the 1980s, the cost of Housing Benefit (HB) rose rapidly at the same time the government tried to cut down on bureaucracy by requiring quick turnarounds on applications. Thus local councils, who pay out housing benefits on behalf of the DWP, were not only faced with higher claims but often allowed verification of claims to take second place to 'quality of service' performance targets (see Doig and Coles 1997).

The DWP has undergone – and is undergoing – substantial organisational change and merger, with the implications of this in terms of tackling fraud clearly noted in the 2003 NAO report (see p 227). Its size and regionalisation has meant issues for coherent strategy and performance: 'the information currently collected by the Department does not give a sufficiently clear view of whether regions' performance on interventions and investigations are improving or not. Nor can the Department track the outcomes of fraud referrals accepted for investigation within each year ...' (NAO 2003a: 10).

The issue of more effective and more cost-effective fraud work has been on the departmental agenda since 1989 when a Fraud Scrutiny report proposed the merger of the Employment Service (ES) and Department of Social Security (DSS) fraud functions. The scrutiny argued that the different organisation of fraud resources made liaison complex, that 'the operational realities of fraud investigation work' led to competition and that there were marked differences between approaches within the ES and DSS, that there were staffing and career development issues, that there was no strategy of proactive fraud work, that information and intelligence were not used effectively, that there were no sanctions if either side failed to deliver on their existing liaison agreement. In considering a client group focus or a benefit focus, the scrutiny opted for a single, independent investigation agency model dealing with cases referred to it by the Employment Service and the Department and resourced by an appropriate framework document.

In 1996 a study initiated by the Conservative Government found that under-investment, poor performance measures, weak incentives and slack monitoring were constraining fraud work. In addition to its proposal for a 'new and powerful inspectorate' (the future Benefit Fraud Inspectorate),[5] the study again returned to the question of different agencies' involvement in fraud work, calling for a greater degree of professionalism (proposing a Head of Profession for investigation), and greater exchange of information. In 2000 the Grabiner report recommended (i) the increased availability of shared data, (ii) joint working where departments (notably the Benefits Agency – now Jobcentre Plus, Inland Revenue and HM Customs and Excise) had common interests, and (iii) the possibility of a dedicated informal economy investigation agency. In 2000, the Scampion Report (Scampion 2000), the first systematic analysis of how the Benefits Agency and relevant agencies were dealing with the fraud threats, based its recommendations on six principles:

- full awareness of the need for the prevention, as well as the detection, of fraud;
- cohesion between strategy and operation;
- an imaginative and innovative use of intelligence;
- a high degree of professionalism;
- a financial regime which supports counter-fraud work;
- joint working between organisations involved in social security counter-fraud work as a fundamental principle of an anti-fraud regime.

Scampion proposed both organisational and strategic changes, including Regional Boards to develop joined-up strategies, promoting joint working initiatives, information sharing and the role of intelligence-led investigation. In the event, a Head of Profession and Chief Investigation Officer post was established with direct responsibility for the area of organised fraud, professional standards and intelligence at a national level. The post did not have direct responsibility for fraud strategy, nor line management responsibility for the area of client/claimant fraud and the operational intelligence units, so that the post-Scampion DWP fraud function was essentially hybrid, split between organised fraud (planned fraud executed on a systematic basis) involving multiple claims, counterfeiting, forgery and theft of Instruments of Payment (IoPs), etc., and claimant fraud. The Scampion recommendations led to an intelligence-led approach to both organised fraud and claimant fraud work, but the claimant fraud function remained firmly within the overall claimant benefits regime which is delivered regionally.

The fraud function was operated through 11 regional services, sharing about 4,000 Counter Fraud Investigation Service (CFIS) investigators, whose workload and intelligence roles were supported by 11 Operational Intelligence Units (OIU). In 2001/02 (NAO 2003a) there were 667,000 referrals received. Of these nearly 400,000 were investigated (58 per cent of referrals received) and recoverable overpayments detected to a value of £123 million. Around 41 per cent (161,000) resulted in an adjustment to benefit and/or the identification of an overpayment (many that are not investigated are referrals of poorer quality, which were considered not to warrant investigation, but which may be appropriate for intervention to ensure compliance). While 40 per cent of cases investigated involved fraud (the average weekly loss is less than £80), most were dealt with by removal from benefits or recovery of amounts defrauded. In 15 per cent of cases, a warning, an administrative sanction (a caution or penalty) or prosecution is also invoked. Local authorities, with some 1,400 investigators, deal with over 200,000 detected frauds, with 800 prosecutions annually.

The responsibilities of the Head of Profession included the National Investigation Service (with some 500 specialist investigators dealing with organised and more serious cases of fraud, including financial investigations and the recovery of money); the Professional Standards Unit (providing legal and policy guidance and responsible for setting and monitoring standards for investigators and training); the Joint Working Unit (promoting joint working between the Department's fraud units, other government departments and local authorities); the Matching Intelligence Data Analysis Service (comparing data held on different benefit systems and with other government departments' data sources); and the National Intelligence Unit (providing specialist advice and support to enable the Department to tackle benefit fraud in areas such as immigration, identity, etc., as well as hosting the National Benefit Fraud Hotline and managing the OIU network).

The effect of the hybrid or partial nature of the reforms, and the mix of dotted line and direct responsibilities of the Head of Profession, was at best a piecemeal or patchwork response and with only partial success. Overall the DWP approach to fraud still mirrored a regional service with a separate resource 'bolted on' to deal with organised fraud, which Scampion did little to change. What changes were introduced, such as the role of intelligence-led investigations and asset recovery, had to work within the existing overall organisational shape. The continuing poor procedural practice – which Scampion had hoped to make more professional in terms of criminal law implementation – essentially required a split in focus and function but was something that the DWP as an organisation took time to assimilate and incorporate into wider reforms.

This took place during 2004 and 2005 with changes to Jobcentre Plus and the delivery of the benefit system and a general reduction of staff. This led to some of CFIS being reorganised within a 'programme protection' approach which shifted the emphasis to the civil side of fraud work in terms of risk-assessing claims and using various interview methods to focus on claimant benefits correction and compliance, with possible sanctions to include penalties, cautions and prosecutions. There is now a focus on working within the national benefits delivery system and concentrating on the rectification of 'error', acknowledgement of any over-payment and a record on file for future reference. Internal research (Department for Work and Pensions 2004: 85) has suggested that those who had been through the sanctions regime believed 'that the experience they have had will deter them from committing fraud again. For incognizant fraudsters the experience has led them to doubly check all information they submit. In this sense the regime can be said to have worked in that people will not offend again and they have a greater sense of what their own responsibilities are. For many people interviewed the experience was shaped not so much by the type of sanction they received but by the fact that they had been subject to the regime in the first place. In essence to many people the deterrent effect would have been the same regardless of whether they had received a caution or an administrative penalty.'

The rest of the staff in CFIS and NIS have been merged into the Fraud Investigation Service (FIS), including its intelligence, professional standards and technical support units to form a national fraud function. FIS has over 3,000 staff (although still located within Jobcentre Plus) allocated regionally and the bulk of whom deal with general benefit fraud. The FIS has proposed to work to a specification agreed with the Department to provide a shared service function across the range of benefits and agencies with an agreed percentage of resource allocated to each activity or delivery agency, as well as having responsibility for joint working across government, in support of their intended outcomes (integrating the activity rather than the resource). Thus the FIS now focuses on both general fraud (drawing on data from the programme protection centres) as well as complex and organised fraud, contract fraud, inter-agency working and collusive employers. The FIS is developing specialist approaches, including professional standards, financial investigations, surveillance, asset recovery, and criminal analysis techniques. Its investigations will be intelligence-led (through a National Intelligence Unit and operational intelligence units) based on the NIM model (using threat assessments, tasking and coordinating approaches). It uses internal data-mining, sharing information with a range of agencies (to see, for example, who is paying tax to HMRC on capital, possession of which they have not revealed to the DWP for assessment of benefits entitlement, or who is in receipt of an occupational pension).

At the end of 2005 the funding relationship with local authorities was proposed for review, with the emphasis shifting to compliance work and away from payments by activity (such as issuing cautions and prosecutions) to a lump sum upfront payment for HB delivery, including fraud work, and performance measures integrated into the Audit Commission's Comprehensive Performance Assessment that operates across all local authority activity. Within the DWP, the Head of Profession aspect was ended in 2005. This may affect fraud policy, training across the DWP and local authorities to ensure common standards, joint working, and intelligence-led work.

NHS Counter Fraud and Security Management Services (CFSMS)

The NHS itself is an industry (and the largest institution in Europe) employing over 1.3 million staff (including 386,000 nurses, 109,000 doctors, 122,000 scientists and therapists and 36,000 managers). With a budget of some £55 billion, 55 per cent of its expenditure goes on staff costs (£31 billion – annual pay awards add another £1.1 billion to the costs each year). 15 per cent of expenditure (£8 billion) goes on medicines. Two-thirds of the expenditure goes on hospital services. Land owned by various parts of the NHS is worth £5.4 billion. The scale of the provision of health care continues, despite the reforms, to be enormous and complex.

The issue of fraud and corruption in the NHS has been on the agenda since 1997 when the Audit Commission published its audit manual (*Protecting the Public Purse 2: Ensuring Probity in the NHS*) as a companion volume to that for local government. This highlighted a number of areas of risk. These included the number of visits that opticians were making to elderly people, and pharmacist fraud, highlighted by analysing the discrepancy between the volume of prescriptions and associated fees remitted to the Prescriptions Pricing Authority by independent pharmacists and by the High Street dispensers like Boots. Later updated, the figures around that time for annual detected fraud was £4.7 million, involving 368 cases. The trend for fraud was significant, with GPs and opticians responsible for two-thirds of the value of fraud. The areas of risk included: doctors' lists; patient prescription fraud through claiming exemption; pharmacist fraud by over-claiming for medicines; home visits by opticians; dental work (such as pre-signing the claim form); mishandling patients' money; procurement fraud. In addition the National Audit Office had issued a series of damning reports during the 1990s over the impact of the organisational changes on regional health authorities, including those on the West Midlands, Wessex and Yorkshire Regional Health Authorities.

Further studies included an Efficiency Scrutiny into prescription fraud (Department of Health 1997) which put patient charge evasion at between £70–£100 million but avoided quantifying the losses by pharmacists, dispensing doctors and frauds involving prescribing in care homes (including those where doctors had financial interests). The report noted that the Prescription Pricing Authority (PPA) had set up its own fraud unit. Like the Audit Commission's 1997 report, the Scrutiny argued for an anti-fraud culture and money spent on the prevention and investigation of fraud. A survey in the same year by the Healthcare Financial Management Association (Healthcare Financial Management Association/CIPFA 1997) reported that fraud was growing across primary care, that fraud was happening across health authorities, that the average loss was over £50,000, that investigation was often complex and time-consuming, and that the police were not always interested. The recommendations were for training for those involved in fraud work, for a central forensic audit support unit to coordinate and investigate cases, for a central database and for efforts to recover lost funds.

By the time the Healthcare Financial Management Association/CIPFA survey returned to the subject a year later (reporting a rise in fraud but a patchy response to its 1997 survey) an NHS 'Fraud Supremo' (the press title for what was to be the Director of Counter Fraud Services) had been appointed in 1998 by Alan Milburn, who was then Labour Secretary of State for Health. This appointment would take responsibility for many of the recommendations. The 'Supremo' – the appointment was just one of a number of 'Czar' appointments to deal with various issues – was to head the Counter Fraud Service (CFS). CFS was from the start a coordinated operation, between policy and other staff within the Department of Health and operational staff – Counter Fraud Operational Services (CFOS) – employed within 'volunteer' Health Authorities. In 2003 CFS was set up as a Special Health Authority and had taken over the PPA fraud unit, created a dental fraud unit and taken on responsibility for general security matters. The current structure comprise 9 Directorates: and includes: the HQ (with about 70 staff), Executive, Communications and Liaison, Training and Skills, Information Systems, Policy, Quality and Research, Security Management, and the Operations Directorate. This latter Directorate covers the dedicated and regional teams (formerly CFOS) with approximately 70 staff, including eight regional teams, a Dental Fraud Team (DFT; five staff), a Pharmaceutical Fraud Team (PFT; 15 staff) and a National Proactive Team (NPT; six staff who deal with complex cases, cases over £75,000 or those requiring surveillance). There is a Patient Fraud Support Unit which provides assistance to Primary Care Trusts in dealing with dental, optical and prescription fraud (for which there are specific penalties, see p 211). There is also an intelligence unit and a computer forensics unit.

The policy of the CFSMS, which now costs £14 million a year and employs some 250 staff, has been to develop a 10-year strategy (during which time 'it would reduce fraud to an absolute minimum') based on assessments of the levels of fraud[6] and the role of its staff in dealing with it. Part of that strategy is delivered through the training of a counter-fraud officer in each Trust or agency through specially created training centres in Reading and Coventry (all CFSMS staff also had to undergo vetting on recruitment), and sustained by secondary legislation that can require Trusts to provide information, cooperate on proactive exercises and receive training, etc. Part is the detailed research and database used to analyse cases, types and cost of fraud undertaken by the Risk Management Directorate, and which also provides the basis of its risk strategy.

The Trust fraud contact people – most of whom are employed in audit or financial functions – are one of the sources of the 1,400 cases the CFSMS has managed to investigate over five years (leading to over 292 successful prosecutions (a 96 per cent success rate). There are over 324 disciplinary cases, as well as an integral use of confiscation and civil recovery processes. Other cases primarily come from the 11,000 anonymous allegations made to the hotline (of which some 49 per cent have been considered to be genuine) and the national exercises (often with the data being processed by the local Trust staff, which has raised issues about the appropriate allocation of audit time).

Much of the CFSMS work – and where the impact of its work has been felt – has been on the tightening up of procedures and forms which have both limited the opportunity for fraud and also discouraged health professionals from becoming involved. These initiatives have included ophthalmic, prescription and dental fraud (see Box 9.1 for an example of the latter).

The CFSMS relies for specific powers on secondary legislation, such as the requirement that PCTs, Trusts, dentists, doctors, nurses

Box 9.1   Dental fraud

A dentist who carried out the biggest single fraud in NHS history has been ordered to pay back £1.3 million. For six years, Mohammed Shiekh, 35, ran an expenses racket based on claiming for thousands of false emergency call-outs. He had 14 surgeries around Nottingham and Derby and used them to devise a fraud based on generous 'recall' fees paid to dentists if they have to reopen their surgeries out of hours to carry out emergency treatment.

However, the high level of expenses he was claiming – in one instance he claimed there were 56 separate call-outs from his practices in one night – aroused suspicion. After an investigation by the NHS Counter Fraud Service, the Dental Practice Board, which pays the 20,000 dentists who carry out NHS work, issued a writ to sue him for the money, the largest case of its kind ever brought.

On Tuesday, at the High Court in London, Shiekh, from West Bridgeford, Notts, was found guilty of conspiracy to defraud between 1994 and 2000 and was ordered to pay back the money, along with £288,000 in costs. A criminal investigation is still going on.

The scheme centred on expenses allowed when a dentist attends an emergency call and needs to reopen a surgery. Sheik was able to claim £32.65 for up to a mile travelled and £53.65 for more than a mile. A dentist can only claim once for reopening the surgery and most of Shiekh's scheme revolved around telling his dentists to leave the surgery and 'drive their car round the houses for at least a mile in between patients' to qualify for another expense claim. Shiekh, who has since moved his operations to Sheffield, said his claims 'were not fraudulent but were made in pursuance of an honest scheme which was intended to maximise income by legitimately exploiting the scales of fees ... while keeping within the terms'.

The court also found his cousin, Jamil Ahmad, guilty of conspiracy to defraud, and he will be forced to pay back a proportion of the money. When talking together about the scheme, they referred to it as 'Jamil's little project'. Another charge against Arun Madahar, a dentist at Shiekh's Greenwood Dale Dental Centre in Nottingham, was settled after he paid £50,000.

Source: *The Daily Telegraph*, 04 April 2003

or health managers who refuse to let counter-fraud officers see their records would face up to nine months' jail or a £5,000 fine (private sector treatment centres and the 'light-touch' Foundation Trusts have such access written into their contracts). CFSMS has also moved into proactive work, seeking to identify areas of risk, promote awareness and act as a deterrent. For example, a 2004 exercise (undertaken by Operations) looked at bank working – the use of agency staff on a pull-down basis. The exercise found that Trusts did not verify the qualifications or eligibility of bank staff, the timesheets were poorly designed and usually incomplete, self-booking was common, there were few guidelines on authorised signatories and few records kept on the wards. In terms of prevention, Policy have addressed the new GP contracts with a number of measures including: random sample checks; detailed visits to selected practices; signed declarations on returns; and a national computerised database for benchmarking and evaluation.

Summary

There is a distinct difference of approach between the two sectors. The private sector is about net profit, minimising risk and complying with regulatory requirements. The emphasis on a managed approach to where anti-fraud work is targeted, the level of resource committed and the balance of risk, markets and preventative controls is offset by the ability to accept a level of loss against levels of business, close down high-risk business, and buy in businesses with dedicated anti-fraud capabilities as and when required. Although the public sector does use the same agencies, it would be impossible for a government body to refuse to accept, or try to withdraw from, a political decision to fund a particular service or activity, just as it would be reluctant to tolerate levels of fraud where the cost of dealing with it may be disproportionate to the losses. Part of the reluctance comes from the fact that Parliament, the Audit Commission or the National Audit

Office would be reluctant to tolerate a public body accepting levels of fraud just because the cost of policing it would be disproportionate. What the public sector spends on anti-fraud work is thus likely to be more than in the private sector, and this is why many public sector bodies now have an internal anti-fraud capability that, in numbers of staff alone, is likely to be greater than that deployed in the private sector or by the police.

Overall, it would appear that, whatever the sector, the issue of fraud is addressed through a range of approaches. However these are increasingly governed by an extensive array of procedural and other requirements. Much of this derives from the impact of the role of human rights in the criminal investigative process whereby any criminal prosecution could constitute an 'interference by a public authority' for the purposes of Article 8(2) of the European Convention on Human Rights (ECHR) and the mere threat of a prosecution may be an interference if it directly interferes with private life. The next chapter looks at the issues that cover criminal investigation and how non-law enforcement investigations are also moving in the same direction.

Notes

1 Known as PEPs (politcally-exposed persons), these are politicians and public officials, and those linked by marriage or in other ways to them, who are involved in corruption and who may be opening accounts for money laundering purposes (see www.wolfsberg-principles.com).

2 National HUNTER is a software service provided by MCL, a Southport-based company whose major shareholder is Experian, the large data and credit referencing agency. Nearly all mortgage lenders license HUNTER which sends to MCL all application information overnight. HUNTER cross-checks the data and returns to users printouts of 'hits', information that within an application or across applications suggests the need for further verification.

3 One of the devolved budget ideas was the minor supplies and expenses credit card. Allocated to local procurement staff to acquire supplies locally, the card is used for 670,000 annual transactions. These are now regularly data-mined for, among other frauds, lapdancing and rollerblading since the data information from the bank identifies the ultimate recipients of payments.

4 The MOD is also one of the largest landowners in the United Kingdom and currently spends over £1 billion per annum on its estate. Defence Estates is responsible for MOD UK and overseas land and buildings

with 1500 staff and operating costs of £214 million. It now also has its own Defence Fraud Unit that runs very much along the same lines as DFAU but only exists for the benefit of the investigation of impropriety or irregularity within the construction industry. They can at any time arrive at any site and undertake 'Blue Sky Inspections'. These vary from DFAU's inspections whose programme is advertised in advance.

5   The BFI reviews the management and procedural arrangements for local authority fraud work, and their relations with the DWP. It is to be merged with the Audit Commission, one consequence of which will be that it will no longer review the DWP aspect of the relationship.

6   Each measurement exercise aims for an accuracy of plus or minus 0.2 per cent and seeks to measure 'before' and 'after' anti-fraud initiatives. The figures identified to date (and including funds 'at risk') total about £250 million and have related primarily to: patient fraud over prescriptions (an initial estimate of £117 million lost annually to fraud, now down to £47 million), eye tests (an initial estimate of £13 million lost to fraud annually, now down to £10 million) and dental treatment (an estimated £40 million lost to fraud annually, now some £20 million). Doctor fraud, fraud in Trusts and authorities, and pharmacist fraud have not yet been calculated. The sample sizes were small – around 3,000–5,000 – but seen as statistically relevant and not dissimilar in size to that of the DWP.

Chapter 10

Investigation frameworks

English law has been developing procedures to govern a more transparent and equitable investigative process, beginning with the 1984 Police and Criminal Evidence Act. Nevertheless it is the rights-based European jurisprudence which is emerging as the response to protection from executive lawlessness against the citizen – particularly in the area of judicial review. The concepts of proportionality, legality and necessity have emerged alongside the traditional doctrines of review, such as 'unreasonableness, abuse of power and irrationality' (see Davis 2003).

That such regulation was deemed necessary was very much a reflection of the English criminal trial which, as Denis Clark points out, 'is not a search for truth but an attempt to do justice within the constraints placed upon it by the law of evidence and the procedural requirements.' Thus much of the recent legislation is intended for a level and transparent playing field and in particular ensure that the disproportionate powers and skills of law enforcement agencies do not prejudice a fair trial. The shift to a rights-based jurisprudence is not yet complete. To whom they apply – as individuals or organisations – is in part determined by the overarching ECHR principles and in part by the legal requirements on who has a general duty to investigate, and who has a duty to investigate with a view to prosecution. In practice these apply to any public sector agency which is increasingly bound by procedural aspects of investigation if the case is likely to end up in the criminal courts.

The legal framework

The 1984 Police and Criminal Evidence Act (PACE) was brought in to regulate parts of the investigative process. It included provision for codes of practice to be introduced (and revised) to add detail to the legislation. Subsequent cases have deemed that the duty to investigate referred to in Section 67(9) of the Act was 'any type of legal duty, whether imposed by statute, common law or by contract.' This means that anyone employed as an investigator and whose contract stipulated they were employed as an investigator was subject to PACE, making them a person 'charged with the duty of investigating offences.' The 1996 Criminal Procedure and Investigations Act sees an investigation as a criminal investigation 'which police officers or other persons have a duty to conduct with a view to it being ascertained whether (a) a person should be charged with an offence, or (b) whether a person charged with an offence is guilty of it.' Full compliance may vary, however, on whether or not those expected to exercise the duty to investigate should also do so to the full extent of a police officer. Thus a social security investigator who failed to tell an interviewee who attended a social security office voluntarily that he was entitled to free legal advice, because there was no such entitlement, was not in breach of the Code but the 1996 Act does advise 'persons other than police officers' to take account of the provisions of the Act in their investigations.

The relativity relates to the fact that, increasingly, investigators work to the higher standard, particularly if there is a later possibility of a criminal prosecution and because most investigators accept that the higher standard reflects current good practice, the potential for a more ethical investigation and less criticism in a tribunal or court context. This means that all criminal investigations now have key components, each of which is now governed by legislation and codes of practice. These include:

The Police and Criminal Evidence Act 1984: covers the conduct of the police and those with a duty to investigate in relation to arrest, interviews, search warrants (including seeking access to confidential personal material and material held in confidence), searches and seizure of material. It makes plain that any court could (rather than will) refuse to allow the prosecution to present any evidence if the methods used to obtain it might have 'an adverse effect on the fairness of the proceedings.'

The Human Rights Act 1998: has a specific impact on investigation in that it concerns the right to respect for private and family life, which prohibits any interference by a public body unless in accordance with the law and for a specific lawful purpose.

The Criminal Procedure and Investigations Act (CPIA) 1996: defines a criminal investigation (leading to a trial) and an investigator (all of those responsible for recording, retaining and revealing information obtained in the investigation). The Act requires 'persons other than police officers' to take account of the provisions of the Act in their investigations. The Act essentially introduced disclosure – all and any information that might appear to have some bearing on the investigation (that is, likely to affect the fairness and thus the outcome of any trial) and detailed the responsibilities of the person designated for handling the administration of disclosure.

Data Protection Act 1998: regulates access to, the protection of, and the processing of, data held on individuals, defines what data is, how it should be kept, and accessed. This also includes data-mining and data-sharing.

Misuse of Computers Act 1990: regulates accessing electronic devices.

The Regulation of Investigatory Powers Act 2000: intended to bring 'lawful' authority to the interception of communications, to carrying out surveillance and to using CHISs (covert human intelligence sources, previously called informants). Surveillance covers monitoring, listening to and observing (and including recording) people (their movements, conversations, communications, etc.). There are extensive codes of practice and procedures that are auditable (for example, payments to informants), with 'necessity' and 'proportionality' playing key criteria. There is also a duty of care to informants.

Overall, what the laws have done is to 'indicate the scope of any discretion conferred on the competent authorities and the manner of its exercise with sufficient clarity, having regard to the legitimate aim of the measure in question, to give the individual adequate protection against arbitrary interference' (Nash and Furze 2002: 50).

Criminal investigations in practice

Much of the activity of an investigation is the same for both public and private sectors; there are a number of laws and procedures that govern anyone with the duty to investigate. Indeed, if there is any likelihood that the case may go to the police or another law enforcement agency and then on to the criminal court, any aspect of an investigation will have to be conducted to criminal standards. Many law enforcement agencies use the National Intelligence Model, a structured approach to intelligence-led investigations which provides a template for planning, tasking and delivering investigations. It includes ensuring that an investigation has access to: sources of information; appropriate personnel; 'knowledge products' (planning and prioritisation models, rules and practices governing procedures, etc.); and 'systems products' (provision of, or access to, the systems and facilities necessary for the secure collection, recording, storage, analysis and use of information).[1]

An investigation itself has a number of key components or aspects, including:

Case management: involves setting up the investigation, tasking, recording and review processes with designated – and trained – staff (such as exhibits and disclosure officers) and case management databases.

Interviews: are conducted under PACE (the law and subsequent interpretations of practice) and cover the recording of interviews, the location of interviews and the conduct of interviews. There are two types of interviewing technique – the cognitive interview and conversation management laid out in the PEACE model for questioning – Planning/Preparation, Engage/Explain, Account, Closure and Evaluation – which structures the interview process around the witness or suspect agenda (what they want to say), the police agenda (the information they wish to elicit – usually using the 5W/H and 'Little TED'),[2] and challenge (reconciling the two).

Search[3] *and Seize*: requires the continuity and integrity of all material taken or used (documents, witness statements, record books, notes of meetings, disks, PCs, etc.) as part of any investigation. The rules (see the Attorney General's April 2005 update: www.lslo.gov.uk/pdf/disclosure) require disclosure of all material being used by the prosecution, and unused material reasonably considered capable of undermining the prosecution case or of helping the defendant. 'Sensitive' material (surveillance material, confidential material from certain agencies, etc.) is still subject to degrees of confidentiality (see the Attorney General's April 2005 update: www.lslo.gov.uk/pdf/disclosure) which stresses the need for prosecutions to undertake an assessment of materiality rather than simply tell the defence that they can inspect all material in the unused schedules.

Technical support: this involves the use of specialist approaches and resources to support investigations, including, for example, forensic computing (the burgeoning use of data-mining and data-matching software to trawl through databases or scanned documentation for links), proprietal software to pictorially represent investigation links and timelines, proprietal software packages to scan different types of computer drives to log information and extract partially deleted information in a way that preserves continuity should the material be required as evidence.[4] Investigators can also call on forensic document analysis which can compare handwriting and signatures (including the distinctive features, and the degree of disguise), identify counterfeited and altered original documents, identify impressions of handwriting from one document onto another, and rebuild shredded, water- and fire-damaged material (see Allen 2005a).

Intelligence and information: intelligence is the use and interpretation of information (although not necessarily 'evidence'). Information in investigations comes from many sources – public or open domain, information obtained by court order and information collected by surveillance or from informants. Legislation governs the sharing of information between public bodies; for example, the 1997 Social Security Administration (Fraud) Act states that the DWP could ask for information held by HM Customs and Excise and Inland Revenue not only for 'the prevention, detection, investigation or prosecution of offences relating to social security' but also to check 'the accuracy of information relating to benefits, contributions or national insurance numbers or to any other matter relating to social security and (where appropriate) amending or supplementing such information.' The Terrorism Act 2000 allows for the transmission of information between the HMRC and the police using similar criteria to Section 29 exclusions under the Data Protection Act 1998. This allows for information to be passed in the prevention or detection of crime or in the prosecution or apprehension of offenders. It is particularly useful in the prosecution of money laundering offences.

Overseas inquiries: for police forces, around 30 per cent of their fraud cases will have an overseas dimension. Obtaining evidence from overseas, as well as extraditing suspects, is governed by a range of Acts and Agreements and a specific procedure through the CPS and Home Office (as well as accessing the information and tracing networks facilitated by Interpol). The operational aspects of law enforcement – collecting evidence, interviewing witnesses, etc. – have been covered by the legal framework which is based on protocols and legislation; for the European context or working through Interpol, this would include protocols on mutual assistance, (such as the European Convention on Mutual Assistance in Criminal Matters (1959 and 1978) or those incorporated into the 1990 Criminal Justice (International Cooperation) Act and its 1998 amendment (see also Murray 2005).

Non-law enforcement investigations

Private sector investigations do not need formal protocols and nor is it necessary to arrange for official permission around the world for UK staff to work in foreign jurisdictions. Many companies have a network of offices which employ local staff, because a global capability is becoming increasingly important (although an investigator may be required to obtain a licence in certain jurisdictions). In this and other areas, the private sector investigation may appear to work like law enforcement but often in a different way and to different ends. Within private sector investigations there tend, however, to be some distinctions between the use of external agencies to deal with loss of assets or dishonest employees, and a company's own internal inquiries (see Goldspink and Cole 2002, for various considerations in the investigative process from both civil and criminal perspectives).

In any case, non law enforcement inquiries follow a different approach where timescales, media handling, confidentiality and cost estimates would influence what is done when, and how, with perhaps an overriding requirement to address the client's expectations although the investigator should maintain their independence so as to properly advise their client. In such circumstances, the investigation will draw upon issues such as the following: 'The source and nature of the allegation, the appropriate case strategy and workplan, budgets, employee rights, investigation techniques, and recovery of any loss, all have to be considered, and important and sometimes critical decisions taken' (Greenhalgh and Coles 2005). A typical private sector investigative framework should work to the five key tests that should be applied before a specific investigation procedure or technique is deployed – see Box 10.1.

Box 10.1 The non-law enforcement investigative tests

Test 1: is the use of the technique permitted by law?
Test 2: is the use of the technique permitted by reference to the employment manual and/or employment contract?
Test 3: does the nature of the client's case justify the use of the technique and is its use proportionate and necessary?
Test 4: has the rationale for the use of the technique been considered and approved by the investigation manager, and been recorded in a transparent fashion?
Test 5: has the use of the technique been discussed fully with the client and written approval obtained?

Source: Greenhalgh and Coles 2005

Many investigations will largely follow the same procedural framework as the public sector (most investigators, for example, are trained in PACE – see Dipple and Ryan 2005). Most non law enforcement investigations will follow the standard case management practices (file management and control, points to prove, permissions, activity logs, etc.), use investigative interviewing techniques,[5] follow similar search, seize and store protocols for documents and in collecting computer evidence (and operating control and continuity procedures to preserve the evidential chain). In addition, they would have the same recourse to computer forensics, forensic accounting, dedicated software and forensic document services and operate to similar good practice on accessing public domain data, and as well as for the use of more invasive techniques such as surveillance and so on, following RIPA practice for informant handling and surveillance work (see Brown 2005; Ormerod 2005; Allen 2005b; Mabey 2005). Additionally there is a range of sources of information – Companies House, Land Registry, commercial and open source databases (such as Experian, Dun and Bradstreet, and Mint), newspapers, Google, the Electoral Roll, court records, bankruptcy records, web and postal addresses, and so on, for gathering information.

Indeed, the issue of good practice – usually emulating that of a criminal investigation – is vital should the client or organisation choose to engage with the police[6] at any time during an investigation:

One of the most relevant of the client's objectives, which will impact upon the case strategy, is whether (subject to the evidence obtained) the client will wish to refer the case to the police, or alternatively to deal with the matter on a civil or internal basis. On occasions, it may be too soon at the outset for the client to decide whether the police should be involved or not. It is important to review the client's objectives as to criminal action at the outset, as if it is required that a police referral option should remain open, what might be referred to as a hybrid investigation will need to be undertaken. This means that the investigation will be performed to the criminal investigation standard to preserve the option of proceeding down the criminal and/or civil route. (Greenhalgh and Coles 2005)

This does not mean that police and civil investigations cannot proceed under different processes and approaches, but the latter should not be in a position to tarnish or compromise the former (see, for example, a 2003 Department of Health practitioner guide). Nevertheless, in relation to, for example, employee issues, 'there is case law to the effect that the employer should still discuss the position with the employee and seek his explanation, notwithstanding police involvement. Similarly, an employer can make a decision based on the evidence he has if the employee refuses to participate in the disciplinary process, provided the evidence available is sufficient for a reasonable belief in guilt to be formed. Therefore evidence of the employee being caught in the act or an admission made to the police can help the employer reach a conclusion if the employee fails to co-operate' (Evans 2005: 47/41).

Indeed, most non law enforcement investigation frameworks will be affected by conditions of employment or by links to general company HR policies on, for example, the circumstances under which searches could take place or the uses and abuses of PCs at work. Further, and despite the apparent absence of law enforcement powers, non law enforcement investigations do have a number of powers they can use through the civil courts to assist with their inquiries (see Thackeray and Riem 2005, Section 55; see Goldspink and Cole 2002), including:[7]

- The use of freezing orders (formerly Mareva injunctions) – going to the civil court with affidavit evidence, almost always *ex parte* (in the absence of or without the prior knowledge of those against whom the order is sought) to prevent the disposal of assets or their removal from the jurisdiction or through an Information Order – to provide information about them;

- Search orders (formerly Anton Pillar orders) – again with affidavit evidence of a strong case, where there is a risk that relevant documents might be destroyed by the defendant(s) if permission is not granted to search premises and seize the documents;

- Disclosure or Information Orders – in the case of Norwich Pharmacal Orders, access to information from another company or organisation to help identify wrongdoers or to trace funds (the case involved a chemical company wanting to be told who was importing a counterfeited version of their product which HM Customs had initially refused to do on the grounds that their interest and information related only to dealing with the importer. They were later told by the House of Lords that they came 'under a duty to assist the person who has been wronged by giving him full information and disclosing the identity of the wrongdoers'). In the case of Bankers Trust Orders, the order is for disclosure of information on funds held by a suspected fraudster or accomplice. This takes precedence over the confidential bank/customer relationship where there is strong evidence of ownership, of fraud and of the possible dispersal of the money before any court case (and where the customer is relying on that relationship to avoid discovery). In the case of both Orders, those caught up in wrongdoing, even innocently, are under a duty at law to assist those who have been defrauded (Goldspink and Cole 2002: 452);

- Tracing – establishing in court a claim over the assets of others in which the claimant can demonstrate an interest or ownership;

- Monitoring – under the 2000 Telecommunications (Lawful Business Practice) (Interception of Communications) Regulations made under RIPA, businesses can record evidence of transactions relating to the business to prevent and detect crime, as well as prevent unauthorised use and to establish 'the existence of facts.' This could include: telephone calls and billing information, e-mails, post, internet use, material stored on a work PC. The regulations governing such activity are as strict as those for the public sector. However, in cases of a suspected fraud they potentially enable the investigator to monitor e-mails or telephone calls, subject of course to the terms of the contract of employment as mentioned above. (Physical surveillance should also take account of civil remedies against the taking of photographs, trespass without lawful authority (including going through someone's rubbish), nuisance, the laws of copyright relating to documents copied without the consent of the rightful owner, and possible harassment under the 1997 Protection from Harassment Act – see Goldspink and Cole 2002: 50–51).

Not unnaturally, such powers and court orders are both costly and open to challenge both during and after the event, as well as being subject to a framework of procedure and precedent as developed as that governing criminal investigations (see Thackeray and Riem 2005). Full disclosure of all material facts (coming to court with 'clean hands') must be given to the court at the outset, especially because the defendant will not be present at the *ex parte* hearing. The orders sought must be proportionate and reasonable given the circumstances, and claimants must be prepared for later actions for damages to business or reputation if the court decides, for example, that a freezing order was wrongly granted.

Outside seeking the criminal punishment of an offender, other investigations may have a focus on disciplinary issues or restitution and damages through the civil courts. While any investigation may give due recognition to the procedural and other issues mentioned above, any case likely to involve a disciplinary hearing or involve employees of organisations must also bear in mind the several pieces of employment-related legislation (see Evans 2005) which, if the matter goes before an employment tribunal or beyond, will be given due attention to ensure the employees' requirements were not breached. These could include: the 1975 Sex Discrimination Act, the 1976 Race Relations Act, the 1995 Disability Discrimination Act, the 1996 Employment Rights Act, the 1998 Human Rights and Public Interest Disclosure Acts, the 1999 Employment Relations Act, the Employment Act 2002 (Dispute Resolution) Regulations 2004 and the regulations governing part-time and fixed-term employees.

The purpose of these various procedures and regulations is to ensure that internal corporate investigations are conducted reasonably, with appropriate procedures undertaken within an appropriate time frame, and recognition of the rights of fairness, proportionality, representation and natural justice for the person being investigated. (Such an investigation also minimises the likelihood of the company's being faced with a claim for unfair dismissal.) This leads to a transparent process which should be detailed in a company disciplinary document covering: acting in good faith, compliance with any statutory procedure (which, since 2004, covers disciplinary and dismissal procedures), informing the employee, assessments, hearings, appeal procedures within a suitable period and so on (although under certain circumstances, an employee can be dismissed for misconduct without notice and before an inquiry). Investigators should then be working to agreed and transparent procedures (see Box 10.2 for examples from Capita's Investigator Code).

Box 10.2 Capita's professional standards code

Standards of Investigation

Investigations shall be conducted in a legal, professional, thorough and ethical manner. The investigator's objective shall be to obtain evidence and validate information that is complete, reliable and relevant so as to enable a client to make a balanced decision based upon the facts alone.

Case investigations shall be subject to proper planning and preparation. This ensures the effective execution of an investigation from receipt through to completion and involves developing strategies and relevant lines of enquiry to guarantee a satisfactory conclusion in a timely manner.

Investigators shall ensure that conclusions arrived at during their enquiries shall be supported with evidence that is objective, relevant and legally acquired. In this regard, an investigator shall give due consideration to relevant law and legislation e.g. The Human Rights Act 1998; The Police & Criminal Evidence Act 1984; The Criminal Procedure and Investigation of Offences Act 1996; The Regulation of Investigatory Powers Act 2000; The Data Protection Act 1998 and the Civil Procedure Rules (the foregoing list is not exhaustive).

Investigators shall conduct all interviews in a courteous and professional manner, giving due regard to ethical interviewing guidelines and techniques. Interviews shall not be accusatory, interrogatory, coercive or oppressive in nature or manner and shall be solely aimed at a search for the truth and not a confession of guilt. At no time will inducements be offered for the disclosure of information.

Source: Capita internal document 2005

Summary

The distinction in the investigative and regulatory world, between duty to investigate and investigations that may lead to court appearances, is slowly disappearing. This is most noticeable in training where the procedural requirements and methods governing criminal investigations, from interviewing techniques to disclosure, are being used for compliance and non criminal work. Overall the focus on transparency and due process, as well as the steady influence of ECHR, is shaping not only how inquiries and investigations are conducted but the competences now being expected of any investigator. No organisation wants to lose a strong case at an employment tribunal for failure to comply with due process, nor have its methods unpicked by defence counsel, nor its approach criticised when sanctions are sought – the subject of the next chapter.

Notes

1   The structured approach to investigations may be mirrored by the skills required of a successful investigator, including: '*investigative ability*: this includes the skills associated with the assimilation and assessment of incoming information into an enquiry and the process by which lines of enquiry are generated and prioritised; *knowledge levels*: this relates to the different types of underpinning knowledge ...; and, *management skills*: these encompass a broad range of skill types that were further sub-divided between "people management", "general management" and "investigative management"' (see Smith and Flanagan 2000: v).
2   5W/H – How, Who, When, Where, What, Why. TED – Tell me, Explain to me, Describe for me. (See Schollum 2005).
3   This section does not go into the mechanics of searching which covers such issues as videoing the search, what type of vehicle might be required to take away seized material, the effect on the business, etc. There are also procedural issues, such as those raised in the 1999 case of *R v Chesterfield Justices*, ex parte *Bramley*, about the police's right to seize and take away to sift for relevant material as opposed to undertaking that function during the search.
4   The ACPO Manual of Guidance provides specific search guidance for computers (see www.acpo.police.uk/asp/policies/Data/gpg_computer_based_evidence_v3.pdf).
5   Although most investigators will emphasise that, certainly in the initial stages, investigations are fact-finding – talking to employees without recourse to PACE or to witnesses, understanding operational procedures,

company HR policies, analysing company data (e.g., data-mining invoices) and securing possible evidence. As Greenhalgh and Coles (2005) note: 'Non-law enforcement agencies have no more legal powers than any other lay person, but that does not mean that they cannot carry out detailed and complex investigations. This is a key fact to consider, and is one of the reasons why the employee manual and any disciplinary procedures outlined are so important to the investigator.'

6 There is no duty to report fraud to the police but there are various money laundering and proceeds of crime offences relating to the failure to report suspicions, or alerting clients, and to helping with or concealing benefits from criminal activity, and so on.

7 Many of which may also be accompanied by a gagging order to avoid alerting or notifying the defendant.

Chapter 11

Punishment, asset recovery and prevention

One of the benefits of, in the public sector, having an in-house capability or, in the private sector, employing professional investigators is the means to control both the investigation and also the outcomes. The DWP, for example, has its own prosecutions department and can thus escalate its range of sanctions from a warning through to a criminal conviction. Indeed, to expand on Dee Cook's point about differential treatment, it may not just be benefits and tax fraudsters who are likely to be treated differently in terms of sanctions or punishments, but the punishment may also depend on who investigates and what is the object of the investigation. This control also allows an organisation to fit such a response to the likely reaction of and impact on its clients or customers, which are likely to be varied. Further, the balance between restitution and retribution is changing, with far more financial penalties being introduced in the public sector from administrative fines to asset recovery, moving it closer to the civil side of fraud. Here the focus is usually less on the fraud process than on its target – the money – and where almost all the procedures and sanctions that are available are predicated on identifying, controlling and ultimately returning the assets, or imposing a financial sanction.

Arbitration, adjudication and punishment

The landscape of remedies against fraud is as varied as the agencies dealing with fraud (Table 11.1):

Table 11.1

Remedy/ Agency	Criminal Prosecution	Criminal Compensation	Confiscation/ Restraint	Disqualification	Civil Debt	Injunction	Insolvency	Settle	Stop Orders	Caution	Admin Fine
CPS	✓	✓	✓	✓						✓*	
SFO	✓	✓	✓	✓						✓*	
DTI/CIB/IS	✓	✓	✓	✓	✓		✓	✓	✓	✓*	
FSA	✓	✓	✓	✓	✓	✓	✓	✓	✓	✓	✓
OFT/TSO	✓	✓	✓	✓		✓		✓	✓		✓
Pensions	✓	✓	✓		✓			✓	✓		
Police			Cash							✓	
DoH/NHS	✓	✓	✓	✓	✓	✓	✓	✓			✓
DEFRA	✓	✓	✓	✓	✓		✓	✓	✓	✓	
RCPO	✓		✓	✓						✓*	
HMRC	✓		Cash	✓	✓			✓	✓		✓
DWP	✓	✓	✓	✓	✓	✓				✓	✓
ARA			✓						✓		tax

Source: Fraud Review Team (2006: 163). [*condtional cautions not yet in effect].

Administrative and Civil cases

Many administrative decisions by public bodies, once taken, are subject to long-standing and accessible appeals procedures through the tribunal system whose remit is adjudication and redress within the context of the rights of the individual. The focus is on the fairness of the original decision, such as assessment of liability, or reduction of benefit, and the appeal tribunals can provide a quick, cost-effective, independent decision-making process which is not overly legalistic. In the case of civil actions, the purpose is to compensate the injured party and not to seek retributive justice against the offender. There is no reason why the civil route should necessarily defer to the criminal route: 'A claimant has a duty to push on with proceedings once they have been issued. The fact that a criminal prosecution may also have begun does not in any way affect this obligation, although defendants can apply for a stay of the civil proceedings'. This is not always automatically granted: 'The civil court has a discretion to stay the proceedings if it appears to the court that justice demands this, having regard to the concurrent criminal proceedings arising out of the same subject matter' (Thackeray and Riem 2005: 55/106–107; 55/109).

Once underway (after being triggered by a claim form), civil cases are governed by comprehensive and often pragmatic rules (CPR or Civil Proceedings Rules), including an overriding intention to ensure, so far as is practicable, that 'the parties are on an equal footing ... and dealing with cases in ways which are proportionate to the amount of money involved, the importance of the case, the complexity of the issues, and so on' (Goldspink and Cole 2002: 479). The rules cover many of the initiatives now introduced in criminal trials – case management meetings, disclosure, witnesses, use of experts, allowing settlements to be reached, attachment of debts, confiscation, and so on. These are, however, more flexible in their application, and in trying to promote an early settlement, than the criminal courts.

Criminal court cases

Indictable-only offences, under the 1998 Crime and Disorder Act, go quickly from the magistrates' court to the Crown Court. Other offences may go to either court[1] although cases dealt with at magistrates' court may still go to the Crown Court for sentencing. Once in the Crown Court a number of procedural requirements, as part of the Criminal Case Management Programme, and including the Effective Trial Management framework and the consolidated Criminal Procedure Rules introduced in April 2005 and mandatory for all criminal cases come into play (only some are discussed here). In particular, for fraud trials that are likely to be complex and lengthy, a preparatory hearing is available. This is intended to improve the effectiveness of pre-trial preparation by resolving evidential/admissibility issues at an early stage and by facilitating the judicial management of serious and complex cases heard in the Crown Court. The procedure was established by Section 7 of the 1987 Criminal Justice Act for serious and complex frauds (see Lucraft and Forster 2005: 16/1–28). The concept was extended by the introduction of Section 29 of the 1996 Criminal Procedure and Investigations Act to encompass any complex or lengthy case which a judge considers would substantially benefit from such a hearing. The purpose of a preparatory hearing is to:

- identify issues which are likely to be material to the verdict of the jury;
- assist the jury's comprehension of such issues;
- expedite the proceedings before the jury;

- assist the jury's management of the case.

Essentially the intention is for prosecution and defence to indicate their case[2] and to agree the facts as far as possible in front of the judge who will also be the trial judge (and no doubt offer the opportunity for informal plea bargaining). Judicial continuity is intended to ensure that the person with an oversight of all aspects of the trial is in an informed position to make binding rulings in relation to technical legal points and in particular with regard to evidential issues, powers and responsibilities specified under the Rules. These also include wider judicial discretion to impose a timetable of actions which is binding on all parties, such as limiting the number of charges or splitting unlinked charges that have been joined together, or to order the prosecution and defence to prepare and serve case statements intended to highlight the key issues in the case. This is to make the trial process more focused, saving time and reducing cost. The trial should then be about the interpretation of the facts and evidence in relation to the charges made.

In March 2005 a Protocol, and three new Practice Directions were handed down by the Lord Chief Justice, Lord Woolf, on the management of complex trials. These add to the programme and the Rules (see Control and Management of heavy fraud and other complex criminal cases; www.dca.gov.uk/criminal/procrules). The intention is to reduce the length of complex trials for fraud and other crimes and introduce improved case management into criminal hearings in the Crown Court and magistrates' courts in England and Wales. This is to be achieved – through a number of pilots – by giving judges more influence over the length of trials through pre-hearings and case management hearings (at which both prosecution and defence explain to the judge the focus of the case and which would allow the judge to get to grips with the detail of the case to – in a trial within a trial – convince, if necessary, the judge that it is necessary for the trial to take longer than the preferred limit of three months). There would also be judicial control over disclosure, the use of surveillance evidence, the use of expert witnesses, the likely length of time given over to witnesses, and, through judicial authority, to vary or discontinue charges. The use of electronic presentation of evidence would also be introduced, as well as keeping the jury informed over the progress of the case – should juries be retained for such trials.

Juries

The 1986 Fraud Trials Committee (the Roskill Committee) is known for a number of successful recommendations, such as the creation of the SFO, the use of 'fraud' judges,[3] use of preparatory hearings and case statements, the use of graphics in giving evidence, and so on, which are common practice today. On the other hand, a number were dismissed, including the call for a Fraud Commission, as well as more resources for fraud and a career structure for fraud squad officers. One unimplemented recommendation, the abolition of jury trials for fraud cases, continues to be the subject of debate today – see Box 11.1.

The Roskill argument was simple: public opinion no longer believed that the legal system was 'capable of bringing the perpetrators of serious frauds expeditiously and effectively to book' (Roskill 1986: 1). Fraud was becoming more complex and the ability to get at the truth more complicated, and jurors chosen at random were likely to be ignorant in terms of the information presented to them, incapable of mastering the volume of material given to them and likely not to want their lives disrupted by lengthy trials. The answer lay in juries chosen from those qualified 'by training, knowledge, experience, integrity or by a combination of these four qualities' ('special' juries) or a judge with two experienced 'lay members' (the Fraud Trials Tribunal).

The discussion on the use of juries – begun in response to the Blue Arrow case (see above, p 76) but also fuelled by the cost and length of other big SFO cases[4] – has continued ever since. Part of the argument against jury trials is the consequence of the Ghosh decision (see p 23) which, in pushing responsibility for adjudging what is dishonest onto jurors, could lead to confusion and variations over what is 'dishonesty', and thus lead to longer trials. It relies on a 'community norm of honesty' among jurors and is 'unsuitable in specialised cases, especially those involving complex frauds where the jury have no appreciation of the propriety of conduct which is unfamiliar to them' (quoted in Omerod and Williams 2005: 1/8).

In 1998, the government returned to the matter with a consultation paper (Home Office 1998) while the 2001 Auld Review of the Criminal Courts virtually repeated the Roskill justifications about the complexity of fraud, the 'unrepresentative nature' of jurors, the ability of jurors to comprehend and understand, the length of trials and the adverse consequence on their working and private lives – none of which, apparently, was 'good for them or for justice' (Auld 2001: para 173). Auld also opted for the one judge and lay panel option.

Box 11.1   Are trials too complex?

A six-month fraud trial costing an estimated £2 million collapsed yesterday when the judge ruled that the evidence was too difficult for the jury to understand. Judge Crowther's decision to discharge the jury of seven men and five women at Newport, Gwent, came after defence barristers argued that the enormous amount of evidence had become 'oppressive and unmanageable'. MPs called for an inquiry into the collapse, which will reopen the debate on whether fraud cases are suitable for juries. Proposals have regularly been made that complex fraud should be tried by a judge alone, sitting with lay assessors.

The case, in which seven businessmen had denied charges of conspiracy to defraud, could not be tried in existing court premises in South Wales and an office block was hired for £160,000. Three weeks and £40,000 were spent fitting out the former Marconi offices as a Crown Court, with pine panelling and computer screens. Four warehouse rooms were set aside to store the mountain of papers.

On discharging the jury from giving verdicts, the judge said that he could not know whether the jury would understand enough evidence to be capable of reaching a proper verdict. Yesterday, one of the defendants, Chris O'Callaghan, an investment broker from Cardiff, claimed the case was so baffling that he had seen two jurors playing noughts and crosses.

The trial, which had another four months to run, centred on an alleged £8.5 million mortgage fraud involving a plot to buy four houses in Belgravia, west London, owned by the Duke of Westminster, as an embassy for the Malaysian Government. The defendants were said to have inflated the values of properties in the area using bogus surveys. All denied the charges.

The Lord Chancellor's Department's costs in running the trial are estimated to be some £1.2 million, with the rest of the £2 million accounted for in legal-aid fees. Judge Crowther admitted that his summing up alone, had the trial continued to its conclusion in July, would have taken 14 days. Before discharging the jury, he said he wanted to avoid an 'expensive disaster', but he said it was his 'very reluctant duty' to direct the jury to acquit the seven. He doubted jurors would comprehend or remember much of the evidence by the time they retired in July or August.

Source: *The Times*, 23 March 1995

His report proposed for serious and complex fraud under the Criminal Justice Act 1987 a number of options, including, as an alternative to trial by judge and jury, the nominated trial judge empowered to direct a trial by himself sitting with lay members or alone. While the overriding criterion for directing a trial without jury should be the interests of justice, either party would have a right of appeal against such decision to the Court of Appeal. For this to work, the report proposed that judges trying such cases should be specifically nominated and trained with the panel of experts, established and maintained by the Lord Chancellor in consultation with professional and other bodies from which lay members would be selected for trials by the judge after representations by both sides in the case. In trials where there was a judge and lay members, the judge should be the sole judge of law, procedure, admissibility of evidence and sentencing; all three should be the judges of fact and that wherever possible their decision should be unanimous, but a majority of any two could suffice for a conviction. (see Auld 2001: para 206).

The problem for the Fraud Review was not just the lightness of any sentence that might come out of an amended court system (see below, p213; the Review wanted the upper sentence limit to be raised to 14 years' imprisonment) but the restrictive nature of the criminal court process itself. It suggested widening the purpose and nature of the process to include elements of deterrence, reparation and prevention. These could range from wider sentencing options (such as compensation for victims, injunctions on convicted defendants or winding up companies) to plea bargaining, within the framework of a proposed Financial Court that would take Level 2/3 cases from a number of agencies, more streamlined procedures for serious and complex cases with specialist judges and better management of time, material and disclosure. The Review suggested that such an approach would mena the use of a single unified 'set' of evidence (that is, one facts hearing with a variety of outcomes) that would reduce inefficiencies, delays, procedural differences and inconsistent findings through parallel and serial hearings in different (criminal and civil) courts. It would also ensure that victims would be more likely to get redress, as well as unifying confiscation, compensation and civil recovery regimes.

The Fraud Review itself avoided the issue of jury trials although it noted the demands that serious and complex cases would have on their use. On the other hand, there are those that would argue that juries may only be one issue. A survey of provincial cases during the 1990s[5] noted that the length of trials was often not one of time taken to explain matters to juries but, for example, holidays, illness (including defendants and witnesses), judicial commitments, and preparation time for the judge's summing up. Other issues included the role of the CPS, how the case was presented, the behaviour of defendants, and so on.[6] Indeed, Levi noted that 'what evidence there is from unsystematic interviews in non-random cases suggests that jurors do approach their task very seriously and most do absorb a good deal of information about the case and change their attitude during the course of the trial' (1993: p188). On the other hand, Honess et al. (1998 and 2003) argued that the potential for incompetent jurors could rise during long trials unless steps were taken to manage trials, juror selection and their pre-instruction 'to establish key terms and ideas.'

Nevertheless, the 2003 Criminal Justice Act introduced the option for the prosecution to request a trial by judge only where the complexity of the trial or the length of the trial (or both) are likely to make the trial 'so burdensome to the members of a jury hearing the trial that the interests of justice require that serious consideration should be given to the question of whether the trial should be conducted without a jury' but only where the judge has seen if there are other ways to address the complexity or length to allow a jury trial to take place (see Ormerod and Williams 2005: 1/26–1/29).

Non-criminal sanctions

Given that civil cases invariably are about assets or money, the civil route has well-developed procedures to enforce judgments. These include:

- Third party debt order – previously known as 'Garnishee Orders', a third party debt order can be used where the judgment debtor is owed money by a third party within the jurisdiction. An application must be made to the court and if successful, the third party owing money to the judgment debtor will be required to pay the debt instead to the judgment creditor. This method is most commonly used against the judgment debtor bank, and can also be used against business owing money to the debtor.

- Attachment to earnings – this order attaches to the judgment debtor's salary and obliges the employer to pay a portion of the debtor's earnings into court.

- Post judgment freezing orders – can be obtained to freeze any of the judgment debtor's assets, most commonly bank accounts, and means that the judgment debtor can no longer move nor carry out any dealings with that asset. An order can be obtained only if there is a real possibility that the judgment debtor may move his assets out of the jurisdiction or dispose of them to prevent the judgment being enforced.

- Charging orders – the party holding judgment may obtain a charging order to secure the debt over any interests in land that the judgment debtor holds. This will rank as an equitable mortgage, but does not directly provide a means of payment. Instead the charge will remain over the property until the debt is paid by the judgment debtor selling the property and paying the debt out of the proceeds, or by paying the money by other means. The party holding judgment may in certain circumstances apply to the court for the charge to be enforced and the property sold.

- Writ of fieri facias (fi fa) in the High Court or warrant of execution in the County Court – the judgment creditor may obtain a writ or warrant from the court which allows him to seize goods belonging to the judgment debtor to sell off to recover the debt owed under the judgment. These are often sought in the High Court because the Court's enforcement office is thought generally 'more effective than a County Court bailiff, as the former is paid by results and will make early and late visits to the judgment debtors property on any day of the week. The County Court bailiff is a salaried public sector employee who is required to tell the judgment debtor in advance of his intention to execute the warrant and can only attend the judgment debtor's property during usual Court hours on weekdays only' (Thackeray and Riem 2005: 55/124–125).

- Bankruptcy or winding-up proceedings – these can be used as a threat to force the judgment debtor to satisfy the judgment. They should be used tactically and with caution, as the party holding the judgment will rank as an unsecured creditor if the judgment is put into bankruptcy/wound up and may not recover the debt in full.

The court can also appoint a receiver to preserve assets pending a trial or the execution of judgment (Goldspink and Cole 2002: 474).

The use of financial penalties as both sanction and deterrent is also growing outside the civil arena. The Inland Revenue have long used the Hansard process to negotiate a financial settlement on outstanding tax, as well as fining those who are late submitting returns, while both the NHS and the DWP operate penalties for administrative breaches. The 1999 Health Act inserted additional sections into the 1997 National Health Service Act to provide the power to introduce the penalty charge by means of regulations. The NHS Penalty Charge Regulations 1999 came into force on 1 November 1999 to allow for penalties to be imposed in respect of unpaid health costs. The penalty charge is a civil fine and may be imposed where a patient fails to pay any amount recoverable from him in respect of any goods or services specified under the Act at a rate of 'five times the recoverable amount, up to a maximum of £100' plus the original charge. This applies to each occasion of dispensing prescriptions, each course of dental treatment, or for each sight test or optical voucher issued where the patient has falsely claimed free treatment. In cases of non-payment the amendments provide for a surcharge of up to £50 to be imposed. In addition, the Act introduced a new specific criminal offence for trial in the magistrates' court. The criminal offence is designed to complement the penalty charge by providing a sanction for alleged cases of repeated or persistent evasion. This offence attracts a fine, on conviction, of up to £2,500.

The sanctions regime adopted by the Department for Work and Pensions (DWP) consists of three main elements: prosecution (usually for serious or persistent offenders) with, on first conviction, a letter warning that any subsequent conviction for fraud within a three-year period will result in their benefit being reduced or withdrawn for up to 13 weeks as part of the 'two strikes' regime; administrative penalties for less serious cases where there are grounds for instituting criminal proceedings but where the suspect may be offered the penalty as an alternative to criminal proceedings being taken against them; a caution where the offence is admitted and where the value of the overpayment is less than £400 (although local authorities can set their own sanction levels). Under the Social Security Act 2001, effective from 2002, where a person is convicted of one or more benefit offences in two separate sets of proceedings within a period of three years they may be disqualified from receiving benefit. This is known as the 'two strikes' provision. Certain benefits can be withdrawn, or reduced by 20 or 40 per cent for up to 13 weeks. Nearly all social security benefits can be withdrawn or reduced.

A growing number of other agencies also have the power to seek criminal or civil sanctions (usually penalties) or to impose civil sanctions. Under Part 6 of the Enterprise Act 2002, which came fully into force on 20 June 2003, the OFT is responsible for investigating a criminal offence punishable by up to five years' imprisonment and/or an unlimited fine for individuals who dishonestly engage in cartel agreements. The Act provided the OFT with certain powers of investigation. The new powers for the cartel offence operate alongside the existing regime that imposes civil sanctions on businesses that breach the Competition Act 1998 prohibition on anti-competitive agreements. Exercising the two powers alongside each other means that the OFT has to operate clear initial procedures because 'it will not always be immediately clear which set of these sets of powers is more appropriate to the investigation' and 'it may be necessary to simultaneously investigate undertakings under the civil powers and individuals under the criminal investigatory powers' but working to ensure that the curtailment of the one does not jeopardise the other (see Wells 2005: 51/7–8).

The FSA has a range of options. It can: issue formal warnings; withdraw a firm's authorisation; discipline authorised firms and people approved by the FSA to work in those firms; impose penalties for market abuse; apply to the court for injunction and restitution orders; issue restraint and freezing orders; wind up companies; and prosecute various offences. The statutory objective of reducing financial crime, however, 'does not require the FSA to adopt any particular means to attain it' (see Gentle and Hodges 2005: 11/3). The FSA can administer a formal caution where there is a realistic possibility of a prosecution but the offender admits to the allegation. A record of the caution will be kept in confidence by the FSA who may use its existence in any future decision whether or not to prosecute the offender if he offends again. If the offender is a firm or an approved person, a caution given by the FSA will form part of the firm's or approved person's regulatory record. The FSA may also operate dual sanctions; in the case of insider trading 'it was felt that the broad definition of market abuse, the lower evidential threshold and the fact that no jury would be required would lead to an increased number of successful outcomes and would send a clear message to those who are active in the market that the FSA would take market misbehaviour very seriously. The criminal penalties of imprisonment (if the conduct is prosecuted as insider dealing) and financial orders are complemented by the power of the FSA to ban wrongdoers from the market, thus removing a person's livelihood, make restitution orders against them and fine them – all draconian powers very much akin to criminal sanctions' (see Gentle and Hodges 2005: 11/4).

Criminal sanctions

In criminal cases, on conviction, the courts may order criminal compensation orders for specific losses to victims, or confiscation orders (see the approach being delivered by the Asset Recovery Agency, see below, p 215), to which restraint orders are linked to avoid dissipation of assets. Once the trial is over, the sentences for fraud often seem light, although the Sentencing Guidelines Council set up by the 2003 Criminal Justice Act does indicate that the seriousness of the offence, the level of 'profit' achieved by the offence, the number of victims and the abuse of trust are all factors that should be taken into account, guidance on which has been given by Appeal Court judges in a number of cases and which will be generally followed in subsequent cases[7] – see Box 11.2

The case of *R v. Barrick* (who in 1981 appealed against a conviction for stealing some £9,000 over nearly two years as a manager of a Cheshire loan company) allowed the judge, Lord Lane, to issue some sentencing guidelines after the court dismissed the case with the warning that 'professional men should expect to be punished as the others; in some cases more severely.' He noted that neither previous good character, the loss of a livelihood nor the unlikelihood of re-offending should preclude a prison sentence. While the amount involved should have a bearing, so should the degree of breach of

Box 11.2   Using the guidelines (or not)

> Solicitor Michael Fielding was able to clear massive debts, fund a palatial London home and buy a luxury hideaway in Florida, stealing more than £5.8 million from client accounts. When one of his victims finally realised what he had been doing and wrote to his firm in 2001, Fielding intercepted the letter and left it, with a letter of farewell, on his boss's chair. In it, he confessed to his three-year crime spree and spoke of his deep sorrow and shame for his betrayal of trust. He fled to America with his wife and spent years spending the money. Police tracked him down and in June he returned to Britain of his own accord. In November 2005 he was jailed for eight years. He sat with his head bowed as Judge Geoffrey Rivlin, QC, told him: 'Put simply, of its type, this case could hardly be more serious … it is off the financial scale of guideline cases.'

Source: *The Times*, 4 November 2005

trust, the status of the offender, the length of the fraud, how the stolen money was spent, the impact on the public, and work colleagues, mitigation on medical grounds, and any cooperation with the police. The length of the sentence would be affected by the amounts lost: up to 18 months for less than £10,000; up to three years for amounts up to £50,000. Over that amount an approximate ceiling would be up to four and a half years. Pleading guilty would result in a lesser tariff.

In a subsequent 1998 case, *R v. Clark*, the Barrick case guidelines were amended to take account of changes to sentencing practice and the length of the maximum sentence for theft, as well as inflation. Clark was the bursar at the Royal Academy as well as treasurer at his Hertfordshire church. Using the chequebooks of both, the former's credit card and cash from church fund raising events, he stole £400,000 from the former and £29,000 from the latter; he received two concurrent sentences of five years. He claimed that the money was to pay mortgage arrears; it also went on home improvements, buying horses and school fees. The court reduced the sentence but did not allow the appeal and took the opportunity to revise the Barrick amounts upwards: stealing up to £17,500 could earn a sentence up to 21 months; up to £100,000 could earn up to three years' imprisonment with a further year for amounts up to £250,000. Up to £1 million would merit between five and nine years, with cases involving more than £1 million attracting a sentence of 10 years or more (see Fletcher 2005: 32/9).

In a 1992 mortgage fraud case – *R v. Stevens* – the Court of Appeal stated that factors taken into account were 'the degree of sophistication of the fraud, the use of false names, properties and values, and the obtaining of loans for commercial purposes under the guise of domestic mortgages', the recruiting of others, the involvement of a professional or semi-professional person, the length of the fraud, the benefits to the defendant, any genuine intention to repay the loans, the amounts loaned and any losses sustained. The factors outlined in Barrick remained in place (see Fletcher 2005: 32/9). In a later 1999 case – *R v. Whitehouse and Morrison* – the Court of Appeal stated that *Clark* provided guidelines only; a sentence outside the guidelines was justified by the aggravating feature that the principal defendant had stolen from his employers out of revenge (Archbold 2003 Digital Edition). A 2001 case – *R v. Roach* – made similar comments where there had been a breach of trust of an elderly and vulnerable victim. Finally, in *R v. Stewart* (1987), guidance was given by the court in relation to both the average offender and the 'professional fraudsmen' when the court, on the basis of nine appeals, felt that the latter would be dealt with severely for making a 'profitable business' from their crimes. To the Barrick considerations the court added that the way in which the fraud started and any repayments should also be taken into account. On the other hand, the court also raised the question of whether imprisonment was the answer for certain frauds when community service, a suspended sentence or a compensation order might be 'of value' (see Sentencing Guidelines Council, 2005, and Council website; also Westlaw accessed 20.06.06).

The Asset Recovery Agency: a new approach?

If recompense and restitution lie at the heart of the civil side of fraud then restitution is an increasingly significant aspect of the criminal side. Taking away the benefits of crime from convicted defendants is not new; the 1889 Prevention of Corruption Act stated that, on first conviction, the court could fine or imprison, bar from public office for seven years *and* order the defendant to pay 'the amount or value of any gift, loan, fee, or reward received by him or any part thereof.' Not surprisingly such sanctions have rarely, if ever, been used (or even known about) although both confiscation or forfeiture – the seizure of proceeds of a crime, or equipment used in the commission of a crime – have long been recognised in the law and by the courts. Of the two, forfeiture could be more effective since it transferred ownership of all the stolen assets away from the defendant while a confiscation order was a fine, with the criminal able to negotiate the way they paid the order and how he or she put together the funds to meet the requirements of the order.

When investigators failed to get their hands on the £750,000 accumulated by the defendants in the Operation Julie drugs case because the House of Lords decided that the existing legislation – the 1971 Misuse of Drugs Act – was about forfeiture and not 'a means of stripping drug dealers of the total profits of their unlawful enterprises', the confiscation regime was reviewed. Thus confiscation got a boost in terms of new legislation following a 1984 report (the Hodgson Report 1984). The 1986 Drug Trafficking Offences Act allowed for confiscation of the proceeds from drug trafficking on conviction (where the assets or benefits were proved to be proceeds from the offences which led to conviction, on a criminal – beyond all reasonable doubt – burden of proof). Confiscation in relation to non-drugs crime was incorporated into the 1988 Criminal Justice Act. Both pieces of legislation were subsequently amended to include aspects of legislation first introduced on the reporting of money laundering in 1993.

By the late 1990s, inconsistencies between the laws were compounded by poor implementation. The courts were reluctant to give time for requests for, or even to grant, confiscation orders. There were perceived delays within the Crown Prosecution Service's Central Confiscation Branch, which was responsible for orders – including processing the affidavits for restraint (or freezing) of assets – across England and Wales. Magistrates' courts were ineffectual at enforcing orders (confiscations were handled like any other court-imposed fine) and the police were little interested in providing the resources necessary to carry out orders. During the 1990s, the number and value of orders dropped and less than half the money due was actually collected.

The UK then looked to the example of Ireland's Criminal Assets Bureau (CAB). A Home Office working party on confiscation in 1998, following similar working parties in 1991 and 1992, recommended a similar agency in the UK. In 2000 the detail was addressed by a Cabinet Office Performance and Innovation Unit report (2000) which saw in confiscation and asset recovery a number of complementary benefits, from tackling local crime to motivating police and disrupting crime networks. The core assumption behind the proposals, however, was that, if criminals were 'taxed' enough so that trying to live from crime became uneconomic, then they might begin to give up crime. The report initiated the 2002 Proceeds of Crime Act (POCA) and the establishment of the Assets Recovery Agency (ARA). The Act focused on three areas:

1 investigating the activity of 'laundering' of assets, with a view to prosecution;
2 investigating benefit from crime, with a view to tracing the benefit and recovery;
3 statutory training in financial investigations under the Act, to accredit personnel to work under POCA.

ARA is *not* responsible for 1. because it does not have prosecution powers, although it can use its powers under 2. to work with any other agency that has prosecution powers. When it carries out its functions under 2. it is looking for assets, not evidence of criminal conduct under 1. or 2. Indeed, if it finds evidence of 1. while undertaking actions in relation to 2. then it will pass that evidence to another agency. Under 2. ARA has three levels of responsibility for cases that occur following the introduction of the legislation:

- Confiscation: following a conviction and an order proposed by CPS to the courts, confiscation will be enforced by ARA whose powers include restraint, customer information orders, account monitoring, and the power of discovery (requiring individuals or organisations to attend for interviews or produce documents);

- Civil recovery: this power resides with ARA because it does not require a court case. Rather it uses the same powers to go to court to request an Interim Receiver be appointed to quantify and value assets. The report would go back to court for freezing and/or recovery;

- Taxation: where the Director has reasonable grounds to suspect that there is income, gains or profits that is chargeable to the relevant tax and which results from criminal conduct, the Director then carries out the tax functions that the HMRC would ordinarily carry out. This is not just limited to the proceeds of unlawful conduct but all the defendant's property. The only difference between the Director and the HMRC is that when the Director is carrying out her taxation functions the source of income does not need to be identified.

ARA is based in London (covering England and Wales) and Northern Ireland; Scotland has its own law and agency which reflects the work and powers of ARA but does not cover taxation. ARA has some 140 staff covering: law, training, performance, policy, civil recovery and taxation (the last two have some 25 staff). It hosts the Enforcement Taskforce, a group of law enforcement and revenue agencies set up to collect assets agreed by the courts for forfeiture or confiscation on pre-POCA cases. Its work is shaped by the Act into a 'hierarchy of action' through which all cases referred to it are considered as follows, by its Case Referrals Group:

- Is the case prosecutable? If so, then the case should go to a law enforcement agency while ARA focuses on confiscation (freezing can be requested at the start of any investigation, in anticipation of a conviction and a consequential confiscation order). ARA can be involved in the evidence-gathering process if it relates to benefits or assets. If the agency has obtained a conviction, it may also then contact ARA in relation to confiscation.

- Is the case likely to lead to a conviction? If prosecution is unlikely to succeed, or fails on a procedural technicality, or is turned down by CPS on grounds of insufficient evidence, then ARA may institute its own civil recovery action, using its own staff.

- Is civil recovery possible? If civil recovery is not possible (and this is based on the link between the asset and criminality, on balance of probabilities), then ARA may institute taxation of assets where the income paying for the asset does not have to be shown.

There are a number of issues in relation to POCA and the work of ARA that are worth noting. First, the money laundering aspect of the Act is not an ARA responsibility. The legislation is intended to police the traffic and transfer of illicit funds by requiring all institutions to whom this part of the Act applies (although there are obvious links between the movement of money and its location for confiscation or recovery) to report the movements to NCIS for analysis and dissemination to law enforcement agencies.

Second, there are a number of powers that allow ARA to introduce previous and current conduct as an aspect of the recovery regime. In relation to confiscation, evidence may be introduced as to criminal lifestyle. After conviction the confiscation statement presented to court will assess what may be confiscated and, in so doing, may make certain assumptions about lifestyle. The lifestyle is determined by the number and type of previous convictions, the number and type of which creates an assumption of a lifestyle that is funded by crime which in turn allows investigators to go back six years into the offender's life. If approved, the statement may lead to the confiscation of all assets in the possession of the defendant (whether or not it came from the specific activities that led to the convictions). Further, under civil recovery, ARA can bring civil proceedings over assets obtained through 'unlawful conduct.' This is conduct that is unlawful under UK criminal law – where the conduct may not have resulted in a conviction but can be demonstrated as relating to illegal conduct (such as living off drugs).

Third, the role of ARA is central to accreditation of investigators wishing to use Part 8 investigative powers under the Act relating to seizure, production orders, etc. There is a Concerted Inter-Agency Crime Financial Action Group (CICFA) which comprises law enforcement agencies – SOCA, HMRC, the CPS and other agencies – to set an asset recovery strategy[8] to ensure a consistent approach and monitoring of the accreditation process. Training also encompasses a range of agencies – DWP, OPRA, DEFRA, CFSMS, etc. – to give them powers to recover assets if the police or other agencies do not, or cannot, do so themselves.

Overall the regime provides wide powers – to order account monitoring to watch patterns of activity or to require financial institutions to search for assets, for example – and double offences (the proceeds of crime and money laundering offences may relate to the same asset). It now makes confiscation mandatory on conviction and does not allow an offender to avoid payment by serving the additional period of imprisonment in lieu of payment. Through both criminal lifestyle and tainted gift sections of the Act it can dispossess a criminal of assets irrespective of family circumstances – and by using the reverse burden of proof to civil standards. The Act, as one police officer put it, is not intended to be fair. To date ARA has dealt with 47 confiscation cases, with £5 million restrained and six confiscation orders worth £2 million issued. It has taken on 97 civil recovery cases with a property value of over £57 million; over £17 millions' worth of assets have been frozen in 32 cases and £7 million taken in. Eleven taxation cases are underway and eight assessments issued to the value of £1.4 million.

The role of ARA has been paralleled by the rise of regional asset recovery teams (RART), which are cooperative ventures between police and other agencies to recover assets but organisationally have nothing to do with the establishment of ARA (and are not, as sometimes assumed, the regional manifestation of ARA) although the officers will have been trained by ARA to use POCA powers. The idea for RARTs came from a joint Customs National Investigative Service and ACPO Economic Crime Committee initiative after a limited experiment in the West Midlands where four forces collaborated on financial investigation work within a drugs team. The initiative was a bid to HM Treasury for £46 million to run similar collaborations in all nine ACPO regions. However, there was funding for only four. Launched in 2003 with initial funding for three years, the RARTs were intended to assist, not supplant, local police, customs and other agencies to target the financial assets of criminals. RARTs and ARA do work together but RART funding has come from a Home Office Incentification Fund to ACPO for a three-year trial, focusing on Level 2 (cross-police borders) criminality.[9] The fund will ensure that, until 2006, the police retain 50 per cent of recovered assets. This explains why police forces are supporting RARTs as well as rapidly establishing internal asset recovery units and boosting Financial Intelligence units (FI), usually at the expense of fraud squads.

Aggregate RART targets are based on confiscation orders, confiscated funds, the number of investigations and cash seizures. Between 2004–2007, this will involve 375 confiscation orders valued at £150 million.

By mid-2005 39 orders had been obtained to a value of over £1 million but there were another 395 cases in process and a further 100 accepted for investigation; £90 million of realisable assets were awaiting hearings and restraint orders had been issued for nearly £50 million. In the same period there had also been 87 seizures to a value of nearly £5 million. The bulk of cases were Level 2 or above. Most cases come from the police (over 60 per cent) and Customs (over 20 per cent).

Prevention and personal responsibility – a forgotten dimension

The squeeze on law enforcement resources and the cost-ineffectiveness of using the criminal route to deal with high-volume, low-cost fraud has persuaded various organisations to promote prevention as the first line against fraud. Certainly, there is a wealth of guidance on internal prevention, primarily grouped around:

- identifying and assessing the fraud risk and vulnerability for a strategic approach;

- promoting public awareness;

- implementing and monitoring compliance with appropriate corporate governance arrangements;

- articulating and promoting appropriate values and standards across the organisation;

- developing, promulgating and monitoring compliance with codes of conduct that advise officials of expected standards of behaviour;

- developing, promulgating and monitoring compliance with standing orders or financial regulations, including the handling of contracts;

- monitoring and measuring anti-fraud and corruption strategies;

- developing and implementing arrangements for reporting, receiving and investigating allegations of breaches of conduct, fraud and corruption;

- using IT, intelligence and joint working;

- applying appropriate sanctions (Public Audit Forum 2001 p 16; see also NAO/HMT 2004).

Within that general framework are a range of control measures (a number of which have been noted above), such as: vetting appointments (and interviews on why people leave), the verification of qualifications, checking information provided in application forms against databases, from claiming housing benefit to mortgage applications, risk-assessed procedures for defining officeholder responsibilities, activity and rotation, sharing information, IT security and monitoring software, due diligence work on contractors and companies, and so on. There are a number of sampling and testing measures: data-matching and data-mining, floating floor analysis, gap point analysis, ratio analysis, benchmarking, profiling, and so on. In addition, there are a number of initiatives to encourage staff awareness, such as codes of conduct, and staff reporting (whistle-blowing or professional standards approaches). In the UK the 1998 Public Interest Disclosure Act (PIDA) is the whistle-blowing Act which is linked to employment rights legislation (cases involving sacked whistle-blowers are heard by employment tribunals and allow for unlimited compensation). The Act is intended to protect any employee, contractor trainee or agency staff who has reasonable grounds to want to report a possible crime, breach of legal obligation, a miscarriage of justice, a health and safety breach (or a cover-up relating to any of these) without fear of victimisation or dismissal. This is known as a 'protected disclosure' to the employer or outside agency, some of which are prescribed as such by law.

To those seeking to develop prevention strategies – from good conduct to reporting the misconduct of others – brings up the question of what makes people honest, reflecting a theme raised by the US National Institute of Law Enforcement and Criminal Justice nearly a quarter of a century ago in relation to corruption:

> Corruption has three main components that are controllable and one that is not. The three controllable ones are opportunity, incentive, and risk; the uncontrollable one is personal honesty. Many public servants over a long period of time have had the freely available opportunity to be corrupt, a large incentive to do so, and little risk of being found if they did, but have refused because 'it wouldn't be honest'. (quoted in Zimmerman 1980)

A comprehensive control environment often abrogates individual responsibility or ignores the contextual, social or cultural framework that may shape such an attitude, with potential offenders claiming that the interpretation of breaches of the rules, or perceptions of misconduct must be determined externally — that is, all conduct is acceptable unless specifically forbidden. In the (as they argue, futile) search for absolute integrity in relation to the US public sector through a compliance environment, Jim Jacobs and Frank Anechiarico warn:

> … we must look beyond the traditional strategies of monitoring, control and punishment … Laws, rules, and threats will never result in a public administration to be proud of; to the contrary, the danger is that such an approach will create a self-fulfilling prophecy: having been placed continuously under suspicion, treated like quasi-criminals or probationers, public employees will behave accordingly. (Anechiarico and Jacobs 1996: 207)

When the Committee on Standards in Public Life first reported, it argued: 'We recommend procedures and institutions that will deter and detect wrongdoing. We seek to restore respect for the ethical values inherent in the idea of public service. Formal procedures have a role to play, but in the end it is individuals' consciences that matter' (Committee on Standards in Public Life 1995: 16). When it returned to the question of public ethics a decade later it sought to focus on the governance arrangements of public bodies in an 'effective and proportionate manner' and improving 'the governance of propriety' through a number of more general requirements. These include: board responsibilities, financial reporting and internal controls and standards, expectations of board members, how bodies are and should be held accountable (including openness, communications, audit and complaints procedures). This would require addressing: general governance issues (board planning and strategy; the board as an employer), financial stewardship (reporting, performance measurement, risk assessments, and audit) and personal conduct (principles of conduct, addressing conflict of interest through the disclosure and registration of such interests, hospitality, dealing with suppliers and whistle-blowing).

The Fraud Review reiterates many of the components of a control environment and uses terms such as 'fraud proofed' and 'zero tolerance'. It suggests the Strategic Authority's role might be through publicity, disseminating good practice prevention and providing links in relation to cross-border fraud. It does raise the interesting issue of whether there should be an assessment of 'an acceptable level of the risk of fraud' based on potential losses and the cost of prevention and detection (2006: 124) but it does not dicsuss people or organisational cultures.

Summary

Clearly, prevention would be a cost-effective approach to dealing with fraud. Investigation and prosecution remain costly and the responsibility of a range of agencies with different agendas and objectives. At one end, the problem of lengthy fraud trials continues to confuse the issue over criminal investigations and prosecutions, even though the problems lie more with the CPS and procedural matters than the capacity of jurors to understand fraud cases. Nevertheless, the question of whether it is worth bothering to prosecute City offenders in return for a few months' imprisonment keeps raising the cost-benefit concerns over retributive justice. Some might argue that restitutive justice – financial penalties – is more effective for and reflective of acquisitive crime. On the other hand, those who can pay, can negotiate a settlement agreeable to both parties and certainly more agreeable than imprisonment. Similarly, if most cases of fraud are prosecuted under the Theft Acts, then it could be argued that neither the method – a white-collar crime – nor the class of the offender – the white-collar criminal – should influence any decision to prosecute or punish. At the other end, leaving aside the question of whether or not the impact of retributive justice is working in deterring fraud, there is the question of whether any emphasis on prevention is making some (potentially erroneous) assumptions about the 'it wouldn't be honest' approach in an increasingly secular society and an enterprise culture where many corporate and individual aspirations become intertwined. The introduction of the Fraud Bill, and thus a specific set of offences that will identify a specific offending group, will also raise questions about sanctions and sentencing policies, and whether this group will still be subject to the current sentencing guidelines. Such issues suggest that the future – or futures – for fraud are, as yet, open for review and reform.

Notes

1 The 1987 Criminal Justice Act allowed for the transfer of serious and complex fraud cases to the Crown Court but did not define 'fraud', 'serious' or 'complex.' The guidelines suggested that transfer on grounds of seriousness should only be considered where the sum at risk is £500,000 or above, save in exceptional circumstances (including where the offence is particularly aggravated or the victim vulnerable) and which endanger the economic well-being of the UK. Complexity included: a large number of defendants and/or charges; the involvement of a large number of

bodies such as banks, building societies or companies; the involvement of financial institutions, such as the Stock Exchange; a fraud involving the use of computers; a large volume of accountancy evidence, asset tracing etc.; a significant international dimension; the need for specialised knowledge (for example of City practices or complex tax provisions) to form an understanding of the case; and where 'it is appropriate that the management of the case should without delay be taken over by the Crown Court.' (www.cps.gov.uk/crowncourtpreparation).

2   Like the prosecution, the defence is also to make disclosure – a statement setting out the defence case and where it challenges the prosecution case, in general terms. Under the 2003 Criminal Justice Act, this is required to be more detailed and to indicate any particular defence on which the defendant intends to rely (see Walbank 2005: 23–26; Trollope *et al.* 2005a, for the defence approach to disclosure).

3   Of which there are a number; they are required to attend judicial training which include fraud issues. The 2001 Auld Report proposed that such training should include, where necessary, familiarisation with information technology, including computer transcription of proceedings, basic accounting and company documents, financial systems of markets prone to fraud, financial practices commonly encountered in serious fraud cases, forensic handling of such cases and the preparation and form of summings-up or judgments in them. There is 'a correspondingly urgent need for the establishment of formal criteria for nomination to and retention on the panel of judges doing such work. There may also be a case for providing serious fraud judges with additional facilities, according to their workload generally or on a case by case basis, for example, specialised information technology and suitably qualified judicial assistants' (Auld, 2001: para 205).

4   For example – Guinness: 188 days and prosecution costs of £2.4 million; Barlow Clowes: 224 days, prosecution costs of £2 million; Maxwell: 234 days, prosecution costs of £11 million; BCCI: 398 days and prosecution costs of £7.1 million; Butte Mining: 347 days and prosecution costs of £2.3 million. The 2005 review of legal aid claimed that over 50 per cent of Crown Court legal aid expenditure is consumed by 1 per cent of cases (high-cost cases); fraud, in legal aid terms, cost about £95 million per year, accounting for 21 per cent of the volume, and 32 per cent of the legal aid cost of all high-cost cases (Department of Constitutional Affairs 2005).

5   For an MA in Fraud Management at Liverpool Business School.

6   The 2005 collapse of the Jubilee Line corruption trial at a cost of £60 million after 21 months in court has again raised the question of jury trials. For only 17 per cent of the time had the jury actually been able to hear any evidence. Apart from trying to retain the jury for such a long period – three became fathers during the period – the case was delayed by poor prosecution practice and thus was less about juries than case management. In September 2005 one co-defendant received a suspended

sentence for conspiracy to defraud after he had pleaded guilty (see also HMCPSI 2006).

7 Sentencing by type of fraud does vary by agency (see Fletcher 2005: 3/21–42) but most mainstream offences generally follow guidance. HMCE offences have similar criteria for duty fraud. The principal sentencing factors relate to the level of duty evaded, the nature of the organisation involved, level of profit, and the defendant's role. Aggravating and mitigating factors include repeated importations, use of violence, use of a legitimate business front, cooperation, pleading guilty, and so on. Sentences can range from £1,000 duty evaded with low profit (a moderate fine) to £1 million and above evaded (five years or more) – see Finnerty 2005: 8/29–30. For corporate offences, the amounts, length of time, persistence, abuse of trust, effect on public confidence and the integrity of public life, loss to small investors, and personal benefit to the defendant are taken into account (see Fletcher, 2005: 32/22 and Sentencing Guidelines Council 2005).

8 Not to be confused with the government's anti-money laundering strategy to which most of the same agencies belong but which is led by HM Treasury, the Home Office and the Foreign and Commonwealth Office (see HM Treasury, 2004).

9 The scheme 'will give police forces a direct financial incentive to recover even more criminally acquired wealth, by giving them a stake in the assets they recover. From 2006/07 a new incentive scheme will be introduced under which all agencies involved in asset recovery will, wherever possible, get back 50 per cent of the receipts they recover' (HM Treasury 2004: 20).

Chapter 12

Conclusion – the futures for fraud?

In July 2006, the Final Report of the Fraud Review Team was published on its efforts to answer three questions: what is the scale of the problem; what is the appropriate role of Government in dealing with fraud and how could resources be spent to maximise value for money across the system? Acknowledging that it could answer the first of these, it did report its concerns that: the information on fraud is poor; that there is no national policy on fraud; that police resources had dwindled, that fraud investigative capacity is spread across organizations, often in ways that are uncoordinated, not cost-effective and do not use the full range of methods or sanctions; and that, as the interim review noted, 'whether a fraud gets investigated can depend on whether the victim can organise and finance the investigation themselves rather than on the harm of the fraud to the economy and society'. The Report made a number of recommendations, some of which are noted in this book, which would be determined within a national strategy that would take a 'holistic' approach, focusing efforts and resources where they are likely to be most effective rather than most attention grabbing, and focussing on the causes of fraud as well as dealing with the effects. The strategy will not replace existing strategies but rather to help coordinate ongoing efforts. Such an approach is likely to emphasise upstream action to prevent and deter fraud, such as educating consumers and businesses on how to avoid becoming victims. Despite these efforts fraud will still happen and the strategy will have to set priorities for downstream investigations and effective ways of punishing fraudsters and obtaining justice for victims. (Fraud Review 2006: 6) Overseeing this would be a National Fraud Strategy Authority. This would be responsible for:

the strategy; the measurement of fraud; helping integrate anti-fraud work and determine priority areas; assessing performance against the strategy; promoting awareness and training; disseminating good practice; acting as an information resource. A Multi-Agency Coordination Group would act as a forum within the Authority for the discussion of operational issues and action plans relating to the priority areas.

In many ways, the Review is going over old ground and half-forgotten initiatives (such as the 'accreditation' of civilian investigators[1]), as well as trying to resolve the wider consequences of what has been nearly two decades if countervailing political, organizational and procedural changes in which, as one Cabinet minister allegedly put it, if the risk of fraud is the price to pay for getting the Government's policies delivered then it is worth paying. Now that that risk is perceived to be getting out of hand, and is funding other, more pressing Government concerns, then action is called for. In so doing, however, it – and the Review – will need to consider a number of themes and trends that have developed as a consequence of those changes.

The current fraud landscape and the need for a strategy?

In the past 25 years, there has grown up a multiplicity of agencies and variations in their powers and approaches to dealing with fraud. In practitioner terms this raises some interesting issues. First, there is continuing 'agency creep' – the establishment of new agencies, sometimes with single functions, and sometimes multi-functional, to address new issues (or variants on a theme) or introducing new powers to deal with existing problems. Thus in their survey of UK agencies dealing with corruption and ethics, Alan Lawton and Michael Macaulay (2004) noted that: 'the regulatory landscape is confusing, being described to us as, variously: "a patchwork quilt of regulatory bodies"; "a multi-piece jigsaw with more pieces by the minute"; "a game of chess with pieces being moved around the board"'.

For many of the organisations fraud is a cost associated with core business; how fraud is addressed, however, often depends on how the business is structured and the delivery of that business. The NAO reported of the DWP that:

The Department is having to manage the effects of major organisational change, arising from the introduction of Jobcentre

Plus and The Pension Service, with new regional structures and new processes for interacting with customers. The complexity of benefit regulations and inadequate computer systems will also continue to be important constraints on the Department's capacity to reduce fraud and error. The Department are working to update their information systems and information technology strategy. They aim to draw on previous experience of implementing major information technology projects and wider experience of other organisations. But successful implementation will depend on the Department overcoming the difficulties inherent in implementing computer systems on such a large scale. (NAO 2003a: 3)

The rate of institutional reorganisation continues, disrupting agencies' attempts to embed core functions, align resources and approaches to maximise anti-fraud work, and retain an institutional memory and individual expertise. Indeed, in the context of decentralised and semi-autonomous organisations, this issue may be as much an internal as an inter-agency issue. Thus the NAO report on the Inland Revenue noted that the Special Compliance Office was having problems receiving referrals from within the organisation and, as a consequence, 'identified working relations between itself and local tax office teams as a key area for improvement. The steps taken to address this issue include regular liaison meetings with local teams, joint working of enquiry cases, mentoring exercises and involvement in training events for local tax offices' (NAO 2003a: 33).

Nevertheless, the fact that there is a multiplicity of agencies dealing with fraud does not necessarily mean that there is overlap and duplication as they have different objectives and timescales for investigations and the pursuit of sanctions. Many also have more than enough fraud in or against their own organisations to deal with. Their response to fraud is also very much focused on the wider objectives of their organisation. While this may lead to differential treatment, impact, sanctions or effectiveness, it does not mean that more reorganisation or mergers or an overall strategy is necessarily the only or most effective way forward. As Levi argues in his review of the concept of the 'Fraud Commission' proposed by Roskill to monitor the overall performance of the criminal justice system against fraud, the objectives of different bodies were so diverse and their accountability mechanisms were so fragmented that it was difficult to see how overall supervision could occur (Levi, 2003).

Who is responsible for the rise in fraud?

It is argued that not only do fraudsters go looking for, or take advantage of, opportunities on offer, particularly patrolling the cracks between common sense, effective compliance, organisational change, and individual, corporate and political ambition, but now so do other types of criminals. Further, such individuals and organisations wishing to commit fraud look for the opportunity and incentive that 'ordinary' citizens may also identify and exploit. Thus organised criminals, terrorist cells and students may indulge in credit card fraud for different purposes. The fact the credit card fraud has been moving in and out of the law enforcement agenda – and has been revived recently with the attention given to identity fraud or theft – is just one example of how areas or activities attract fraud in a way that can be both systematic and organised or opportunist. Any response to fraud must therefore ask why, apart from professional criminals who exploit anything from businesses to benefits to extract funds (and in that sense are operating no differently than if they were running protection rackets or selling drugs), those who commit fraud set out to do so. Do they become involved with fraud through changing circumstances, and do they commit fraud regularly? This raises then further questions as to who encourages the opportunity for fraud? Does the impetus come from external drivers, such as cultural changes, the rise of e-commerce and IT, demographic changes, etc., or from internal changes such as re-engineering, professional trust, introducing private sector approaches and practices to the public sector, marketing, competition, profits and perks, and so on? And how far has opportunity facilitated fraud by those who don't need specialist fraud competences, opened up fraud to those who previously might not have become involved, or encouraged the migration of fraudsters from one area to another? In other words, as a society, are we more fraud-prone, are providers of goods and services making it too easy to commit fraud and are we talking about an expanding but common fraud pool, or disaggregated and diverse fraud groups? Is the problem structural or cultural, longer-term or transitional? In other words, who would a strategy be aimed at?

What is the harm caused by fraud?

Answers to such questions leads to the issue of the cost or harm of fraud. Is fraud, in relation to Leigh's comment, a threat or an absorbable cost or, in the contemporary jargon about organised crime, the 'harm' to society? Certainly the warnings are now becoming more explicit. The FSA considers that 'the incidence of fraud in the financial sector is significant and rising'. Fraud is in the NCIS UK Threat Assessment and the Home Office has two fraud websites as part of its crime reduction strategy. The question should be – is fraud in itself a harm to society or does fraud facilitate harm to society?

In February 2005, the Welsh Food Fraud Co-ordinating Unit was announced. Financed by the Food Standards Agency through the Welsh Assembly, its intention is to share intelligence between the various agencies that were tackling the problem of food fraud, especially the sale of unfit meat, and to establish joint working arrangements because previous inquiries into illegal meat fraud had identified the importance of building strong communication channels to counter the activities of organised criminal gangs. In 2006, the Food Standards Agency announced its own Food Fraud Task Force to help tackle the trade in illegal food and protect consumers. Nearly a year earlier, in June 2004, Mr Justice Jackson told the defendants in the Versailles case that their fraud was 'clearly the most serious fraud before this court. It was carried out over a period of some eight years. It gave rise to losses exceeding £150 million … in my judgment, the Versailles fraud is one of the worst cases of conspiracy to defraud which is likely to be encountered in practice.'

The latter was a 'straightforward commercial fraud that 'involved a massive deception of the London Stock Exchange', 'gross breaches of trust' and a 'gross deception of many other people and institutions'. It was a duty of the court 'to uphold certain basic standards of honesty on the part of company directors who are handling tens of millions of pounds of other people's money'. On the other hand, the 'harm' to the reputation of the City or to society in general may be debatable. Was the case typical or did it reflect effective regulators and investigative agencies in uncovering the wrongdoings and achieving a successful prosecution? In the case of the new Food Fraud Unit, deception and misrepresentation may lie at the heart of the activities being investigated but, despite the inclusion of the word 'fraud' in the new agency's name, the unit is less about fraud than about the 'criminal gangs' producing and supplying the food that threatens health and would bring immediate harm to society.

Thus not only does fraud as an activity need to be assessed for 'harm', as opposed to financial loss, but also whether those involved are committing fraud as an end in itself or are using fraud as a vehicle to fund or facilitate more harmful outcomes. Such a perspective may explain why the government would view with concern frauds associated with pension liberation schemes and dishonest pension advisers. With an increasing emphasis by government on personal responsibility for pension provision, and the ending of final salary settlements in the private sector, the state is aware of the need of some supervisory role to protect the integrity of the pensions marketplace, and thus consumer trust, as well as provide cover when schemes collapse. While the frauds may not yet be significant, and the recent industry-funded pensions protection fund a visible safety net, the harm to society and its faith in government assurances is likely to receive more attention than, say, investment frauds like Versailles.

What do agencies really want? The future of policing and mapping the landscape of fraud through information

In 1970 a circular from the Home Office (No. 115/1970) defined the roles and composition of fraud squads:

> The primary purpose of a fraud squad should be the efficient handling of those investigations, often complicated and long drawn out, in which specialist knowledge of the elements of company law is necessary. The complement of a fraud squad should reflect the need for such investigation in the area; and those forces in which a fraud squad is not likely to build up enough experience to become expert should arrange for the work to be done with the assistance of a more experienced fraud squad in a neighbouring force.

Just over 30 years later a fraud victim received from the Sussex police 'inspector of incident management' the explanation that 'public consultation has shown that priority must be given to residential burglaries, violent crime and vehicle crime. Other criminal matters must be assessed carefully to calculate time spent in investigation and the likelihood of a successful prosecution. Fraud may be investigated in certain circumstances but falls way down the list of crimes we can justify committing resources to, particularly when the alleged offences often involve protracted inquiries and rarely result in prosecution' (*Daily Telegraph*, 13 February 2001).

It has been clear that Chief Constables have responded rapidly and comprehensively to successive governments' populist agendas to increase recruitment, put police on the streets and focus on public order and public safety, burglary and street theft priorities. This has compounded the previous Conservative governments' agenda for decentralised delivery and streamlining of management ranks (see Doig, Johnson and Levi 2001). That has not hurt the public sector significantly, since not only do a number of organisations have a substantial in-house fraud capability, but also they conduct their own prosecutions. Where it has hurt, has been in the private sector, when organisations seek a law enforcement solution to their problems. Whether or not the police themselves can recover their former resourcing is problematic. Now that fraud is back on the agenda, there is a concern over the dwindling expertise (reinforced by the reaction to, for example, the Bichard inquiry into the Soham murders which has seen the shift of experienced detectives into murder, rape and gun crime priorities) and the type of frauds officers currently deal with (which continue to be focused on professional criminals).

On the other hand, of the priorities that have emerged from the organisational shifts in the past decades, the issue of a national or regional fraud squads would not be at the top. What public and private sectors seek are networks and shared information – understanding the landscape or jigsaw of activities, groups and individuals to facilitate the development of *their* approach to fraud.[2] Thus the British Banking Association has a number of its own anti-fraud working parties and committees – the Fraud Liaison Group, Banks-Police Liaison Working Group, Anti-Fraud Strategy Panel – and is a member of 13 committees led by such agencies as APACS, the Royal Mail, the FSA, the Home Office and the Police. The SFO has stated that it 'participates in wider networks of public and private sector organisations that have joint interests in tackling frauds – it is increasingly common that in individual fraud cases more than one organisation will have an interest. Such networks help ensure that members are aware as soon as possible of any changes in the number or size of cases that may be referred to it, and that each case is dealt with by the most appropriate organisation, (NAO 2003c).

Most would support the proposals of the Grabiner Report (2000: para 6.1) which noted that: 'as with data sharing (which is an issue here too), the key is to make it happen effectively. Beyond the obvious obstacles, such as different organisations being based in different locations, there are several barriers to overcome. Incompatible IT systems, different departmental cultures and working methods, and any possible lack of resources and funding ... all need to be addressed. It is important that the commitment to joint working must come from the entire organisation, not just from the top or from investigators at the front line.'

The futures for fraud – culture and honesty?

Finally, as the Fraud Review Team moves towards a full assessment of the scale and cost of fraud, the appropriate role of government, and the value-for-money approaches available to dealing with fraud, the question of how fraud in the future will be addressed, may require further rethinking if the only answer so far is based on a crude correlation between the apparent rise and pervasiveness of fraud and the range of agencies and procedures set up to address it. It may be necessary to look at less exciting but much more fundamental issues of self-regulation and prevention. In discussing white-collar crime in general Hazel Croall has already anticipated concerns noted by the Fraud Review: 'given the complexities of many white collar crimes and their location in occupational and organisational settings, the criminal law is ineffective and inappropriate. Ultimately, self-regulation and persuasive and cooperative strategies are likely to be more effective means of protecting the public, particularly from the harms of corporations and organisations. The criminal law is seen as costly and cumbersome and ill adapted to deal with the problems of organisational offences. Sentences which appear to be insufficiently stringent can also be seen as an inadequate deterrent' (Croall 2001: 150–51). If the criminal route is problematic, then how should reform address what Levi has termed 'the combined pressures of the envy and greed produced by the huge salaries in some sectors; of conglomerates which make it hard to maintain independence of judgment; of conspicuous consumption in the fast lane; and of the need to move all that money which has been borrowed from depositors and has to make a profit' (Levi 1987: 356). This thus raises the question, is the rise in fraud the consequence of issues beyond the reactive control approach of the Fraud Review Team? Would wider societal changes support a belief that prevention and internal controls will be effective to encourage the 'it wouldn't be honest' approach? In other words, is prevention still viable and achievable or is it a consequence of a different era, and how far is it relevant to contemporary threats? Is it possible to seek to have responsibility as the key to an effective ethical environment and revive the 'wouldn't be honest' attitude as the norm in public or private sectors?

Maybe the future for fraud is futures – a range of responses depending on circumstance, activity and agency?

- If, as Weisburd and Waring suggest, financial penalties rather than imprisonment would be more effective inhibitors, then the development of the confiscation regime is clearly energising both the current response to fraud as well as general responses to acquisitive crime. In its 2004/2005 report the SFO states that 'the emphasis on removing the benefits of crime from convicted fraudsters is greatly to be welcomed'.

- Maybe the answer also lies in more effective and more cost-effective fraud work through some form of joined-up approach beyond legal gateways, formalisation of previous multi-agency work (along the lines of the creation of the Northern Ireland Organised Crime Task Force), or the integration of existing agencies with identified overlapping operational focus?

- Maybe the answer lies in compliance and personal responsibility that would create the 'it wouldn't be honest' attitudes that the 1991 Cadbury Committee called for through its Code, underpinned by the principles of openness, integrity and accountability, or that the 1995 Committee on Standards in Public Life expressed in its seven principles (selflessness, integrity, objectivity, accountability, openness, honesty, leadership) supported by a Code, independent scrutiny, and guidance and education?

This book is being published 60 years after Home Office circular No. 115 informed all Chief Constables in 1946 about the establishment of the Metropolitan and City of London Fraud Squad, nearly 50 years after C. Wright Mills wrote: 'Whenever the standards of the moneyed life prevail, the man with the money, no matter how he got it, will eventually be respected' (Mills 1959: 146), and nearly 25 years since the 1992 Cadbury Report called for 'a sharper sense of accountability and responsibility all round' and the 1994 House of Commons Committee of Public Accounts proposed 'effective systems of control and accountability and above all responsible attitudes on the part of those handling public money'. The book would suggest that major assessments and initiatives are now necessary as the moneyed life continues to prevail, as fraud becomes an integral part of other crimes as well as a significant crime in its own right, and as current agency and other resources reflect past political and organisational objectives – all pointing to new and challenging futures for fraud that will require new and challenging answers.

Note

1   Partners Against Crime was a proposed initiative between the Confederation of British Industry (CBI), the Metropolitan Police and the City of London Police, and forensic accountants and accredited private investigation firms. Intended to begin on 1 April 2000, fraud investigations in the Metropolitan and City of London police areas were to have been 'subcontracted' to approved organisations, with the police 'accrediting' investigators as competent to investigate complex fraud cases. These investigators would sign a contract with the police for each individual case they investigated. As yet the scheme has not been approved.

2   While much of the public sector information-sharing is done through legal gateways, and usually carefully monitored to avoid public criticism and Data Protection breaches, there are information exchanges. One is FFIN (the Financial Fraud Information Network, housed in the FSA). The private sector has a range of commercial companies providing corporate and personal data checks, such as Experian, Equifax and Dun and Bradstreet, while CIFAS (the Credit Industry Fraud Avoidance System) was set up in November 1988 as a not-for-profit agency by the major retail credit lenders in the UK consumer credit industry to warn each other of suspected frauds. It is expected that the public sector may participate in the near future.

Annex

Scotland

There is also no succinct definition of the crime of fraud in Scotland; it is a common law offence with the elements of falsehood, fraud and wilful imposition being present. The offence is investigated by the police who will report their findings to the Procurator Fiscal Service or, where the crime is one of a more serious nature, such as a complex fraud, to the Crown Office. The Crown Office can and often do direct the police to carry out investigations, where they have had an offence reported direct to them or to other agencies who have no investigative capability. Criminal law and procedure in Scotland differs from that in the rest of the United Kingdom. The main distinction is that Scots criminal law is based principally on a common law tradition which means that much of Scots criminal law relies for its authority on past decisions of the courts and on the writings of respected legal scholars (called institutional writers) rather than on Acts of Parliament. For a crime to be committed there has to be independent corroborative evidence. Various laws apply, mainly in the area of human rights (such as ECHR, Freedom of Information, Data Protection, RIPSA – the Scottish equivalent of RIPA) but, on the other hand, the requirements of PACE and CPIA do not apply. Suspects can be detained and interviewed for up to six hours, without a lawyer present, after which time the suspect must be charged or set free for further investigation. Interestingly, a suspect cannot be detained a second time for the same offence. Consequently there is a need to use the limited detention time with great forethought. (This is why Scottish police may delay arrests or even detention until inquiries are well underway.) If charged, however, there are strict deadlines by which committal papers must be served and the trial started.

The Crown Office and Procurator Fiscal Service provide Scotland's independent public prosecution and deaths investigation service. They provide the prosecution service for the police and a number of 'specialist' agencies, such as the Health and Safety Executive, the Scottish Environment Protection Agency (SEPA) and the Maritime and Coastguard Agency, as well as Local Authority departments such as Environmental Health and Trading Standards.

The Procurator Fiscal is a qualified solicitor and member of the Law Society for Scotland who has responsibility at local level for the investigation and prosecution of crime in the public interest. The prosecutor in Scotland has a statutory power to direct the police in the investigation of crime; for serious cases, which will be considered by a jury, the Procurator Fiscal can interview witnesses and gather and review the forensic and other evidence before a decision to prosecute is taken and, if so, in which court. At the centre is the Crown Office – the HQ which has Policy, Management Services and Operations divisions; the last consists of four main Units:

- The Fraud Unit – a team of lawyers and support staff, who investigate complex fraud cases, deal with major confiscation cases, deal with extradition and provide mutual legal assistance to foreign jurisdictions;

- A Unit dealing with money laundering cases (Scotland has its own version of ARA which does not have the taxation requirements);

- The High Court Unit – a team of lawyers and support staff who prepare cases for the High Court;

- The Appeals Unit – a team of lawyers and support staff who prepare cases for the Court of Appeal;

There is also the Scottish Charities Office – a team of lawyers and support staff who deal with concerns regarding alleged misconduct or mismanagement relating to the administration of charities.

References

Adams, J.R. and Frantz, D. (1992) *A Full Service Bank*. London: Simon and Schuster.

Albrecht, W.S., Wernz, G.W. and Williams, T.L. (1995) *Fraud*. New York: Irwin.

Allen, J., Forrest, S., Levi, M., Roy, H., Sutton, M. and Wilson, D (eds) (2005) *Fraud and Technology Crimes; Findings from the 2002/03 British Crime Survey and 2003 Offending, Crime and Justice Survey*. On-Line Report 34/05. London: Home Office.

Allen, M. (2005a) 'The Forensic Examination of Documents' in A. Brown, L. Dobbs, A. Doig, G. Owen and G. Summers (2005) *Fraud: Law, Practice and Procedure*. London: LexisNexis.

Allen, M. (2005b) 'Handwriting and Signature Evidence' in A. Brown, L. Dobbs, A. Doig, G. Owen and G. Summers (2005) *Fraud: Law, Practice and Procedure*. London: LexisNexis.

Anechiarico, F. and Jacobs, J.B. (1996) *The Pursuit of Absolute Integrity*. Chicago: University of Chicago Press.

Appleby, E. (1995) *The Inquiry Report of Miss Elizabeth Appleby QC*, London Borough of Lambeth, July.

Archbold (2003) *Archbold Digital Edition*. London: Sweet and Maxwell.

Arlidge and Parry (1985) *Fraud*. London: Waterlow Publishers Ltd.

Ashe, M. and Counsell, L. (1990) *Insider Trading*. London: Fourmat Publishing.

Association of British Insurers (ABI) (2005) *UK Commercial Insurance Fraud Study 2005*. London: Association of British Insurers.

Audit Commission (1994) *Protecting the Public Purse: Ensuring Probity in Local Government*. London: HMSO.

Audit Commission (1997) *NHS Fraud and Corruption Manual*. London: Audit Commission.

Audit Commission (2004) *Crime Recording*. London: Audit Commission.

Audit Commission (2005a) *Ethical Governance in Local Government in England: A Regulator's View*. London: Audit Commission.

Audit Commission (2005b) *Public Interest Report: Manchester City Council*. London: Audit Commission.

Auld, R. (2001) *Review of the Criminal Courts*. London: TSO.

Auleta, K. (1986) *Greed and Glory on Wall Street*. London: Penguin.

Barchard, D. (1992) *Asil Nadir*. London: Gollancz.

Barnes, P. and Allen, S. (1998) *The Fraud Survey*. Leicester: ACFE.

Bose, M. and Gunn, C. (1989) *Fraud*. London: Unwin Hyman.

Bower, T. (1991) *Maxwell: The Outsider*. London: Mandarin.

Brown, A., Dobbs, L., Doig, A., Owen, G. and Summers, G. (2005) *Fraud: Law, Practice and Procedure*. London: LexisNexis.

Brown, A. (2005) 'The Forensic Accountant' in A. Brown, L. Dobbs, A. Doig, G. Owen and G. Summers (2005) *Fraud: Law, Practice and Procedure*. London: LexisNexis.

Byrne, J.E. (2002) *The Myth of Prime Bank Investment Scams*. Maryland: Institute of International Banking Law and Practice, Inc.

Cabinet Office: Performance and Innovation Unit (2000) *Recovering the Proceeds of Crime*. London: Cabinet Office.

Cabinet Office (2002) *Identity Fraud: A Study*. London: Cabinet Office.

Clark, D. (2004) *The Investigation of Crime*. London: Butterworths.

Clarke, M. (1981) *Fallen Idols*. London: Junction Books.

Clarke, M. (1986) *Regulating the City: Competition, Scandal and Reform*. Milton Keynes: Open University Press.

Clarke, M. (1990) *Business Crime*. Oxford: Polity Press.

Clementi, D. (2004) *Review of the Regulatory Framework for Legal Services in England and Wales*. London: Department for Constitutional Affairs.

Comer, M.J. (1985) *Corporate Fraud*. London: McGraw-Hill.

Comer, M.J. (2003) *Investigating Corporate Fraud*. Aldershot: Gower.

Committee on the Financial Aspects of Corporate Governance (1992) *Report*. London: Gee/Professional Publishing Ltd. (The Cadbury Committee).

Committee on Corporate Governance (1998) *Final Report*. London: Gee.

Committee of Public Accounts (1988) *35th Report: Ministry of Defence: Procurement Irregularities*. HC 450. London: HMSO.

Committee of Public Accounts (1991) *37th Report: Fraud and Irregularities at Defence Establishments*. HC 442. London: HMSO.

Committee of Public Accounts (1993) *48th Report. Irregularities in the 1991–92 Accounts of Forward Civil Service Catering*. HC 558. London: HMSO.

Committee of Public Accounts (1994a) *8th Report: the Proper Conduct of Public Business*. HC 154. London: HMSO.

Committee of Public Accounts (1994b) *7th Report: the Department of Employment: The Field System*. London: HMSO.

Committee of Public Accounts (2003) *10th Report: Individual Learning Accounts*. HC 544. London: TSO.

Committee of Public Accounts, (2004) *32nd Report: HM Customs and Excise Standard Report.* HC 284. London: TSO. See also NAO (2001) *Losses to the Revenue from Frauds on Alcohol Duty.* HC 178. London: TSO.

Committee on Standards in Public Life (1995) *First Report.* London: TSO.

Committee on Standards in Public Life (1998) *Fifth Report.* London: TSO.

Committee on Standards in Public Life (2005) *Tenth Report.* London: TSO.

Commons Education and Skills Committee (2002) *3rd Report: Individual Learning Accounts.* HC 561. London: TSO.

Commons Education and Skills Committee (2005) *UK e-University.* HC 205. London: TSO.

Cook, D. (1989) *Rich Law, Poor Law: Different Responses to Tax and Supplementary Benefit Fraud.* Milton Keynes: Open University Press.

Cooper, T.L. (1998) *The Responsible Administrator.* San Francisco: Jossey-Bass Publishers.

Copisarow, R and Barbour, A. (2004) *Self-Employed People in the Informal Economy – Cheats or Contributors? Evidence, Implications and Policy Recommendations.* London: Street UK and Community Links.

Cox, B., Shirley, J. and Short, M. (1977) *The Fall Of Scotland Yard.* London: Penguin.

Croall, H. (2001) *Understanding White-collar Crime.* Milton Keynes: Open University Press.

Davies, P., Francis, P. and Jupp, V. (eds) (1999) *Invisible Crimes.* London: Macmillan.

Davis H. (2003) *Human Rights and Civil Liberties.* London: Willan.

Dean, H. and Melrose, M. (1995) "Fiddling the Social": Understanding Benefit Fraud', *Benefits*, 14.

Dean, H. and Melrose, M. (1996) 'Unravelling Citizenship', *Critical Social Policy*, 48.

Dean, H. and Melrose, M. (1997) 'Manageable Discord: Fraud and Resistance in the Social Security System', *Social Policy and Administration*, 48.

Department for Constitutional Affairs (2005) *A Fairer Deal for Legal Aid*, Cm 591. London: TSO.

Department of Health (1997) *Prescription Fraud: An Efficiency Scrutiny.* London: Department of Health.

Department of Health (2003) *Countering Fraud in the NHS: Applying Appropriate Sanctions Consistently.* London: Department of Health.

Department for Work and Pensions (2004) *In-house report 149: a review of the DWP benefit fraud sanctions scheme.* London: DWP.

Ditton, J. (1977) *Part-time Crime: An Ethnography of Fiddling and Pilferage.* London: Macmillan.

Dipple, D. and Ryan, T. (2005) 'Investigative Interviewing and the Recording of Interviews', in A. Brown, L. Dobbs, A. Doig, G. Owen and G. Summers (2005) *Fraud: Law, Practice and Procedure.* London: LexisNexis.

Doig, A. (1984) *Corruption and Misconduct in Contemporary British Politics.* London: Penguin.

Doig, A. (1993) 'Retreat of the Investigators', *British Journalism Review*, 3 (4). See also Doig, A. (1997) *'The End of Investigative Journalism?'* in Michael Bromley (ed.) *Journalism: A Reader.* London: Routledge.

Doig, A. and Coles, E. (1997) 'Local Government and Housing Benefit: Cost and Control of Fraud', *Local Government Studies*, 23 (2).

Doig, A. (1997) 'The Privatisation of the Property Services Agency: Risk and Vulnerability in Contract-Related Fraud and Corruption', *Public Policy and Administration*, 12 (3).

Doig, A., Levi, M. and Johnson, S. (2001) 'Old Populism or New Public Management? Policing Fraud in the UK', *Public Policy and Administration*, 16 (1).

Drummond, H. (2003) 'Did Nick Leeson Have an Accomplice? The Role of Information Technology in the Collapse of Barings Bank', *Journal of Information Technology*, 18.

Duffield, G. and Grabosky, P. (2001) 'The Psychology of Fraud', *The Australian Institute of Criminology: Trends and Issues in Crime and Criminal Justice*, No. 199. Canberra: Australian Institute of Criminology.

Edelhartz, H. (1978) 'The Nature, Impact and Prosecution of White-collar Crime' in J.M. Johnson and J.D. Douglas (eds), *Crime at the Top.* New York: J.B. Lippincott.

Evans, D. (2005) 'Employment Law and Disciplinary Procedures' in A. Brown, L. Dobbs, A. Doig, G. Owen and G. Summers (2005) *Fraud: Law, Practice and Procedure.* London: LexisNexis.

Fay, S. (1996) *The Collapse of Barings.* London: Arrow Business Books.

Financial Services Authority (2006) *Firms' High Level Management of Fraud Risk.* London: FSA.

Finnerty, N. (2005) 'HM Customs and Excise' in A. Brown, L. Dobbs, A. Doig, G. Owen and G. Summers (2005) *Fraud: Law, Practice and Procedure.* London: LexisNexis.

Fitzwalter, R. and Taylor, D. (1981) *Webb of Corruption.* Manchester: Granada.

Fletcher, R. (2005) 'Sentencing' in A. Brown, L. Dobbs, A. Doig, G. Owen and G. Summers (2005) *Fraud: Law, Practice and Procedure.* London: LexisNexis.

Fraud Advisory Panel (2005) *The Human Cost of Fraud: Seventh Annual Review, 2004–2005.* London: Fraud Advisory panel.

Fraud Review Team (2006) *Final Report.* London: The Legal Secretariat to the Law Officers. http://www.lslo.gov.uk

Fuller, J.G. (1962) *The Gentlemen Conspirators.* New York: Grove Press, Inc.

Geis, G. (ed.) (1968) *White-collar Criminal.* California: Atherton Press.

Geis, G. and Meier, R.F. (eds) (1980) *White-collar Crime.* New York: The Free Press.

Geis, G. and Stotland, E. (eds) (1980) *White-collar Crime*. California: Sage.

Gentle, S. and Hodges, L. (2005) 'Regulatory Offences' in A. Brown, L. Dobbs, A. Doig, G. Owen and G. Summers (2005) *Fraud: Law, Practice and Procedure*. London: LexisNexis.

Giacalone, R.A. and Greenberg, J. (eds) (1997) *Antisocial behaviour in Organisations*. California: Sage.

Gill, M. (1994) *Crime at Work*. Leicester: Perpetuity Press.

Gill, M. (2005) *Learning From Fraudsters*. London: Protiviti Group.

Gill, K.M., Woolley, A. and Gill, M. (1994) 'Insurance Fraud: The Business as Victim?' In Gill, M. (ed.) *Crime at Work*. Leicester: Perpetuity Press.

Gillard, M. (1974) *A Little Pot of Money*. London: Private Eye/Andre Deutsche.

Goldspink, R. and Cole, J. (eds) (2002) *International Commercial Fraud*. London: Sweet and Maxwell.

Gorta, A. (1998) 'Minimising Corruption: Applying Lessons from the Crime Prevention Literature', *Crime, Law and Social Change*, 30 (1).

Gorta, A. and Forell, S. (1995) 'Layers of Decisions: Linking Social Definitions of Corruption and Willingness to Take Action', *Crime. Law and Social Change*, 23 (4).

Grabiner, Lord (2000) *The Informal Economy*. London: HM Treasury, p. 7.

Greenhalgh, S. and Coles, L. (2005) 'The Investigator' in A. Brown, L. Dobbs, A. Doig, G. Owen and G. Summers (2005) *Fraud: Law, Practice and Procedure*. London: LexisNexis.

Gunn, C. (1992) *Nightmare on Lime Street*. London: Smith Gryphon Publishers.

Hamadi, R. (2004) *Identity Theft*. London: Vision Paperbacks.

Harrow, J. and Gillett, R. (1994) 'The Proper Conduct of Public Business', *Public Money and Management*, 14 (2).

Healthcare Financial Management Association/CIPFA (1997) *Probity in Primary Care*. London: Healthcare Financial Management Association/CIPFA.

Hemraj, M.B. (2005) 'The Regulatory Failure: The Saga of BCCI', *Journal of Money Laundering Control*, 8 (4).

Henry, S. (1978) *The Hidden Economy: The Context and Control of Borderline Crime*. London: Martin Robertson.

Herring, J. (2004) *Criminal Law*. Oxford: OUP.

HM Crown Prosecution Service Inspectorate (2006) *Review of the Investigation and Criminal Proceedings Relating to the Jubilee Line Case*. London: Corporate Services Group, HMCPSI.

HM Inspectorate of Constabulary (1999) *Police Integrity*. London: Home Office.

Hodgson, G. (1986) *Lloyds of London*. London: Penguin.

(The Hodgson Report) The Profits of Crime and Their Recovery, The Report of a Committee Chaired by Sir Derek Hodgson (London: Heinneman Education Books, 1984).

Home Office (1998) *Juries in Serious Fraud Trials: A Consultation Paper*. London: Home Office.

Home Office (2002) *Entitlement Cards and Identity Fraud*. Cm 5557. London: HMSO.

Home Office (2004a) *Fraud Law Reform*. London: Home Office.

Home Office (2004b) *Legislation on Identity Cards*. Cm 6178. London: HMSO.

Honess, T.M., Levi, M. and Charman, E.A. (1998) 'Juror Competence in Processing Complex Information: Implications from a Simulation of the Maxwell Trial', *Criminal Law Review*, November.

Honess, T.M., Levi, M. and Charman, E.A. (2003) 'Juror Competence in Serious Frauds since Roskill: a Research-based Assessment', *Journal of Financial Crime*, 11 (1).

Hosken, A. (2006) *Nothing Like a Dame*. London: Granta.

Howson, K. (2005) 'The Salvation Army, Aspects of their Financial Administration: Success and Failure', *Managerial Auditing Journal*, 20 (7).

Huntington, I.K. (1992) *Fraud: Prevention and Detection*. London: Butterworth.

Huntington, I.K. and Davies, D. (1994) *Fraud Watch*. Milton Keynes: Accountancy Books.

Hyland, M. (2005) *Fraud: Fraud Manager's Reference Guide*. BBA Enterprises and MHA Compliance and Training.

Jennings, A., Lasmar, P. and Simson, V. (1991) *Scotland Yard's Cocaine Connection*. London: Arrow Books.

Johnson, J.M. and Douglas, J.D. (eds) (1978) *Crime at the Top*. New York: J.B. Lippincott.

Johnston, M. and Wood, D. (1985) 'Right and Wrong in Public and Private Life', in R. Jowell and S. Witherspoon (eds), *British Social Attitudes: the 1985 Report*. London: Gower/Social and Community Planning Research.

Jones, G. (2005) 'Identity Fraud' in A. Brown, L. Dobbs, A. Doig, G. Owen and G. Summers (2005) *Fraud: Law, Practice and Procedure*. London: LexisNexis.

Jones, P. (2004) *Fraud and Corruption in Public Services*. Aldershot: Gower.

Kirk, D.N. and Woodcock, A.J.J. (2003) *Serious Fraud: Investigation and Trial*. London: LexisNexis.

Kochan, N. and Pym, H. *The Guinness Affair*. London: Christopher Helm.

KPMG. (2003) *Report on the Review of the Regime for Handling Suspicious Activity Reports*; accessible on www.ncis.co.uk

Law Commission (1996) *Offences of Dishonesty: Money Transfers*, 243. London: Law Commission.

Law Commission (1997) *Legislating the Criminal Code: Corruption*. Consultation Paper. No 145. London: Law Commission.

Law Commission (1999) *Legislating the Criminal Code. Fraud And Deception – A Consultation Paper*. London: Law Commission.

Law Commission (2002) *Fraud*. LC276. London: Law Commission.

Law Reform Commission (1993) *Scrutiny of the Legal Profession Complaints against Lawyers*. Report 70. New South Wales, Australia: Law Reform Commission.

Lawton, A. and Doig, A. (2006) 'Researching Ethics for Public Service Organisations: the View from Europe. *Public Integrity*. Vol 8(1).

Lawton, A. and Macaulay, M. (2004) *National Integrity System: UK Country Study*. Berlin: Transparency International.

Leigh, L. (1982) *The Control of Commercial Fraud*. London: Heinemann.

Lever, L. (1992) *The Barlow Clowes Affair*. London: Macmillan.

Levi, M. (1981) *The Phantom Capitalists: the Organisation and Control of Long-Firm Fraud*, London: Heinemann. (Cambridge Studies in Criminology Series – to be republished by Ashgate with new introduction, 2006.)

Levi, M. (1987) *Regulating Fraud: White-Collar Crime and the Criminal Process*. London: Routledge.

Levi, M., Bissell. P and Richardson, T. (1991) *The Prevention of Cheque and Credit Card Fraud*. Crime prevention unit paper no. 26. London: Home Office.

Levi, M. (1993) *The Investigation, Prosecution, and Trial of Serious Fraud*, Royal Commission on Criminal Justice Research Study No. 14. London: HMSO.

Levi, M. (1994) 'Masculinity and White-collar crime' in T. Newburn and B. Stanko (eds), *Just Boys Doing Business*, London: Routledge.

Levi, M. and Gold, M. (1994) *Money-Laundering in the UK: an Appraisal of Suspicion-Based Reporting*. London: Police Foundation.

Levi, M. (1995) *The Reporting of Suspected Money-Laundering Transactions*. Home Affairs Committee. Third Report: Organised Crime. London: HMSO.

Levi, M. and Handley, J. (1998) *The Prevention of Plastic and Cheque Fraud Revisited*. Research Study 182. London: Home Office.

Levi. M. (1998a) *Prevention of Plastic Card Fraud*. Research Findings No. 71. London: Home Office Research and Statistics Directorate.

Levi, M. (1998b) 'Organising Plastic Fraud: Enterprise Criminal and the Side-Stepping of Fraud Prevention', *The Howard Journal*, 37 (4).

Levi, M. (1998c) *Reflections on Organised Crime: Patterns and Control*. Oxford: Blackwell (Edited Book).

Levi, M. (ed.) (1999) *Fraud: Organisation, Motivation and Control: Vol. I and Vol. II*. Aldershot: Dartmouth.

Levi, M. (2000) *The Prevention of Plastic and Cheque Fraud: A Briefing Paper*. London: Home Office.

Levi, M. (2003) 'The Roskill Fraud Commission revisited: An assessment', *Journal of Financial Crime*, 11 (1).

Light, P.C. (1993) *Monitoring Government: Inspectors General and the Search for Accountability*. Washington, DC: The Brookings Institution.

Lucraft, M. and Forster, T. (2005) 'Procedural Considerations' in A. Brown, L. Dobbs, A. Doig, G. Owen and G. Summers (2005) *Fraud: Law, Practice and Procedure*. London: LexisNexis.

Mabey, V. (2005) 'Forensic Computing' in A. Brown, L. Dobbs, A. Doig, G. Owen and G. Summers (2005) *Fraud: Law, Practice and Procedure*. London: LexisNexis.

Mancuso, M. (1993) 'The Ethical Attitudes of MPs', *Parliamentary Affairs*, 46 (2).

Mars, G. (1983) *Cheats at Work: an Anthropology of Workplace Crime*. London: Unwin Paperbacks.

Martin, R. (1981) *New Technology and Industrial Relations in Fleet Street*. Oxford: Oxford University Press.

McLagan, G. (2004) *Bent Coppers*. London: Orion.

Middleton, D.J. and Levi, M. (2004) 'The Role of solicitors in facilitating "Organised Crime"', *Crime, Law and Social Change*, 42 (2–3).

Middleton, D.J. (2005) 'The Legal and Regulatory Response to Solicitors Involved in Serious Fraud', *British Journal of Criminology*, 45.

Mills, C. W. (1959) *The Power Elite*. New York: Galaxy Books.

Morgan, J., McCulloch, L. and Burrows, J. (1996) *Central Specialist Squads: a Framework for Monitoring and Evaluation*. London: Police Research Group, Police Department; Home Office.

Murray, C. (2005) 'Mutual Legal Assistance/International Co-operation' in A. Brown, L. Dobbs, A. Doig, G. Owen and G. Summers (2005) *Fraud: Law, Practice and Procedure*. London: LexisNexis.

Nash, S. and Furze, N. (2002) *Essential Human Rights Cases*. Bristol: Jordan.

(NERA) National Economic Research Associates (2000) *The Economic Cost of Fraud*. London: NERA Associates.

NAO (1989) *Department of Employment: Provision of Training through Managing Agents*. HC 569 London: HMSO.

NAO (1991) *Fraud and Irregularities at Defence Establishments*. HC 134. London: HMSO.

NAO (1995a) *Department of Employment: Financial Controls in Training and Enterprise Councils in England*. HC 361. London: HMSO.

NAO (1995b) *Ministry of Defence: The Risk of Fraud in Defence Procurement*. HC 258. London: HMSO.

NAO (1996) *Inquiry Commissioned by the NHS Chief Executive into Matters Concerning the Former Yorkshire Regional Health Authority*. HC 280. London: TSO.

NAO (1998) *Special Compliance Office: Prevention of Corruption*. HC 1058. London: TSO.

NAO (2000a) *The Millennium Dome*. HC 936. London: TSO.

NAO (2000b) *The Risk of Fraud in Property Management*. HC 469. London: TSO.

NAO (2001) *Giving Confidently: The Role of the Charity Commission in Regulating Charities*. HC 234. London: TSO.

NAO (2002a) *Agricultural Fraud: The Case of Andrew Bowden*. HC 615. London: TSO.

NAO (2002b) *Individual Learning Accounts*. HC 1235. London: TSO.

NAO (2002c) *Winding-up The New Millennium Experience Company Limited*. HC 749 London: TSO.

NAO (2003a) *Department for Work and Pensions: Tackling Benefit Fraud*. HC 393. London: TSO.

NAO (2003b) *Tackling Fraud Against the Inland Revenue*. London: TSO.

NAO (2003c) *Managing Resources to Deliver Better Public Services*. HC 61-I and II. London: TSO.

NAO (2004) *HM Customs and Excise: Tackling VAT Fraud*. HC 357. London: TSO.

NOA and HMT (2004) *Good Practice in Tackling External Fraud*. London: NAO/HMT.

NCIS (2003) *UK Threat Assessment.* London: NCIS.

Ormerod, D. (2005) 'Voice Identification Evidence' in A. Brown, L. Dobbs, A. Doig, G. Owen and G. Summers (2005) *Fraud: Law, Practice and Procedure.* London: LexisNexis.

Ormerod, D. and Williams, D. H. (2005) 'Introduction' in A. Brown, L. Dobbs, A. Doig, G. Owen and G. Summers (2005) *Fraud: Law, Practice and Procedure.* London: LexisNexis.

O'Shea, J. (1991) *The Daisy Chain.* London: Simon and Schuster.

Osse, A. (1997) 'Corruption Prevention: A course for police officers fighting organised crime'. *Crime, Law and Social Change,* 28 (1).

Parkinson, S. (2005) 'Corruption' in A. Brown, L. Dobbs, A. Doig, G. Owen and G. Summers (2005) *Fraud: Law, Practice and Procedure.* London: LexisNexis.

Phillips, E., Walsh, C. and Dobson, P. (2001) *Law relating to Theft.* London: Cavendish Publishing.

PricewaterhouseCoopers (2005) *Global Economic Crime Survey 2005: United Kingdom.* London: PricewaterhouseCoopers.

Punch, M. (1996) *Dirty Business: Exploring Corporate Misconduct.* London: Sage.

Public Audit Forum. (2001) *Propriety and Audit in the Public Sector.* London: Public Audit Forum.

Raw, C., Page, B. and Hodgson, G. (1972) *Do You Sincerely want to be Rich?* London: Penguin.

Raw, C. (1977) *Slater Walker.* London: Coronet Books.

Rezaee, Z. (2002) *Financial Statement Fraud: Prevention and Detection.* New York: John Wiley and Sons, Inc.

Robb, G. (2002) *White-collar Crime in Modern England: Financial Fraud and Business Morality, 1845–1929.* Cambridge: Cambridge University Press.

Robinson, P. (2004) '*The FSA's New Approach to Fraud – Fighting Fraud in Partnership.*' Speech in London: 26 October 2004.

Roskill, Lord (1986) *Fraud Trials Committee Report.* London: HMSO.

Rowlingson, K., Whyley, C., Newburn, T. and Berthoud, R. (1997) *Social Security Fraud: The Role of Penalties.* London: TSO.

Scampion, J. (2000) *Organised Benefit Fraud.* London: DSS.

Schollum, M. (2005) *Investigative Interviewing: The Literature.* Wellington, New Zealand: Office of the Commissioner of Police.

Searle, G.R. (1987) *Corruption in British Politics, 1895–1930.* Oxford: Clarendon Press.

Sentencing Guidelines Council (2005) *Guideline Judgements Case Compendium.* London: Sentencing Guidelines Council.

Serious Fraud Office (2004) *Annual Report 2003–4.* London: Fraud Office.

Sharp, K. (2005) *Stamping Out Corruption.* London: Corporation of London/City of London Police.

Slapper, G. and Tombs, S. (1999) *Corporate Crime.* London: Longman.

Small Business Council (2004) *Informal Economy*. London: Small Business Council.

Smith, N. and Flanagan, C. (2000) *The Effective Detective: Identifying the Skills of an Effective SIO*. Police Research Series Paper 122. London: Home Office.

Smith, S. (1986) *Britain's Shadow Economy*. Oxford: Clarendon Press.

Sommer, P. (2005) 'CyberCrime' in A. Brown, L. Dobbs, A. Doig, G. Owen and G. Summers (2005) *Fraud: Law, Practice and Procedure*. London: LexisNexis.

Sutherland, E.H. (1983) *White-collar Crime: The Uncut Version*. Yale: Yale University Press.

Thackeray, S. and Riem, A. (2005) 'Freezing Injunctions and Related Process' in A. Brown, L. Dobbs, A. Doig, G. Owen and G. Summers (2005) *Fraud: Law, Practice and Procedure*. London: LexisNexis.

Thompson, P. and Delano, A. (1991) *Maxwell: A Portrait of Power*. London: Corgi.

Tomkinson, M. and Gillard, M. (1980) *Nothing To Declare*. London: John Calder.

HM Treasury (2004) *Anti Money Laundering Strategy*. London: HM Treasury.

Trollope, A., Wong, N., Beynon, R. Samat, D. and Kurzner, E. (2005a) 'Defending Cases' in A. Brown, L. Dobbs, A. Doig, G. Owen and G. Summers (2005) *Fraud: Law, Practice and Procedure*. London: LexisNexis.

Trollope, A., Wong, N., Beynon, R., Samat, D. and Kurzner, E. (2005b) 'Frauds on Investors' in A. Brown, L. Dobbs, A. Doig, G. Owen and G. Summers (2005) *Fraud: Law, Practice and Procedure*. London: LexisNexis.

Van Duyne, P. (2003) 'Organised cigarette smuggling and policy making, ending up in smoke', *Crime, Law and Social Change*, 39.

Walbank, D. (2005) 'Prosecution Disclosure' in A. Brown, L. Dobbs, A. Doig, G. Owen and G. Summers (2005) *Fraud: Law, Practice and Procedure*. London: LexisNexis.

Weisburd, D. and Waring, E. (2001) *White-collar Crime and Criminal Careers*. Cambridge: Cambridge University Press.

Wells, R. (2005) 'Competition Law Considerations: OFT Powers of Investigation' in A. Brown, L. Dobbs, A. Doig, G. Owen and G. Summers (2005) *Fraud: Law, Practice and Procedure*. London: LexisNexis.

West, H. (1987) *Fraud*. London: British Institute of Management.

Widlake, B. (1986) *Serious Fraud Office*. London: Warner Books.

Wojciechowski, T. and Newiss, G. (2002) 'Fraud' in Crime in England and Wales 2001/2002: Supplementary Volume. London: Home Office.

Zimmerman, J.F. (1982) 'Ethics in the Public Service', *State and Local Government Review*, 14 (3).

Index